BETWEEN LOSING AND FINDING

BETWEEN LOSING AND FINDING

The Life of an Analyst

FRED PLAUT

FREE ASSOCIATION BOOKS

First published in 2004 by
FREE ASSOCIATION BOOKS
57 Warren Street
London W1T 5NR

www.fabooks.com

A CIP catalogue record for this book is available
from the British Library.

ISBN 1 85343 719 0 pbk

Designed and produced for the publisher by
Chase Publishing Services, Sidmouth, EX10 9QG, England
Printed and bound in the European Union by
Antony Rowe, Chippenham and Eastbourne, England

Contents

Foreword by Andrew Samuels   vii

Acknowledgements   xii

Preface   xiii

Illustrations   xix

1   Losing–Finding   1
2   Childhood in Germany, the First World War, School   2
3   The Rise of Nazism   16
4   A Major Journey   19
5   Johannesburg in the Thirties and Medical School   26
6   South Africa, Races, Locums, Quacks and a Witchdoctor   32
7   Sailing as to War, the War Years, Victory   40
8   Still Young in Post-War London, Moving out to Jordans
     and back again   50
9   On Training within a Human Context   57
10   How My Practice Has Evolved and Some General Reflections
     on Analysis as Therapy   71
11   Meeting Famous Colleagues and Other Notable Figures   83
12   Hobbies, Old Maps, Gardening and Painting   96
13   Reflecting on Various Kinds of Love   105
14   Not So Young in Berlin (1986 to the present)   118
15   Recent Travels   124
16   On Getting Very Old   136
17   Memories and Remembering   140
18   Still Searching   147
Appendix: What is the Difference between Freud and Jung?   156
Glossary   161
Chronology   168
Publications by Fred Plaut   170
Index   171

Foreword

Andrew Samuels

I have known Fred Plaut since 1971 when I was twenty-two years old – hence for most of my adult life. He has been a challenging teacher, loving friend, supportive and forgiving father-figure and, sometimes, errant adolescent son. I consider him to be perhaps the most intelligent and deeply reflective person I have ever known. Sometimes, he gets into awful depressions and then he can be truly horrible. Because of the longstanding complexity of a thirty-three-year relationship involving an age gap of thirty-six years, I was really grateful for the publisher's invitation to write a Foreword. After all, it will help me clarify some things for myself, won't it?

These are some of the themes you will find in this remarkable and brutally honest autobiography: an acute account of the limits of memory and remembering and autobiography itself (and hence, by extension, of psychoanalysis); mature reflections on the various kinds of love and their vicissitudes; a frank account of the bound-to-fail struggle for full self-acceptance tempered by the realisation that a good-enough level can be achieved; devastatingly perceptive accounts of the virtues and vices of the world of Jungian analysis and psychoanalysis written by one "who was there"; a balance – really very rare to find in an analyst writing outside the sanitised field of professional publication – between a reductive approach to life ("it was due to my father dying when I was six") and taking responsibility for the "present moment" (to use the latest buzzword from the professional literature). And all of it wrapped up in a damn good story of one man's journey from Germany to South Africa to Britain to Germany – never forgetting the inner journey that you'd expect to travel in the company of an analyst.

This is clearly much more than an account of an analyst's professional life. In fact, I would describe the book as a valuable cultural document. For example, the chapters on life in South Africa in the 1930s and 1940s, post-war London and present-day Berlin give an excellent snapshot of those milieux that is lively and interesting. Fred has mastered the use of "the selected fact" (Poincare) whereby a small detail opens into a larger exploration. Not many people can claim to be intimately involved with the Mandela-revolution in South Africa as well as the fall of the Berlin Wall. As you might expect of a travelling man, Fred's hobby is collecting maps, and this has led to publication in specialist cartographic journals. In the book, this particular love of Fred's is presented in terms that illumine what the collectors' bug is about as well as linking up with the general desire to know where one stands.

From my personal experiences of him, Fred has a tendency to eschew the direct approach in favour of a more tangential one. This, too, gives the book a wide non-specialist appeal because, when Fred is writing about his profession, he often utilises raw material of a general nature. For example, when I first met him in the selection interview for training at the Society of Analytical Psychology, he stunned me by asking me by what method I paid the rent or mortgage on my flat. What on earth did this have to do with anything?, I felt. As I explained my not very unusual situation, so many interconnected issues emerged that I was amazed and remain so to this day at the way the question organised so much stuff. To what extent was I dependent on my family still? Did the many part-time jobs I was doing say something significant about a failure to integrate and cohere? Was I alone or partnered? What was my conception of the future? Where did I stand in relation to social realities, in the sense of an emotional response or "feeling" (in Jung's sense of evaluation or judgement).

Later on, we both developed an interest in incorporating this "feeling" about the world in which an analytical treatment was being conducted into the analysis itself. Fred's ideas about "the third" in analysis deserve to be up there with those of Jacques Lacan, Jessica Benjamin and Charles Spezzano. But they never will be – and this is due to several factors that I'd like to contextualise for the reader.

The first is that Fred was, is and will ever be a Jungian analyst. The fact that he is extraordinarily conversant with psychoanalytic (i.e. Freudian and post-Freudian) thought should not obscure this. Hence, in his professional writing to date, he has voluntarily limited his readership, despite being published from time to time in important psychoanalytic journals. That this remains the case more than ninety years after the Freud–Jung split is both a tragedy and a total joke. But there it is. In this book, he has the chance to leapfrog these petty professional turf wars and reach a much wider readership.

The second is that Fred's role in the Jungian world, certainly from the 1950s to the end of the 1970s, was to demystify and deromanticise (if there is such a word) much of Jungian psychology. For example, he wrote a paper asserting that the "luminosities" (Jung's word for the little building blocks of imagination in the psyche) were sometimes as important as the great big impressive and decorous self (or Self). Parts can be as important as wholes, as any post-modernist knows. Earlier, he slashingly attacked Jungian analysts who "educated" rather than analysed their patients. These thunderous interpolations into ongoing debates about the true nature of Jungian analysis (was it a "symbolic" or a "clinical" process, as the question was absurdly put at that time), tended to obscure other offerings that presented Fred as less partisan – for example, a paper bemoaning the lack of meaningful rituals in the contemporary world and a brilliant exposition of the centrality of the shadow in human and political affairs.

Putting these two particular features of Fred's position in the Jungian world together, one can see how it is that, whilst commanding universal respect, his is not one of the household names in the depth psychology field.

And there's something else to add to this, which Fred touches on in his book but spoke more fully about in an interview with him that I conducted for the

Journal of Analytical Psychology in 1989. There, he spoke frankly about his relationship with Michael Fordham who was still alive at the time. I think this is important to bring up in my Foreword because, all too often, I find that Fordham and Plaut get muddled up as if Fred was Michael's rottweiler in the Jungian and post-Jungian wars. This is what Fred said to me then: "Fordham is, of course, the greatest figure on the post-Jungian horizon, certainly in this country. His weakness in professional terms, has always been that he found it hard to tolerate that anybody was ahead of him one little bit. That's to say, he could tolerate it if it came from outside Jungian analysis, but within his own Society he was, like Jung, eager only for support."

In the Society of Analytical Psychology, as I experienced it during my training and have done so ever since, there was always the power of the Fordham clan to contend with. You were either one of them or not. Because I was associated with Fred, and for other awful sins, I was never a Fordhamite and so my version of the history of analytical psychology in Britain has inevitably differed from that put forward by the followers of Fordham.

Why did Fred not start a school of analysis and therapy of his own? Why are there relatively few Plautians? The man is both modest and sceptical about his work. The modesty has led to a reluctance to invent new terminologies for old ideas or to insist that what he once memorably called "ad hoc" theories were truly revelatory. The scepticism means that Fred sees analysis as a perspective on the world or *Weltanschauung* and not as the religion he accuses some Freudian psychoanalysts of making it. These "religious" Freudians know the answers before they find them, seeking only confirmation from the patient. Fred abhors this and throughout his career he has stood out against there being any kind of orthodoxy, against the analytical thought police that are not figments of anyone's imagination. One can only say that the faction-ridden professional field of psychoanalysis would be better off if there were more Plauts amongst the established and senior contributors and fewer great founders.

There were some other insights in that interview that I would like to include in this Foreword. Fred talked about "faith" and the role it plays in the making of discoveries. In the autobiography, one constantly gets the impression that Fred is discovering obvious things time and time again – the *telos* or unconscious goal of losing things is to *discover* them again as well as merely to find them. It is a special and perhaps indefinable faith that drives Fred – "relentlessly", in his own word. Shorn of the capacity to engage in conventional religion, suspicious of the degeneration of mysticism into sentimentality that he sees around him (though not losing a mystical vision), Fred's faith is just that – faith.

Connected with this is what Fred has had to say over many years (not only in the interview) about "individuation". This concept of Jung's is making a real comeback from having been conveniently equated with ordinary development and maturation and thereby subjected to conventional, bourgeois mental health values as well as losing any specific meaning at all. Fred was in the van of this particular "return to Jung" in which individuation is released from its developmental prison and, thankfully, his particular "discovery" of Jung's concept is not in an elitist and exclusive form (which is the weakness of Jung's account) but instead is something open to Everyperson. Fred stresses the presence of psychopathology and suffering in the processes of individuation: "There is no possibility of coming anywhere near to individuation, *or even to the end of your life*, without suffering." I have added the emphasis because, although there is much joy and humour herein, there is also a helluva lot of pain and suffering, much of it worked through but some destined never to be because the author is ninety-one years old as I write. In the interview, Fred stated that his clinical values have shifted and he no longer seeks to ameliorate or eradicate symptoms. If this should happen, then it is as a by-product of the search for self-knowledge and not as a goal of the analysis. As Fred says, analysis does not depend on success any more than religion depends on miracles (a point made powerfully in his book *Analysis Analysed* (1993)).

I want to use the personal knowledge I have of Fred and his family to comment on his relations with his children. I can't be too specific but one thing that has moved me over the years is the way that Fred and his offspring have come to terms with disappointment, betrayal and rupture, managing to establish decent lines of communication and developing mutual respect. I think this comes out in the book but it might need highlighting. Part of Fred's credo is always to admit his own desire(s), and this means admitting and accepting (and forgiving himself) to as great an extent as is possible for the destruction that eros sometimes bestows. I think his children realise that this is an unordinary man in many respects and that they have to learn to take the rough with the smooth. There is a kindness in Fred that he sometimes struggles to express.

On several occasions in my life, I have experienced this kindness to a very great degree: when my then partner was having a miscarriage, when I lost a whole series of professional elections, when an important relationship broke up, when I had a sudden, terrible gastro-intestinal bleed (actually on the way to Berlin to deliver the oration at his ninetieth birthday party – as I was leaving to go home, he embraced me and said quietly into my ear "Andrew, you are a very ill man, get to a hospital." He was right. I did and survived).

Fred's current interest is in learning to paint and draw and, in taking up these arts, I feel he is returning to the theme of one of his greatest papers 'Reflections on being unable to imagine' (1966). In this paper, Fred enters the world of those individuals who have, quite literally, had to learn how to fantasise. In their early lives, or for whatever reason, the faculty of imagination has been cut off.

As I read the manuscript, my own fantasy image began to emerge. This was the image of the Wandering Jew. Any slight ambivalence Fred might have about this should be allayed by the way in which many people can see that this image stands in for the generally unsettled state of Western urban people today, well beyond what might be true for the Jews. This is particularly true in the early years of what has already been called the "century of migrations". In spite of this macro version of Fred's life, in which the resonances to collective experience are highlighted, I still do see Fred as a carrier of what I would term Jewish perspectives in the following senses. First, he knows that nothing is fixed or permanent and that to pretend that things are safe leads only to catastrophe. Next, without eschewing the irrational dimensions of life to the slightest degree, there is a ubiquitous love of "working it out" – of knowledge and reason, in all their tropes. Third, there is always a moral confrontation for both Fred and his reader: how betrayal can lead to repentance and apology and how forgiveness and the creativity that attends it can then come on stream. Finally, there is the drumbeat of the theme of being less than one's ideals, how one has to settle for losing and then finding them again.

References

Plaut, Alfred (1966) "Reflections on not being able to imagine". In *Analytical Psychology: A Modern Science*, ed. Michael Fordham, *et al.* London: Heinemann (1973).

Plaut, Alfred, (1993) *Analysis Analysed*. London and New York: Routledge.

Samuels, Andrew (1989) "Fred Plaut in conversation with Andrew Samuels". *Journal of Analytical Psychology*, 34:2, pp. 159–84.

Acknowledgements

My greatest thanks are due to my secretary, Claudia Böttger, without whose interest, orderliness and devoted help this book would never have seen the light of day. Being extremely untidy myself her qualities supplement my wish to look back at my long and eventful life in amazement. Claudia has been more collaborator than secretary. In both capacities she did splendid work for which I cannot thank her enough.

I am extremely grateful to Andrew Samuels for agreeing to write the Foreword. He is worldwide probably the best-known Jungian writer and speaker in our day. The demands made on him as professor, practising analyst and supervisor, as well as a family man with a young child would be overwhelming for any lesser person. Thank you Andrew!

Special thanks are also due to my nephew Martin Plaut, who provided me with many photographs from his father's archives.

The letters to me from C.G. Jung dated 27 March 1952, 22 September 1953 and 5 February 1957 are copyright © the Estate of C.G. Jung and are reproduced here with kind permission.

I want to express a different kind of thanks to my wife Helga Anderssen-Plaut who patiently stood by during the two-and-a-half years gestation that this book required.

To all the other persons who helped, like my agent Leslie Gardner of Artellus and Trevor Brown of Free Association Books, my heartfelt thanks.

Fred Plaut
Berlin, May 2004

Preface

Wanting to hold on to the long and eventful life that began on 8 February 1913 is my main reason for writing. By doing so, I hope to make it public that there can be joy in still being here, despite knowing for certain that all is ebbing away and that what is left can never be found again.

My far-flung and numerous offspring have also given me reason to think that they will be interested in the story the old man has to tell and get a picture of what he was like in his day and age. Just as important is my hope that I too will get to know why I am where I am today and what has become of all the other persons I have been. There were hardly any contemporaries left at the turn of the twenty-first century who could tell me. No one at all who has lived through two world wars and their aftermaths and was at home in three different countries. My life has included four marriages, four children, eight grandchildren and great-grandchildren of an as yet unpredictable number. Then there is my work in a fairly rare occupation. Psychoanalysis in all its versions and evolutions still fascinates me as much as it did at the start, fifty years ago. Work that began that long ago has become an inseparable part of me. Everybody knows that analysis has something to do with gaining self-knowledge, so a person could not be blamed for thinking that I should know myself sufficiently by now without having to write an autobiography. However, communicating knowledge by writing is different from private knowing. But the capacity for self deception is as inexhaustible as the realm of the unconscious or the presently unthinking part of the mind that emerges, unbidden, in dreams and other moments of truth, only to sink into oblivion again. Yet another cycle of finding and losing. Like life and death.

In the first place this means how much of the truth to tell or, for example, what not to tell about sex and the involvement with partners who were of more than fleeting importance. How much can one tell about encounters that were not just dependant on lust and the spice of the clandestine or illicit? Was it curiosity or seduction? Was it love, did it enter, was it mutual, did it last? How did it seem at the time, how in retrospect? The reader is entitled to be curious, the writer must give replies that at the time and for the purpose must be truthful enough. An autobiography that does not contain omissions, whether deliberate or unwitting, is unthinkable. Selection is inevitable. The criteria for it are the subtext, an unsung score as individual as one's signature.

Questioners in search of the place of love in another person's story might feel disappointed if the scent does not lead on to the trail of gratifying details. If it is sex and not love that readers are curious about, their splitting could be justified on the grounds that "love" is a word with a range of meanings so wide that its message is at once too easily understood and misunderstood. I cannot think of another word that for its meaning depends so much on the context. Why else should it have to be repeatedly declared unless a steadying word is needed to cover all contingencies in a constantly fluctuating emotional climate? Is love declared to man, woman, child or parent? Is it the love of God or gods that is meant, of nature at work, of one's family, lover – or oneself? Is it all of that? Above all, is it true, is it real? No matter: we want to hold on to it as if it guaranteed a safe anchorage.

Then again, how "real", how lasting is the reality of a relationship? Surely not as in the fairy tale's ending "they lived happily ever after," implying permanency, an outcome to which every loving couple aspires. First of all, the capacity to love has to evolve and become strong enough to withstand the ordinary disappointments. Later, the lovers, not as sure in their heart of hearts as they would like to be about the permanence of their feelings need repeated incantations of the traditional formula. This despite all vows and in the case of marriage contracts witnesses, rituals and ceremony, rings of gold, symbols of permanence, imperishability. All unreliable, as everyone knows. Reality is more like the legend about the treasure that once found after much hardship, is lost again. Were it otherwise, much of poetry, many novels, plays, operas and fairytales would never have been written and more eagerly consumed than the permanence of love would warrant. Few poets have given such clear expression to the time link between Eros and Thanatos, sex and death, as Andrew Marvell did in his poem *To his Coy Mistress*. It opens:

Had we but World enough, and Time,
This Coyness Lady were no crime.

Undaunted by such sobering realities as biological drives, ageing and material necessity, the hope remains that immaterial "love" will last forever and so bestow on the loved and loving person a degree of security. The experience of time passed has been sufficient to tell me that nothing remains as it was and now is. Every love object and relationship must float in the medium of time, vary in degree and mode of expression and finally cease to be, except, perhaps, beyond death in "loving memory". And yet, in the face of all sober reflections about the realities, the myth of enduring love has been re-enacted countless times between couples as if contracts, marital security and procreation were of no account. Since the religious promise of a continuation of life on the other side is not taken seriously anymore, generation after generation all over the globe has sought to incarnate the hope of everlasting love. Such is the strength of the longing for eternal love, so intense the investment in it that just occasionally it even seems to become a life-time reality. More often love means for the time being, a phase or temporary model for living without feeling unwanted and alone.

The most personal urge for my writing is to bring back and highlight some magical moments that were evoked by people and events. By no means all these highlights and anxieties had to do with love and happiness. On the contrary, the uncertainty caused by various excitements seems to have been the common ingredient of the moments that "transported" me beyond everyday life. Only in childhood was each ordinary day extraordinary enough to be vibrantly alive.

Reflection and focussing on the past have been my main tools. Journal notes, particularly photos and letters which I accidentally came across have helped as much as the process of writing itself. Of greatest help have been the detailed images that were entraced in my mind's eye and became recallable. Wanting to let the past rest as much as trying to revive it has determined the limits of the harvest.

My daily life revolves around two languages, German and English. I write mainly in English. Have done so for the last sixty-eight years. It comes to me most easily. It is the language in which I have lived the longest span of my life, the language of my four children and their mothers and of my grandchildren. It was the language of my first adult love. It is still the language of my closest surviving friends, of the majority of my former colleagues, patients and pupils. It remains the language in which I learned and practised medicine and had my training as a psychiatrist and analyst. But it is not my mother tongue. There is also more than a pinch of gratitude to the land that has adopted me in my fatherland-less state, so I call English my father-tongue.

"So you have gone back to Germany" people say. "Sie sind also nach Deutschland zurückgekehrt." This is true in an obvious way. It is less obvious in as much as I had never been as completely at home there like my gentile friends. Not even at a time when it would never have occurred to me that "home" could be anywhere else. I think that was because even as a child did I feel the difference between us who lighted candles in a seven-armed candelabra and our neighbours who decorated and lit their Christmas tree. It was not a trivial detail. It began to dawn on me, I cannot say at what time in my childhood, that I was, that we were, different from the other children. It certainly was brought home to me when I did not attend religious instruction at my first school. This was in Düsseldorf where I was born and went to school up to matric (Abitur) before going to university to study medicine. After the first war, that was in 1919, there seemed to be utter chaos about schooling as well as in the political climate of a defeated nation. One of my first schools was a Catholic school. We were rewarded with small colourful pictures of saints. I loved them more than I hated the ruler which was used, however lightly, for punishment. The saints deserve mentioning here because of their images which I am convinced are the "language" whether visual, acoustic, tactile, or olfactory, in which my recallable memories are stored before they can become words. Later they link up with the words, sounds and rhythm of the language all around me, even before I understand their exact significance. Aura, melody, rhythm before vocabulary and syntax.

The having "returned" so late in life is also less than true because I have not left the part of me that feels at home in England where my sons Adrian and David as well as my brother's children and a granddaughter live and where we had a family home for twenty-five years until Evelyn, their mother, died. I had come to England from South Africa where I had emigrated to when it was still a "Dominion". That was in 1933. I became a British subject before the Second

World War broke out in 1939. I had to swear "allegiance to King George V, his heirs and successors". Although I have never thought of myself as a Royalist, "allegiance" was no empty phrase.

The bilingual state of living is a different matter from being able to speak several languages, or even being a professional translator. I think of that as a skill, an act of supreme control in later years, best acquired when young. I compare it with the art of a juggler who can keep many balls in the air at the same time until at the end of his act they are caught and he becomes an ordinary person who wants his beer. Linguists, "sworn" translators and official "interpreters" are professionals like the juggler. Whereas the bilingual state of being eats deep into the person who cannot change back. A fusion has taken place between the private person and the two places and languages where I have or had a home. Is it a fusion, is it a split? I don't know.

The husband of a friend of mine was brought up in conditions that made him English as much as French. Sitting far enough away from him not to be able to hear what he said she still could tell with certainty by his posture and movements what language he was conversing in. It goes to show that living in or between two languages is quite different from putting on the translator's act. Certainly, control over the language you decide to speak is an achievement. But the bilingual person has much less control over the language that he comes out with spontaneously as compared with a deliberate juggling act. Although there is fun in the mastery of getting a translation exactly right, the test comes at unguarded moments of emotional stress that punctures the persona when the difference between the person who lives in two languages and the juggler-multilinguist is liable to show up. Suddenly a word wants to obtrude from the "other" language, whether he succeeds in guarding his tongue is a matter of discipline.

In war-time such punctures were made use of to unmask spies. No matter whether he spoke the enemy's language as well as a native speaker, if you would suddenly and unexpectedly hit him in the face, his spontaneous reaction would most likely be an earthy exclamation in his mother tongue. Of course, alcohol and other depressives would also help to reduce conscious control. I am not sure what language I would come out with on such occasions. I know that I swear in English. The language I happen to be in is more like the gear of a car. If the car suddenly were brought to a halt, the gear I had previously been in would probably decide the language in which my engine would restart. My wife, Helga and I speak German at home in Berlin. Except when I come off telephoning in English or when I have just come out of my writing. My childhood recollections I first wrote down in German.

Looking at the list of contents I notice once more how much of my life and writing shows that the person I am is inseparable from the profession I have pursued for fifty years. It is obvious in the chapters that deal with it. Especially the chapter on famous colleagues and even more so the chapters on training and practice. I cannot leave these out because their influence has shaped the person I have become. I know that many people in different walks of life have such models stored up inside them whether they are aware of it or not. I believe that I do not consciously emulate any of these. Their influence has been subtle and in some cases negative. Oftentimes during working and leisure hours I found that I was silently asking myself what would so and so have said to this situation. Without actually formulating the question, the imagined answer just comes to mind. But then, it might also be a quote from Shakespeare, Blake or Goethe. In retrospect I realise that they were all searchers like myself, only they were sure and talented enough to have found answers they were able to communicate while I am still searching, as I shall describe in the last chapter. The other fellows all had a father. Mine remained almost an unknown entity.

1 "The dear horse" – "Das liebe Pferd" 1915.

2   Family during the First World War.

3   With brother Erwin 1923.

FORM P 101

BRITISH OVERSEAS AIRWAYS CORPORATION

PASSENGER CLEARANCE

SERVICE No. 2526 . . . which please quote when making enquiries.

DATE OF DEPARTURE . . 9 . 6 . 46 . . . .

Journey by B.O.A.C.:
From: JOH To: LONDON. Ultimate Destination: LONDON.

Sponsor:		Rebate:	Invoice Fare to:	
Personal Wt. Kgs.	Baggage: Free Kgs. Excess "	Excess Baggage Allowed: Kgs.	Invoice Excess Baggage to:	

CAMERAS	✓	FIREARMS	—	CUSTOMS DECLARATION FORM:	✓	CUSTOMS EXPORT FORM:	✓	CIVILIAN CLOTHES:	✓	CURRENCY RESTRICTIONS:	V
CURRENCY COUPONS	✓	TRAVELLERS CHEQUES	—	INSURANCE	✓						

NAME OF PASSENGER: as shown on passport **MR. A.B.J. PLAUT.**

NATIONALITY: **S. AFRICAN.**

ADDRESS UNTIL DEPARTURE: **CARLTON HOTEL, JOH.**

TELEPHONE NUMBERS: Day

PERMANENT ADDRESS: if different from above **18 CECIL AVE., MELROSE, JOH.**

Night **42-4520.**

PASSPORT REQUIREMENTS	PASSPORT S. AFRICAN	NUMBER: 55866	PLACE OF ISSUE: PRETORIA.	DATE OF ISSUE: 7.6.46.	DURATION OF RESIDENCE 13 years.

Endorsements for: *Kenya, Sudan, Egypt, France, U.K.*

Visas for:

EXIT PERMIT: ENTRY PERMIT FOR:

HEALTH REQUIREMENTS	Yellow Fever: Date: 22.5.46.	Vaccination: Date: 22.5.46.

Other requirements:

EMBARKATION ARRANGEMENTS *Zanzut leaves Mauritine Horse 0400 hrs.*

REMARKS:

IT IS MOST IMPORTANT THAT YOU SHOULD READ THE "ESSENTIAL INFORMATION" BOOKLET PROMPTLY AND CAREFULLY, OTHERWISE YOU RISK NOT ONLY INCONVENIENCE BUT MAY ALSO BE SERIOUSLY DELAYED.

PLEASE LOCK **ALL** YOUR BAGGAGE.

NEXT OF KIN	Full Name: *Mrs. E. P. PLAUT,*	Relationship: **WIFE.**
	Full Postal Address: **18 CECIL AVE. MELROSE, JOH.**	Telephone No.: **42-4520.**

Interviewed by . . .

Telephone . . . . Extension . . . .

A copy of "Essential Information" booklet is acknowledged.

Time . . . . Hours L.S.T.

Date 8/6/46 :194 . . . .

Passenger's Signature . . . .

A COPY TO BE RETAINED BY THE PASSENGER THROUGHOUT JOURNEY.

4 Passenger Clearance to London in 1946.

5   Post-War London ruins.

6   The Thames at Westminster shortly after the war. Liquid history indeed.

7　Four "displaced" persons awaiting transport back to
the roof of Regency Terraces, London 1948.

8　The Sculpture Exhibition 1951.

9   With my mother, Regent's Park Gardens 1952.

10 Wedding 1949.

11   Evelyn with Adrian and David 1957.

        KÜSNACHT-ZÜRICH
SEESTRASSE 228

March 27th 1952.

Dr.A.Plaut,
25, Park Crescent,
London W.1.

Dear Dr.Plaut,

        Dr.Jung asked me to let you know that he will be glad
to make an exception and to see you when you come to Zürich.
This could be almost any time between the beginning of May and
the end of June.

        If you will write again when your plans are more
definite I will let you know about the exact possibilities.

                    Yours sincerely,

                    Mari-Jeanne Schmid.

                    Secretary.

     KÜSNACHT-ZÜRICH   22 IX 1953
SEESTRASSE 228

Dear Dr Plaut,

I have read your paper with greatest
interest. Thank you! It is most circumspect and
therefore apt to help our colleagues in the understanding
of archetypes. An English edition of "Synchronicity"
is underway. By mentioning the acausality of symbolic events you lead the reader dangerously close to
the witch's cauldron or to the creator playing dice,
Einstein's bogey. Will somebody is going to be surprised.

           Gratefully yours C.G. Jung.

KÜSNACHT-ZÜRICH
SEESTRASSE 228

5th February 1957

Dr. A. Plaut
10, Devonshire Place
L o n d o n   W.1

Dear Doctor Plaut,

The address you want is as follows: Dr. John
J. Gruesen, 2122 Mass. Ave., NW Washington 8, D.C.
As you know the mandala i.e. more strictly the quadratura
circuli is a pattern which plays the most essential
rôle in arranging psychical contents in an orderly
fashion. Accordingly you encounter mandalas very frequently in states of disorientation and chaotic confusion as a compensation. These states are based upon
strongly emotional factors reaching right down into
the spheres of the instincts. That is the reason why
I surmised that the pattern arranging emotional contents
must be localised in brainstem. It was in the case
of epilepsy where in a vision the quadratura circuli
was observed as a prodromal symptom. By an electric
stimulation of a certain place in the brainstem it became possible to elicit the same vision artificially.
It is indeed an important discovery if this find could
be confirmed. I got the news on May 18th, 1955 and I
acknowledged it on June 4th, 1955. Since then I have
not heard from Dr. Gruesen any more. Gruesen is not
the man who has made this discovery. He quotes it from
a book by Wilder Penfield and Herbert Jasper "Epilepsy
and the Functional Anatomy of the Brain" (1954).
I think you will get all the necessary data from the
book mentioned above.

Sincerely yours,

C. G. Jung

12   Letters from Jung in 1952, 1953 and 1957.

13 Onkel Joseph 1957.

14   Mosuto woman witchdoctor interviewed and photographed by
Erwin Plaut in 1957.

Telephone: WHITEHALL 4488
Telegraphic Address:—
For Inland Telegrams:
"OPPOSITELY LESQUARE LONDON"
For Overseas Telegrams:
"OPPOSITELY LONDON WC2"

SOUTH AFRICAN EMBASSY,
TRAFALGAR SQUARE,
LONDON, W.C.2.

October 12, 1964.

Dear Dr. Plaut,

I hasten to reply to your letter dated October 8, 1964, asking for a copy of the Immorality Act. This Act, No. 23 of 1957, was a consolidating Act and there have been no amendments.

Copies of Acts are not kept at this Embassy for sale or distribution but they can be obtained from the Government Printer, Pretoria. The cost of a copy of the Act - including airmail postage would be 2/6d plus/minus.

However, you would be very welcome to read the Act at your leisure and make notes in the Embassy Reference Library during normal business hours. The Embassy is open to the public from 10 to 12 and 2 to 4 p.m. from Monday to Friday.

May I remark that you have a most interesting subject to deal with. Race relations and prejudices, for the want of a better term, differ so greatly according to so many factors, including the numerical differences of the racial groups in given areas. There is, naturally one supposes, a higher or lower degree of tolerance, wishful thinking, and general moralisation according to how intimately any particular circumstance concerns the protagonist. One of the many fallacies that are propagated is a comparison between the negro problem in the States and our own problems in South Africa. There is no comparison at any stage. It is really a fascinating question and, I should have thought, quite inexhaustible in theories and ingrained prejudices and, above all perhaps, instinctive reactions. South Africans, at least speaking for myself, are surely actuated to a great extent by the instinct of self preservation backed by the white man's three centuries of intimate contact with the Bantu. It is a source of wonderment to me how, even the best meaning people, however intelligent they may be, can interpret, or pretend to interpret, the workings of the minds of other people thousands of miles away in connection with matters which are really vital to their existence. Theoretical knowledge and theories, so often based on emotionalism, make nonsense of practical problems associated with day to day existence.

Of course, your own knowledge of South Africa must be extremely helpful in discussing so important a subject. I wonder if you would agree with me that colour prejudice is

not / .....

is not synonymous with racialism?

May I ask if your paper will be published and, if so, would it be possible to obtain a copy?

With best wishes,

Yours sincerely,

H. Maclear Bate
for Director of Information

15 Letter from South African Embassy in 1964.

16 London – Berlin – Conference 1996.

17   A drawing from Andreas' art classes.

1
Losing-Finding

"It was lying here on the table and now it's gone!" Aunt Mali, all anger and despair, was storming through my grandmother's house in Detmold, where my brother (seven) and I (ten) were staying for our summer holiday – yet again. The "it" could have been different things but today it was her purse, as usual when it was most needed, just when we wanted to go out. Aunt Ella, her older sister, was incautious enough to try and calm her down. When did she last use it, had she looked in her bedroom, would she not think for a moment where she had really seen it last.

It looked as if all these appeals to reason made Mali rage even more. Tears were flowing down her red face. She started screaming. Had she not worked hard enough to earn her money and now it was gone. I was probably not the only one in the family to feel himself accused of having stolen the purse. Ella, pale in the face and trembling went on a search through the house. Mali followed her wailing that it was useless. She knew where she had put it. Time was pressing. Outside the coachman and carriage were waiting. The high point of our holidays had come, the trip to the Hermann's Denkmal, a memorial to the king of the Cheruscans, a Germanic hero who at the supposed spot on a hill overlooking the woods had defeated the invading Roman legions.

In writing this down I become aware that my grandmother kept out and left the scene to the sisters. Perhaps she knew from past experience how it would go on and left it to them to sort out. My slightly retarded Uncle Manfred, the youngest of six, put on his sympathetic face and murmured suitable words, how could something like this happen. My brother, Erwin, had escaped into the garden and was playing with the dog. I sat spellbound in the living room from which the purse had disappeared.

Suddenly Ella, close to collapsing, had a brainwave. She came back and pulled the purse out of Mali's handbag which had been lying on a chair under the table. Showing it to Mali her hand holding the purse was like an accusing finger. Far from apologising Mali was all beaming with delight like a child that had been discovered after hiding itself. Wasn't the weather nice, now we should really go at once. Manfred reflected her cheerfulness. Grandmother distributed the waiting bags and parcels that everyone had to carry to the picnic and off we went. Once in the coach, Ella put on her sunspecs and got a migraine. The coachman had to stop twice so that she could get out to vomit while Mali supported her head. Not before evening had she fully recovered.

I am not sure whether this and similar episodes point to a genetic factor but I am affected with both migraine and frequently "losing" things. My mother only lost things rarely but thoroughly. When the loss lasted for some time she became distraught and asked her Catholic friend to burn a candle to St Anthony. She often regaled us and whoever would listen to the strange and wonderful story how after this emergency measure had been taken the lost Bonds had been brought to her door by a complete stranger. That could never have happened in Detmold where my grandfather had been teacher and chairman of the Jewish congregation. The family there had no friends outside the congregation, although they were on friendly terms with all their neighbours.

I don't think my grandmother had ever heard of Bonds or Shares and kept what little money she had in the form of gold coins in a safe place for which she had chosen a beautiful coffee-can in the locked vitrine that stood in the best room of the house with exquisitely carved and upholstered chairs. To my knowledge neither the room nor the chairs nor the coffee-pot were ever used. The air there was stuffy, the atmosphere almost holy. Surely, no thief would ever think that this sanctum could also be a hiding place.

The loss of things which are needed and were "there" until a moment ago are part of my daily life. That cannot be changed. Of that I am certain. None of the psychoanalytic interpretations I have received over many years and by different analysts have made any difference. I have accepted the habit as unalterable, a pattern of behaviour, like one of Wagner's "Leitmotifs", Jung's archetype, or a signature tune. I would not be "me" without it. In the course of my long life I therefore designed ways of dealing with this endlessly repeated losing and nearly always finding. These are practical measures. As I know that some of my fellow beings are similarly affected I shall mention some steps I found useful. I regard myself as something of an expert in the matter.

As things seemed to have a will of their own and played "hide and seek" with me, I had to take countermeasures which have been so effective that I want to hand them on to fellow sufferers, although they will already have made their own inventions. I found the following useful:

- Lift your eyes and let them go round like a periscope or radar.

- Keep the colour of the lost object in mind, it can be a guide. My note books are red, present writing is in yellow folders, past in brown or green.

- Lift all papers that could serve the lost object as a hiding place. See to it that the light is good. Go round the desk and room to alter the angle from which you are looking.

- Repeat this process before getting angry or panicky and tearing open drawers or cupboards.

- Thinking "where did I last see it" is useless as I already know, see Aunt Mali. What you think you know is frequently where you *second* last saw it or left it.

- The use of hearing is obviously limited to objects that can respond to whistles or electronic impulses like my cordless telephone. How often have I wished that keys, spectacles and books could be similarly equipped. Surely this invention must already exist especially for blind people. Sometimes it seems as if I were blind too.

• When the first wave of actively searching has abated and you get out of your mini-panic as Mali in the story never did, you could, taking a deep breath, ask yourself "where would I never have left X?" Occasionally this helps. In this way I once found my cup of tea in a cupboard. More often it is more by good luck that you come upon it. This takes time. Meanwhile use a substitute, like a spare key. You may have to invent a substitute. Doing so calms me down.

• If I have difficulty in getting out of a Mali-like state I remind myself that I must treat the matter benignly, without anger. So I talk to the lost object, in my head of course, knowing full well that this is animism. "Don't think I am running after you. Just let me know when you want to come back. I have got a substitute and can do something else in the meantime." When an Aunt Ella is about, I might additionally ask for help.

• Although as an analyst I realise that with my animism I deny my fear of helplessness, I still use it much in the way my mother asked for St Anthony's assistance.

• When all the searching and thinking and the helpfulness of others has abated and I have, in a manner of speaking, given up, I may, possibly just before falling asleep, see an image of the lost article against a hitherto unsuspected background. It is like an afterthought. Then I only need to go to the place and the article believed lost is, of course, there, waiting for me. At that moment, after all the tumult and the shouting has died, a feeling of joy and gratitude floods over me so intense that I almost feel the losing has been worth it.

• Last of all I return to being an analyst and ask myself what my specific unconscious motive for losing could have been. I rarely get an answer. Getting one is no guarantee against recurrences. The reverse of finding what is lost is that some objects I additionally come across recall forgotten memories. Particularly photos and letters.

There is something between finding and losing and that is not finding what one expected yet finding it, only somehow changed. My grandmother's house, the Wehrenhagenstraße 16, Detmold, I knew as a child was situated in a modest street. It had a well looked after garden as well as a vegetable garden including fruit trees. My grandfather, Abraham Plaut had already been dead for two years before I was born. However at fifty-six he had already begotten seven children, none of whom were still alive when I recently visited the house with my wife

Helga. An invitation of the Heinens, Eugen and Sabine, had brought us to Detmold. Eugen had been to Berlin to interview me in connection with a biography he is writing about my Uncle Joseph.

The house had undergone a complete change from the one I remembered from childhood, only the facade facing the street had remained the same. That and the fence. But even that had shrunk. The high iron lances, black and silver tipped were now only half a metre high. Or was it because I had grown? That's how it is with growing up. Even the street had changed. It had been on a steep rise and cobblestoned, leading to another street at rightangles where there had been a smithy specialising in shoeing horses. The smell of burnt horn hung constantly about. Of course, it had disappeared and the Wehrenhagen had become an ordinary slightly-rising street. The daring downhill chases my brother and I had enjoyed in grandmother's garden trolley could not have been as fast as they seemed in my recollection. Gone and built over was the field that had been there before one came to No.16. Gone too was the gate consisting of even higher lances and the brass plate bearing grandfather's name. What had happened to it? Where was it now?

The entrance to the property had been moved up to the other end. Entering it one passed the wall where the morello cherry grew, protected against the birds with old net curtains. It led to the impressive new entrance door and hall. On the right of it rose a new wood-clad wing with a music salon on the first floor. On the garden floor, where the green kitchen with the zinc bath tub under the table had been there was now a white modern kitchen. The coal and potato cellar had given way to a central heating boiler and laundry. The newer used front room on the first floor had become one with the one-time living–dining room, "open daily to the public". Higher up the many small bedrooms with iron bedsteads, horse-hair sunken mattresses, marmor topped tables for porcelain water basins and cans had given way to but two modern bedrooms, hot and cold running water and bath-shower equipped. Following bourgeois manners the owners' bedroom was not on show to visitors. It might have evoked "wrong" fantasies.

Obviously Uncle Joseph after his successful return to Germany and after him the present very pleasant, welcoming couple had remodelled house and garden. What had become of the old grandmother's house in my memory? It had become part of the "me" I had been and partly remained.

2

Childhood in Germany, the First World War, School

Nose pressed flat against the window I watched the horse that had fallen and the coachman who was trying to get it onto its legs again. It was a bitter winter, icy roads. The window got misted by my breath. I was standing on a stool the better to see. The coachman had put sacking in front of the horse's hooves and was trying to pull the horse up by the reins while his mate was spanking its behind to spur it on. At last they were successful. As a reward they tied a sack full of oats around its neck. It had taken several attempts because the horse having half got up slithered down again. From early childhood the horse has been my favourite animal. I first had a small wooden horse; later I got an upholstered one on wheels on which I could ride through our flat. Like its predecessor it was known as "the dear horse" (see Plate 1).

In those days there were fewer motor cars than horsedrawn vehicles in the street and, of course, also a tram. Quite the most exciting horses were the greys. They drew the fire-engines as they galloped through the streets while a fireman rang the bell to clear the traffic out of the way. What a wonderful job! When I asked why the fire-engines were drawn by greys I was usually told: "because the others are at the Front". Only much later did I understand that white was more visible than dark and therefore the greys would be more exposed to enemy fire. Much later still, during the Second World War, I learned that new wars usually start with the technical equipment with which the previous war had ended. The first had ended by the invention of tanks and planes. At the end of the Second World War air superiority seemed to be decisive.

The next time I saw dark horses was when a squadron of Ulans trotted by, lances held high in their left hand, black and white pennants fluttering at the top. It was a beautiful sight, their smiles suggested victory. The children's nurse accompanying me smiled back. Together we offered a box of cigarettes. The Ulans bent down from their saddles and skilfully helped themselves without having to come to a halt.

The bells of the church at the end of our road had rung more frequently than usual. I had been used to their ringing from birth and also their striking telling us the time. Earlier they only rang on holidays and Sundays, or special occasions like funerals. When I asked why they now rang more often, I was told it was because of yet another victory. When the war had ended my mother said: "We have been victorious unto death." She was bitterly disappointed as probably the whole population was. Soon my father returned from the war. But he was ill having contracted a bad throat infection, followed by rheumatic fever. Half a year later he suddenly died of an embolism. My father's return and death as well as my mother's mourning have all become one and of equal importance with the end of the war. As a child and a man who grew up without a father I recognised that these events have been of far reaching importance in my life. I shall go into that more fully.

I had regarded my childhood as having been an averagely happy one. Retrospection adds a note of sadness to what it must really have been like at the time. Although the circumstances were not all that extraordinary, when taken together with the social expectations and historical events, there remains an air of tragedy in the way that past generations with many children on both sides of the family have been reduced from a lively stream to a mere trickle. The numerous tribe has been reduced to a few survivors of which I am the eldest.

There exists a photograph showing my father, Hermann Plaut, in uniform working apparently in an office with his comrades and smoking a pipe. How solid, *bodenständig, gemütlich* pipe-smokers have always struck me. Maybe it is the caring relationship between themselves and their pipes that gives that impression. It is not unlike the love with which gardeners look after their garden. I never smoked a pipe, the idea did not occur to me.

I can show another photograph (Plate 2), a highly conventional piece, showing my father and the whole family, probably dating back to 1917. I also possess a family tree dating back to 1758 showing that all the Plauts come from a small village, Willingshausen in the province of Hessen, pretty near the centre of Germany, and had the then usual large number of children. My father was the forth of seven. My grandparents belong to the first generation who did not live and die where they were born. I belong to the fifth.

My mother, née Friederike Wolf, got married rather late in life, I think around the age of thirty-five or thirty-six. It must have been a year or so after her partner in business, Clara Brender, had got married when the original firm and partnership, which was called "Wolf and Heller," both their maiden names, came to an end. My mother retained the name as that of her firm. I have often wondered how it was that she got married at all. She had plenty of character and humour but was not beautiful, as I realised even as a child. She was determined to make our childhood, my brother's and mine, a happy one because, as she often said, hers had been unhappy. Her father must have died when she was about 10, possibly earlier, but the point was that, after his death, her mother never did another stroke of housework. Mother used a German phrase that meant her mother stopped all caring and cooking. It conveyed that she had gone into a deep depression from which she never recovered. I was not told the cause of death and I, with the tactfulness peculiar to children when they sense that there is a dark secret, did not press the question. There would have been plenty of opportunity when I accompanied her on her frequent Sunday visits, weekly at first, to my father's grave and after that to her mother's. I never knew where her father was buried. In much later years I wondered whether her mother had committed suicide.

I never knew enough about my mother's own parents. Nor did she. But with the certainty with which children can sniff out what they are not supposed to know I knew that there was a skeleton in the cupboard. Perhaps even two. The reason I was given was good enough to explain why my mother and her brother had to be adopted, although not formally, by relatives. She into the family of her great-cousin, the redoubtable matriarch Aunt Lina whose husband had also died early. Lina's mother, the still more formidable and witty Aunt Rosa, source of many wise and humorous sayings and sagas, was no longer about – at least not in the flesh – when I was born. Her husband had also died prematurely but that may be the wrong word. On both sides of my family, perhaps all families at that time, the husbands died when they had generated some half-a-dozen children. Nature's own way to stop a population explosion? Perhaps, but it certainly produced many capable and stern mamas.

My other uncle, Joseph – my mother's brother – was nearly the same age. He was a solitary bloke. He had married, was childless. Almost a recluse outside the family that had brought him up with my mother, he seemed to have no-one but his wife and must have done some humble clerical job in his foster-father's firm. But all that seemed entirely irrelevant. For as far as I could see, and that was infrequently, although they lived in nearby Cologne, most of his waking hours he was wrapped up in the endless rituals of his religion. What changes there were, were connected with the phases of the moon and, of course, the seasons. Christianity adopted a new calendar with fixed dates for its festivals; Jews stuck to the calendar year according to the moon. In the Christian Gregorian Calendar only Easter and Whitsun remained set by it. In comparison with her brother and other relatives my mother was a heathen. She ate forbidden food and worked, if necessary, on Saturdays. But she had a conscience about not going to the synagogue on high holidays and would have liked us to do the same. We refused. My brother first.

It was her sense of humour and her bravery in hard times that made my mother remarkable. First, my father's absence during most of the first war, his illness and death shortly after it. Before she met him she had managed her modish made-to-measure tailoring salon alone and successfully employed some eight seamstresses. After her partner's marriage she was alone again as she had been during and after the war. At the time of the rampant inflation of the twenties most of her dress materials were stolen when thieves broke in while we were on holiday. Insurance covered a roll of yarn. Ten years later her customers had to leave her because of the Nazi regime. Emigration had meant a new life for me. She and others of her age and older lost the ground from under their feet to regain it only at their burials. To become fluent in another language after sixty had not come easily. In Cape Town mother had lived in a furnished room not far from my brother, his wife and my daughter. But she ended up like my aunts Mali and Toni in the Jewish Old Age Home in Johannesburg. I was in England looking after a young family. But Mother Rieke had deserved a medal and much more love than I gave her. When I realised it, it was too late.

I remember very clearly the day my father died. It was on 4 April 1919, shortly after my sixth birthday. After he had returned from the war, I saw him mainly in bed. It was the twin bed next to my mother's that I had slept in while he was away. Whenever he had been home on leave I was of course moved out into another room, which I shared with the maid. My father had only been drafted in 1915, having at first been declared unfit for service because of his partial deafness following an attack of measles in childhood. It was also due to this deafness, at first not recognised in the small principality of Detmold, that I think he had been regarded as not very bright. At any rate, he had been apprenticed to a tailor. On account of his deafness he had been excused from the year of military service that any healthy German of his age would have had to do. The peace-time service would have qualified him later on to become either a non-commissioned officer or officer in case of mobilisation. As it was, he only became a private soldier in the Reserve. He seemed to have had a very bad time of it because, according to my mother, he swore that he would see to it that his sons would never have to go to war. I also recall vividly the parcels, the tinned conserves of meat which my mother used to send him via the Red Cross to wherever he was stationed.

Among my childhood recollections a particularly bright picture turns up of a Sunday morning. I might have been four or five. I am lying in my father's bed which means it was during the war. My mother is sorting out fresh linen. She has loosened the golden silk ribbons which held each staple together. The sun is shining through the linen curtains with their flowery bands. I cannot see enough of the fine dust which has taken on the colours of the rainbow and is whirling about in the sunbeam. My mother is humming a tune to herself. I have already asked her to bring out the box containing her jewellery. Now she brings it out from its hiding place where no thief would ever have discovered it. It is made of Japanese lacquer, shining black, discretely decorated with a little golden paint. The doors of this miniature cupboard had of course been locked. Now they are open and reveal six drawers. I take one after the other out and admire the rings and necklaces, but I know already what it is I want to see most. It is the finest work of art that had ever been created, a silver brooch stuck on a small cushion of lilac silk. How is it possible that this shepherd with his long flute blowing above the backs of the sheep of ever decreasing size has come to life, although I know it is only a silver brooch. Do they move when I am not looking? I am wrapped in these reflections when my mother says it is long past getting up time. She seems to ask herself whether it is a bad thing to get up so late. The time must have been near ten o'clock.

A different kind of recollection from a later age stands out in equal detail. It happened when Mother and I visited Father one Sunday – I was about three – at Ürdingen, the place where he was in barracks, presumably in training before being sent to the front. I was shown where he slept in a dormitory with rough bunks, three, one above the other. I was taken for a walk by one of his comrades while he and my mother obviously had intercourse in the empty barracks. I could sense the air of complicity and their happy smiles when I came back and could guess the rest. It nevertheless was a slightly mystifying experience, which had made me jealous of their togetherness. My anxiety not to let my mother out of my sight was, I assume, dating back to this episode. After my father had died, I suffered from nightmares. Murderers everywhere. Predictably, the light switches would not work.

To the eye signals "not in front of the children" I responded by pretending not to have noticed what she and the children's nurse talked about. Children still play the same game, although the sexual behaviour of adults is no longer a guarded area. It was not only tact that made me adopt the "see not, hear not, speak not" posturing. The aim was to make them reveal more, if "they" believed that I was blind and deaf and apparently engrossed in playing. Occasionally it succeeded. Seldom did they remember that "little pitchers have big ears". Had they forgotten their own childhood? Later the grown-ups became more careful and spoke French. I only knew why.

One does not have to be an analyst to realise that a son's jealousy of the father can be displaced and added to that of a brother, even though mine was the younger. He was the upstart, the rival that I had been during my father's short presence. On one occasion, when I was about eight, I had knocked my brother out in a fight and had the fright of my life, fearing that I had killed him. The maid sprinkled water in his face and alarmed my mother, who came running upstairs. Fortunately, Erwin had already regained consciousness. But the fear of having killed him was still alive when he died at the age of eighty. During the last years of his life, we had got on famously which remains a great comfort and I still miss him, although during most of our adult lives we were separated by the distance between Cape Town and Johannesburg, later London.

The scene of all the early events was the house where I was born at Blumenstraße 7. It was an apartment house purpose built, like many others at the beginning of the century. It was divided into spacious flats. There were shops on the ground and offices on the first floor, where my mother's business was situated. It consisted of a large atelier in which dresses were made to measure, later assisted by more than half-a-dozen girls, some highly specialised, and one "directrice", comparable to a manageress, and also apprentices. Mother had been trained in Düsseldorf by a Herr Scheuer, who himself had been trained in Paris.

The other apartment on that floor was occupied by the office of a solicitor, Dr Lucas, a very nice man indeed, a widower who became a friend of my mother's. He was always very protective and kind to her and to us. She had hired a pantry, or storage room, in his flat, which played a vital part during the first years of my life in the First World War. I remember little about cans and jars on the shelves, which were much higher than me, but a blue and grey stone jar on the floor containing eggs in a kind of jelly forms a very clear image. The cellar was also the laundry for the whole house. A very large iron kettle was heated from below. On washing days steam filled the air like fog accompanied by an unmistakable smell. Upstairs in the loft the washing would be hung up and dried just under the roof. The maids of the house had their small bedrooms next to it. I must have been about four when a siren went off in the night. It probably was towards the end of the First World War. According to the grown-ups, this meant "Englische Flieger" (English planes). One night one could hear the thump of a distant explosion. But nothing further happened and when we were ready to go down into the cellar, the siren sounded the all-clear and we went back to sleep.

My mother earned enough to keep us in middle-class style, fee-paying schools and holidays included. She did so by copying and cutting out of dresses and costumes that she had seen or designed herself. After the war, she went to Paris twice a year to see the new collections of the big fashion houses. The public was strictly forbidden to sketch while the models paraded as they still do. Nevertheless my mother made notes and sketches. Then came the measuring and fitting of her customers, some of whom I still remember because we were called downstairs to say hello and shake hands with the corpulent ladies, who exclaimed how much we had grown. We hated it. A fair bit of gossiping must have been going on between my mother and her customers. One of them told her that we, my brother and I, were her best capital investment. This too was repeatedly quoted. The message was clear, repayment for all the "happiness" would be expected. The happiness expected of us consisted particularly of being taken on holidays, sending us to fee-paying schools, seeing that we got good food. My mother even made some of our clothes, for instance the sailor suits in which we were photographed (Plate 3).

Mother had of course to employ people for the household and us children all the time because she could not be looking after her business, fitting her clients, do the necessary buying and travelling as well as looking after the household. On Sundays, she did the cooking herself. I most particularly remember the home-made ice-cream – I can still see the machine that worked by turning the handle. It seemed to take ages before the milky fluid changed into stiff ice-cream. The ice around the cylindrical container had been delivered in huge blocks which had to be broken up. Half a block was enough for our icebox, where it slowly melted, keeping cool the contents in the zinc-lined compartments on either side. Daily a tap would be turned to drain off the ice that had melted. The icebox was situated in the passage near the kitchen, where a coal-fired oven and later a gas cooker stood. The kitchen itself was lit by gaslight, the mantle of which always glowed and became bright when one pulled a chain above the kitchen table. The other rooms in the house were lit by electricity, the staircase by an extremely dim carbon-filament bulb. The house was not very beautiful. I realised that even at an early age although the windows on the staircase were of stained glass, matching the outside with an Art Nouveau mosaic design laid into the cement screed. The front entrance was guarded by an iron gate that was wound up from the cellar by the caretaker at night. I don't know what all this anxiety was about. I think a lot of it was based on a medieval superstitious fear of darkness. The burglary I mentioned remained a horrible memory especially as the *directrice* was under suspicion because it looked like an inside job. I dreamed about burglars for many years. Anyway, it seemed a great tragedy, which no doubt brought my mother to the verge of bankruptcy.

My brother Erwin was born on 1 December 1915. The date confirmed my suspicions that he was conceived on the occasion I mentioned just before my father left for the war. I had insisted that I would get a sister and not a brother. My mother quoted me as saying "they say it is a little boy, but I insist that it is a little girl". In the end I compromised by deciding that it was an "it". I remember standing on my toes by his crib, looking down and remarking to my mother "It has already got fingers!" Seeing those little fingers sticking out of the white knitwear, I marvelled at this work of art. Something adorable anyway. The relation to my brother became difficult early on because we were very different personalities and of course we picked on each other's weaknesses terribly easily. I know that he both looked up to me as well as being extremely jealous of me because I was the first born and my mother's favourite. This became a terrible burden and responsibility after my father had died because I felt that my mother regarded me as a substitute for him and that is what I both wanted to be and refused as it threatened me being myself. A pattern that was repeated in later marriages.

My brother remained very jealous of me and made no bones about it. Later I realised that I in turn envied him his freedom to be cheeky to our mother. He could make her laugh when she tried to be angry. As we grew up, mother made her plan known whereby she would run the household for my brother and myself until she felt that her days were numbered when she would choose wives for us. She often complained later on in life – I still feel guilty as I remember it – that she had expected her old age to be so much nicer and so much kinder to her and that she was bitterly disappointed especially in me. I had by then removed myself to England. That is another story but the fact remains that I left both my mother and my first wife behind in South Africa.

My brother's wife, Faith, had turned very much against my mother and my brother was much too weak to do anything else but to follow his wife's feelings. I did nothing to come to the rescue, pleading small children and a living to be made abroad. My mother died feeling unloved and unwanted. I think she got a lot of satisfaction during her years in Cape Town where she cared about my younger daughter Helen as she had done in Johannesburg for Geraldine while her mother and I were in Kenya. The close bond between the three of them is gratefully remembered to this day. Geraldine had gone with her architect husband to live in East Africa.

As I focus on my childhood other episodes come to mind. One of the nursemaids discussed with her fiancé on our walk how she should word the notice she would give my mother. They agreed that "mein Mann trägt des Kaiser's Soldatenrock" ("my fiancé wears the Emperor's uniform") should come into it. Sure enough when we got home the formula was repeated when she gave notice.

On another walk with another nanny a soldier began to chat her up. He must have persuaded her to continue the walk with me while she went shopping. It began to rain. We stood under a tree on the "Napoleonsberg". Standing behind me he slipped his hand down into my trousers. I remember that he was a very small man. I don't remember any sensations, only my astonishment. When I talked about it at home, my story was called "eine Räuberpistole" (a cock-and-bull story). It may well be that I was not believed because I told the event in a distorted way and the children's maid who had left me in the tender care of the homosexual was more eloquent in covering up her mistake.

The French soldiers of the army of occupation in the Rhineland were rather short. By contrast their bayonets were long which was very striking when they were fixed on top of their rifles. They paraded with short quick steps with an exaggerated swing of the free arm to the sound of a military band. My friend and

I were fascinated and did our best to imitate the parade, marching, trumpets and all. I heard the same monotonous tune at a village fête some forty years later when I visited the Loire district with my son Adrian. It seemed to go on all day. We were in fits of laughter.

The French uniform and helmets were a bluish-grey, in contrast to the Belgians on the left bank of the Rhine who wore a kind of khaki-green. We were intrigued by the tassels that hang down from the pointed tip of their caps almost to the root of their noses swinging to and fro with every step they took. As I am writing I wonder whether they were designed as a kind of fly-swish for soldiers serving in what had been the Belgian Congo. About that time too I remember a fantasy on my way home from school that I was a giant with an enormous broom sweeping both the French and Belgian armies into the Rhine. The analyst whom I told this 80 years later interpreted it as an early sign of my omnipotence. I had hoped it was an expression of patriotism or at least of an identification with the Fatherland. So let us call it a projected form of omnipotence that would have received praise at that time.

Children become fascinated by the sensational events reported in war times. The imagination of boys finds expression in play and drawings. I observed it in my own sons when they were little and I also saw it when I worked as child psychiatrist in a child guidance clinic and in private practice. The rattle of machine guns, their falling down dead, the enemy's planes being shot down in flames. Girls seem comparatively immune to this identification. There is no glamour for them in killing as such but war-heroes are romantically admired.

In my childhood I had been fascinated by two books. One from when I was around four, a picture book with captions. It was called *Vater ist im Kriege* (Father is in the war). It illustrated and glorified all the various regiments of imperial Germany. I remembered the one about "Landwehr im Schützengraben" (homeguard in the trenches). The accompanying verse had stuck in my mind, probably because it referred to my father's regiment. Eighty three years later I confirmed my recollection. To my surprise the book could be found in the Staatsbibliothek, Unter den Linden, Berlin. It was obviously a children's book, sponsored by the Union of German mothers for "Kriegskinder". The cover was almost Victorian, the illustrations and words were crude but just as I had remembered. The librarian was helpful and attested that the text I had written down before I had opened the book corresponded word for word to the printed text: "Bärtige Männer alte Knaben, Landwehr liegt im Schützengraben" (Bearded men, old boys, homeguard entrenched). The other regimental picture and verse referred to the pioneer corps. I had also remembered it correctly but had omitted the opening line to the effect that the words followed had been spoken by the Kaiser himself. He, as it seemed was not needed in my recollection.

"Es sprach der Kaiser mit Vertraun: / Wenn alles stürzt und fällt, / was deutsche Pioniere baun, das hält."
The emperor spoke with confidence, / Though everything else may collapse and fall, / What German pioneers have built will hold.

I knew that I had a good memory and realise that childhood memories last when much more recent events are forgotten as is the case with old people.

The second book was called: *Aus Tsing-Tao entkommen.* It could also be found in the library, a bigger tome of some two hundred pages, written for adolescents it included some badly staged photographic illustrations. The selection my memory had made was specific. It centred around one single sentence to the effect that the landmine, laid in preparation of the enemy's attack, was ready, "Herr Oberleutnant". Would I have remembered this particular sentence so clearly if I had not been thrilled by it at the time? The officer so addressed by his Sergeant, remarked that this sounded like music in his ears. Actually, the text said "angel's music". The mine's explosion was of course timed to kill or wound as many enemies as possible. "Angel's music" indeed. Of course, I heard the same sentiments expressed in much coarser language during the Second World War when I had been thrilled by Churchill's speeches and horrified by Hitler's.

Shining the torch light of memory into early childhood, brought back a third book, one of my early reads that I read over and over. My memory had been in error though when I attributed it to Graf von Spee who had indeed been one of the German sea heroes. A battleship in the Second World War was called after him. But the title *Seeadler* was right and my secretary Claudia using the internet found the right author, Graf von Luckner. There it was. The picture of a sailing ship on the cover that had stayed in my memory. Not suspecting that such an old fashioned sailing ship could be an armed raider, much allied tonnage became her prey. How thrilling for boys whose minds are in any case easily captured by war-time heroics. Luckner, always a gentleman towards his captured enemies, took them aboard or saw to it that they had a chance of survival before sinking their ships.

Reflecting on my rediscovery of early childhood reading, I am again astonished by the strength and ruthlessness of the aggressive drive from the beginning of life on. The extremely complex ways by which our memories work, including of course, falsification, are obviously influenced by the emotional impact made, whether repeated or repressed. It is not as if I had recited these fragments to anyone during the intervening eighty years. The words came back as I focussed on writing about my childhood.

Some fifteen years after the Second World War when I lived with my wife Evelyn and my family in Jordans, Buckinghamshire, we all watched the hilarious BBC television serial "Dad's Army". It centred on a reserve battalion, the Home Guard, and was very funny. I don't think that German film makers would have had much success with a film that made fun of one of their own military units. So much for one suspected difference in national characteristics.

My brother and I had shared my mother's love of light opera, the music of Humperdinck and Offenbach as well as Weber and Meyerbeer. Nearer to adolescence Richard Tauber's sentimental (schmalzige) voice made us dream of things to come.

In our teen years my friend Ernst was the one I was sent to because I would not eat and he had a healthy appetite. Later we played war together with all the make-shift accessories we could lay our hands on. A few years on we exchanged fantasies about Karl May's books about Winnetu and the Red Indians. After that phase our heroes became the leaders of polar expeditions. The names of Nansen, Amundsen, Scott and Shackleton still come to mind. Our children would find it strange that the conquest of the poles had only just happened when I was born, just like our grandchildren will find it strange that the first man to set foot on the moon was the cosmic event in the childhood of their fathers. My elder son, Adrian, was not yet one when Mount Everest was conquered.

In our adolescence, radio with crystal sets and earphones had become available and we listened spellbound to the ringside reports of the heavy-weight stars. Schmeling, Dempsey, Tuney come to mind. Later our parents arranged for tennis lessons. Tennis and especially the highpoint, Wimbledon, became our obsession. Borotra was the absolute star in our day. He was French and called "the bounding Basque" because of his leaps. His athleticism was admirable at a time when tennis was played in long white trousers, but nothing compared with Boris Becker in our age, who catapults the whole of his body horizontally into the air to play the ball. All that became small fry as puberty turned our heads to dancing lessons and the pursuit of girls, girls, girls.

Far and away the most famous member of the Plaut family was Onkel Joseph (see Plate 13). One of the three first names my parents gave me is after him. A glance at the family tree shows that he and I are not the only Josephs. The other name my ancestors could think of was Hermann. One Biblical, the other typically German. Up to the catastrophe the Plauts were one of the oldest Jewish families in Germany. Joseph was my father's older brother, the third of seven surviving children. Born 1879, died 1966.

The Plaut family lived then in Detmold, which was a small principality in the heart of Germany. Joseph's local patriotism paid off handsomely in the form of a song dating back to the 1870/71 war with France. It is a sad-sentimental and at the same time tragic-comic ditty about a soldier from Detmold who was first wounded and then killed by bullets. Joseph made it famous. He sang it with the local dialect. Later many other accents became one of Joseph's strong points. In his second book called *Das heitere Plaut Buch* (The Cheerful Plaut Book) he tells us how in the Army during the First World War he had the unique opportunity to get to know local dialects and expressions of various moods. The purpose of his art, so he wrote, was to make people forget their everyday worries. I had the satisfaction to witness his success on several occasions. A grateful town has named a street after him. His high school (Gymnasium Leopoldinum) recently dedicated an evening of its 400th anniversary celebrations to my uncle.

Onkel Joseph was a complete extravert, from childhood on determined to be taken notice of. In his book *Hille-Bille* he describes how he achieved fame among the boys of his neighbourhood by swallowing live flies. Having hidden his self-disgust, he then proceeded to entertain his public by burning his arm with the help of the sun and a magnifying glass pretending to the admiring youths that he felt no pain.

Apparently he was a good scholar but instead of completing his studies there, he took up singing lessons and soon got on to the stage as a singer. When I was a child I saw him twice as such. Once as the swineherd in the *Gypsy-Baron*, the other time as the prison-warder in *The Bat*. I did not recognise Onkel Joseph in either part which was as it should be. Later still Joseph gave up opera singing and for a short while became an actor. But that too cannot have been his true metier. He really found himself as an entertainer with a unique mixture of humour, sentiment and drama. He travelled all over Germany in a chauffeur-driven car giving "Joseph Plaut Evenings". I remember a large Buick and also standing next to him at the Hotel Four Seasons ("Vier Jahreszeiten") looking down. Seeing the Buick he said: "A car to be proud of." His was the art of a storyteller, an art that has become rare in our time.

Joseph was not alone among the artists I got to know to be supremely selfish. When after the First World War rationing was severe, he came on a flying visit and had a meal with us but he also ate the whole of the family's butter ration. He must have noticed the looks that passed between my mother and our nanny, for he felt it necessary to explain "my body needs fat".

I admired my uncle for his vitality and guts. During the war years as a refugee in England he had made a meagre living by giving singing lessons, and the occasional "evenings" to the German-speaking community, mainly refugees. He returned to Germany immediately after the war. Then aged sixty-seven, he resumed his career and did extremely well appearing also in films and on the radio. He reconstructed his parental home and lived again with his wife. Being an "Aryan" she had obtained a divorce. I found this rather dishonourable but she may have acted under duress.

Joseph and his sister Mali whom I had mentioned at the beginning had admired one another. Judging by the correspondence, their relationship came close to being a life-long love-affair. And indeed they had much in common. In addition, they resembled each other facially much like twins which was to Mali's disadvantage. They were completely alien to my nature. My kind of love for them was that of the exploring "otherness" type, as I shall describe in the chapter "Reflecting on various kinds of love".

3

The Rise of Nazism

How can I explain that when I told my friends and former classmates "Only a war can end this", they were without exception of the opinion that the rule of National Socialism was a temporary affair. Three months, perhaps six, then the officer's corps would restore order, bureaucracy and democracy, but whatever would happen "this" could not last. We had met shortly after Hitler had become chancellor in January 1933 when I was already a medical student.

During the time of the occupation of the Rhineland I had observed both at schools as well as in my own fantasies that there was a widespread denial of defeat. Germany had not lost the war and would soon show the world once more that it was *"über Alles"* as the national anthem went. Hitler explained the loss of the First World War as the result of "treason". A popular myth. At the Gymnasium it had been customary that, before breaking up for Christmas holidays, the teacher would offer us a choice between reading or telling us a story. The year was 1923, almost five years after the end of the First World War. We were unanimous about wanting them to tell us something of their war-time experience. Their personal accounts did not make out that things were any better than they had been. I remember some gruesome details. We listened enthralled and enacted some events with toy bayonets and pistols when we got home.

At my own school, steel helmets with a swastika made their appearance on blackboards and as miniatures in buttonholes from the mid-twenties on. Later a classmate appeared clad in a brown shirt with a swastika armband, some three or four years before Hitler became chancellor. At the time of writing, another world war and more than fifty years later, the same phenomena can be observed in some public places of Germany. Emigrants are being attacked and occasionally murdered. Jewish cemeteries and synagogues are being desecrated. The government is seriously worried on account of the German image and the possible economic consequences. Also, public memory of genocide is still too close for comfort. Neo-Nazis declare that concentration camps never existed. Something drastic as well as educative had to be done. In fairness, I must add that I have never been personally troubled; on the contrary, teachers and fellow pupils and German colleagues accepted me as one of their own or, at least, as a long-lost brother. It has generally been my experience that when people really get to know each other on a friendly basis, the anti-race, anti-religion, anti-national feelings diminish. Nothing more effective than to see at close quarters the personal suffering and bereavement of the "other" that the media cannot convey.

I therefore had to ask myself two questions. How is it that anti-Semitism in Germany took and still takes on a more violent form than anywhere else in the world? And: What made it possible that during the bitter trench warfare of the First World War, the enemies for a brief and sentiment-laden moment celebrated Christmas together before returning to their killing duty? I arrived at a multicausal answer. The love of order, in itself a flight from threatening chaos, seemed to me only part of the answer. Even in concentration camps the authorities responsible kept inventories about all the details of their victim's mobile possessions, such as their wedding rings and gold teeth, of which they were divested. In no other field of human activity finds this love clearer expression than in militarism, where the aggressive drives are channelled by order and discipline, where timing and rhythm, often accompanied by music, give a thrill to those who watch spectacles like the changing of the guards, or the fly-past of fighter planes that require total machine-like co-ordination and the carrying out of "orders". The quasi-religious adoration of flags, insignia uniforms and decorations; the liberation from one's personal conscience and individual responsibility is another essential constituent; so is the joy of belonging to a group of comrades all with the same unquestioning loyalty and submission to a leader. Here the individual status of modern men and women is suspended as the unique human being becomes a "detail", as a single soldier in the British army is called. A cog in the machine. Add further the relief from having to think and judge for oneself, now replaced by the absolutely clear distinction between "us" = "good" and "they", the enemy, = "bad". The might of propaganda will teach and nurture this regression to a childlike single track of mind when self-preservation or self-sacrifice rule the day and the killing of enemies creates heroes, the equal of media stars in peace-time.

Now apply all these constituents to the hidden "enemy of the people", the usurper and traitor within one's own country whose existence is as insidious as it is parasitic and all at once genocide begins to make some horrific sense. The habitation and property that the alien race had acquired by stealth and cunning could now be handed back to the rightful owners, "the Aryans". This return of their "stolen" poverty became "*Arianisierung*". Add to this the stirred-up anger, the love of order, the punctiliousness of carrying out instructions and the keeping of records like the number of gold teeth removed from corpses and you have some of the ingredients that were required to create concentration camps, extermination machines. Even a visit to a former camp is enough to shake one's belief that man is superior to animals. Nobody could have foreseen this in the twenties and not even at the beginning of Hitler's reign. The unbelievable becomes only analysable in retrospect. Despite my multicausal answer to the question why anti-Semitism in Germany exploded in a more violent form than elsewhere, the Holocaust remains in the end an incomprehensible phenomenon. I had unwillingly taken in the ingredients mentioned and knew that I myself would as a German have been vulnerable to these influences of propaganda. Today I ask myself how any Jew who heard the brown-shirted demonstrators sing in the streets:

"Und wenn's Judenblut vom Messer spritzt, dann geht's nochmal so gut"
"And when Jewish blood spurts from the knife, all will be twice as well"
and the chorus shouting:

"Deutschland erwache! Juda verrecke!"
"Germany awake! Jews perish!"
could have been so deaf and blind as not to prepare for emigration. The main source of disbelief was not so much the understandable reluctance of established people to uproot themselves, but the extraordinary degree of assimilation of German Jewry, of which I shall presently give an extreme example.

The patriotism of the majority of German Jews was well established in my own family. My mother voted Deutsche Volkspartei, which was a right-wing party. Her clients, mostly gentiles, mainly voted Deutsche National Partei, the party closest to Adolf Hitler's Nationalsozialistische Deutsche Arbeiterpartei (NSDAP). Its members were predominantly Lutherans; Catholics in those years voted often more Zentrum. I remember when as a youngster my mother took me to Synagogue the Rabbi prayed to God: *"Sei mit unserem schwer geprüften deutschen Vaterland."* "Be with our severely tried German Fatherland." Several years later the rabbi was beaten up in front of the tabernacle.

The event I am about to describe remains for me an extreme example of the assimilation of German Jewry. It took place at Freiburg when I joined one of the student clubs, not unlike the American fraternities and sororities except for the origin and traditions on which the German *Verbindungen* are based. Their nationalism was historical. I had joined one of the Jewish student clubs called "Neo-Friburgia". I would probably have joined another had they not excluded Jews. This too was by tradition. It was laid down in their statutes which distinguished them from similar clubs in other countries where exclusion is by tacit agreement. The German love of order makes paragraphs obligatory. I joined the Neo-Friburgia because it had a ski hut where members could stay for a time during the season. I wanted to take advantage of this facility and intended to quit the club again before it came to the other peculiarity, namely that it was a *schlagende Verbindung*, meaning that the members went in for duelling by sword, resulting in scars in the face, called *Schmisse*, an easily recognisable lifelong honourable wound. The men so marked would regard themselves as an elite. The Neo-Friburgia's rites, including their initiation and beer-drinking rituals, their student caps and coloured bands worn obliquely across the chest were an exact replica of their German Christian counterparts. But the ultimate caricature of assimilation consisted of an imitation: a paragraph in the constitution of the Neo-Friburgia excluded Christians from becoming members. This is still as shameful as it was ridiculous, because there was not the remotest chance of it ever being put to the test.

As for the second question, the enemies celebrating Christmas together, how it could be that the hatred could suddenly subside and almost turn into the opposite. The answer seems to be that under the sway of equal deprivation and dangers and with the help of a common ritual a strange kind of neighbourliness is created. Both sides can see, as if through a tear in a thick curtain of fog that human suffering and hopes are alike on both sides. The official enemies can exchange tokens of love before returning to the duty of killing each other. It was like an ecumenical Service between Jews and Mohammedans.

4

A Major Journey

Against the opposition from the side of my mother's influential relatives, I succeeded finally in getting their blessings and my mother's support to study medicine. One of their daughter's had become a doctor and had studied in Bonn. My first lodgings there were with the same family. I was happy to have got away from home, to have loafed as students were free to do in pre-war Germany, made friends and had generally a good time.

The study of the first two and a half years, or five terms (semesters), included anatomy, physiology, physics and chemistry. One was free to study for as many semesters as one wished at as many universities as one liked. Only if one wanted to present oneself for examinations, did one have to have the professor's and other faculty members' signature, that you had been to their lectures. Provided a person had enough to live on they could become "eternal students". I chose to study for two semesters at Freiburg before returning to Bonn to sit for the pre-clinical examination (*Physikum*), the passing of which entitled one to begin with the clinical or bed-side medicine. Already in 1933, a new regulation was introduced that a person had to have a "Certificate of Prussian Citizenship" to study further at Bonn, thereby excluding all foreigners. My American friends had to go home. It became certain that I had no future in Germany.

My first and most important major journey took place when I was twenty and emigrated to South Africa having stopped over in England. It was at the beginning of November 1933 after I had passed the Physikum at the end of the summer term. In the correspondence that preceded my emigration my passing was the condition the university in Johannesburg (University of the Witwatersrand) had made of crediting me with two years of preclinical studies. I had actually been at university the usual two-and-a-half years so I lost only half a year. All arrangements had been made beforehand by correspondence. Accordingly I could begin my third year in January 1934. But the intervening journey and waiting time had been tense and anxious. In the end all went according to plan.

The details of my good-byes from Düsseldorf, my former class-mates, friends and family have, significantly, escaped my recollection. I am pretty certain that my mother and brother were already in Berlin where my mother worked for Aunt Mali and Erwin underwent an apprenticeship with a carpenter. All travel documents had been put at my disposal by the South African relatives. I was already in possession of a German passport with a brown paper cover imprinted in black with an eagle. At that time the emblem did not wear an imperial crown or a swastika nor did the word *"Jude"* appear on the cover as would have been the case later on.

Virulent anti-Semitism was already visible in the streets, on posters and in national socialist newspapers like *Der Völkische Beobachter*, public attention was drawn by warning notices on the windows of Jewish-owned shops. Worst of all were the songs of the brown-shirted SA marching through the streets, shouting their anti-Semitic slogans. A man called Streicher edited the paper *Der Stürmer* (related to storm but in the context "The Angry Man"). In sadistic detail it reported the castration of a Jew who had slept with a Christian ("Aryan") girl.

I was aware that the police, who, in my childhood fantasies had so often rescued me from thieves and murderers, would now have been powerless to protect me from being attacked in broad daylight. It was a nightmare that could become reality at any moment.

Then one evening my train from Düsseldorf to Hoek van Holland got up steam and departed. It seemed to stop at the customs for hours. Various officials walked or ran up and down the train. I was alone with my luggage in the compartment in semidarkness. After an endless time the train set in motion again. First station Arnhem. Safety at last. I took a deep breath and relaxed. Not until then had I let myself become aware of the excitement of an adventure from which there would be no home coming. Today people say to me "you have come back". It may look like that. But I have not. Although I have a home in Berlin but I am not at home as I was in Düsseldorf, the Rheinland, of my youth.

The gentle rocking of the ferry during the night crossing to Dover made me happy. That my mother and brother had remained in Nazi Germany did not worry me. As I shared the cabin with three young Englishmen, my country and the past were forgotten. I was over the top. When my companions complimented me on speaking English so well already, I was almost angry; that was not good enough!

I had not shut an eye when my cousin Charlie, Dolly's brother, met me at Waterloo Station. It was a grey, drizzly November morning when he took me to a miserable hotel in the vicinity of Euston and St Pancras Station. No sooner had I got to my bed when I fell asleep. Later Charlie came round to collect me in his small open-top car to show me a bit of London. Ten years earlier he had come to visit us in Düsseldorf. He had been in the British Army at the time when the whole South African family was on their first visit after the war. Seen from South Africa, England was "overseas", seen from England Germany would have been the "Continent". Charlie showed me Speaker's Corner and, at the other end of Park Lane, Hyde Park Corner. Buzzing around in his little car in the circulating traffic there made me quite giddy.

The lifts at Liberty's impressed me more than anything else I saw. It was that one apparently did not walk into a lift at all but into another room, panelled like the rest in dark wood. After waiting for a while the door would shut and the room would begin to shudder and swing slightly as it slowly ascended. The very opposite of the small cells of the dangerous "paternoster" in the recently built high-rise office block in Düsseldorf that not many years ago my friend and I had played in.

A few days later Charlie took me to the boat train going to Tilbury Docks where the SS *Gloucester Castle* was waiting for her passengers. With her 8,000 tons she was a relatively small ship. In Hamburg I had seen the *Bremen* that later was given an English name. According to our guide she was part of the post-war "reparations" handed over to the Americans as a condition of the peace treaty of Versailles. I think she was about four times the size of the *Gloucester Castle* which was a ship of the Union Castle Line that specialised in the South Africa passenger service. She was only an "intermediate vessel", stopping at small harbours and taking nearly three times as long as the Royal Mail boats to and from Cape Town. In our case we called at Tenerife, Ascension Island and St Helena where we delivered a soldier with his wife and rifle. He had been sent there to do guard duties, so that another soldier could go home. I asked myself whether an equally monotonous job in a more boring environment could be found anywhere else.

We were six to the cabin situated just above the stern of the ship, the steerage class. It had one porthole. Its location became very noticeable in stormy seas when the propeller came out of the water and made the whole ship shudder, but especially the deck. One had got used to the regular revolutions and engine noise. Only the silence was loud when the engines stopped. But then again my three weeks' passage only cost £25 which even at that time was cheap. I found the life on board so exciting that I hardly noticed the discomfort and the boring food. We third class passengers had to organise most of the entertainment ourselves, for instance a boxing match all quite professionally organised by a fellow passenger who also acted as umpire. My opponent was well matched for weight and age and, probably, experience too. (I had gone to a class when I was a student at Bonn.) He happened to be Rosemary's brother. I had fallen in love with her at the time. The family came from Northern Rhodesia, now Zambia. The fight ended in a draw. Rosemary and I corresponded for a while. Our umpire knew his job as he gave a good imitation of a professional. He had introduced me as representing Germany which even at the time appeared ironical to me.

No-one in the third class and probably on the whole ship knew a word of German. Most fellow passengers were Cockneys, from the East End of London, and a few were Scots or Irish. That gave me the opportunity to increase my vocabulary and knowledge of the language and different accents.

But not only that. On board I had my first taste of the British working-class style of life, as determined by mealtimes, games and other rituals. Even in our part of the ship, "the steerage", were we woken up by the steward with an early morning cup of tea. "Specially sweet this morning", said the steward who knew all that went on when he came to the bunk of one cabin mate who had spent most of the night on the boat deck. The boat deck was high up and a place of ill repute, almost like a redlight district because that is where couples met after dark. The main meal of the day took place towards evening, English working-class people's "high tea". Other rituals consisted of the shipping line's traditional entertainment programme, in which the stewards and occasionally other members of the crew took part. There was the daily sweepstake, betting about the mileage the ship had sailed during the past twenty-four hours. As we approached the equator the sailors changed from navy blue uniforms into white tropical gear. The "crossing of the line" was something special for passengers, especially those who had never crossed the equator before. Neptune and his masked assistants came on board to "baptise" us by tilting the barber's chair so that the person in it tipped over into the swimming pool, much to the enjoyment of the experienced travellers and onlookers. The pool was a small crudely rigged-up affair of scaffolding, ropes and waterproofed canvas. Afterwards, we got a certificate protecting us from further baptisms at future crossings.

I had no fears about the future, no home-sickness as I was standing alone at night on the deck above the stern where I had my first sight of the starry southern sky. And what a sight it was! The long awaited Southern Cross had replaced the Great Bear. The milky way seemed like a solid arch across the sky. The depth of blue gave luminosity and a three-dimensionality such as I could never have imagined. On a few nights the sea itself was phosphorescent, alive with myriads of microbes stirred up by the ship's propeller. Other spectacles were provided by shoals of flying fish and by the native coin divers at one of the Canary Islands who were already awaiting us when we called.

The sight of the "starry heavens above" that had inspired Kant has remained a source of awe and comfort to me ever since. At that time it helped not to feel singled out as an alien and refugee. The irrelevance of an individual life was made obvious by the sight of eternity, as was also the puniness of the human race dreaming of immortality. From that perspective time was forgotten. Then back again into the turmoil and excitements of daily living. Timelessness found once more when in mourning.

Anyhow, the show must go on; the fancy-dress ball for adults and children. All classes took part. Prizes were allotted by a special committee. Everybody got some sort of prize. Another occasion was the gala dinner, when the captain or maybe one of the officers, who usually dined in first class, joined us steerage passengers. Deck games, like table tennis and deck quoits, were a daily feature.

With so many people to a cabin and the sexes in our class separated even if they were respectably married people, it was difficult for those who found the boat deck too uncomfortable. On one occasion we had all agreed to stay away from our cabin so that an elderly – they seemed much too ancient to me for such things – couple could have intercourse. How could they possibly, I asked myself. I guess they must have been at least twice my age, that is over forty!

Indeed the journey seemed a long one. It took even longer than the expected twenty-one days. The more surprising when one considered that "the Scot" had made the journey in 1891 in the record time of fourteen-and-a-half days, a record that remained unbroken for forty-three years. When I was a child my grandmother in Detmold allowed three or four weeks for her letters to reach "the children" in Cape Town. When I moved to London in 1946 airletters from and to my mother and the family in South Africa took a week; now we have e-mail.

I digress here about the accelerating means of communication from my early youth on up to today's instantaneity. It helps me to remain aware of the length of time I have lived. Other reminders are, of course, the growing up of children, the birth of grandchildren and great-grandchildren. Most effective, however are the decrepitude of age and the death of loved ones, contemporaries and friends, colleagues and patients all younger than myself. Time and again this comes as a shock. Unfortunately, in common with the starry skies and other awe-inspiring spectacles, even shocks are repeatedly lost sight of and I go on living as though there was no tomorrow. Just one more cycle of finding and losing, until the losing becomes final.

The ship's progress was especially slow during the last two days when she pitched and rolled as we were tossed about by the "Cape rollers". Just at that point, the engines had stalled. I was one of the few passengers who was not sea sick. Tables and chairs in the dining room were bolted down. Things that were not rolled around. The smell of vomit was everywhere. The ship's engineer was the most wanted person. He was called "Mac", generically because he was nearly always a Scot. (Much like in the army, the electrician was called "Sparks".)

At long last, one morning there it was, the Cape of Good Hope, a sight for sore eyes. Table Mountain was in bright sunlight with its "tablecloth", white clouds pouring over the top, blown by the notorious Southeaster. It looked like milk that was boiling over. The pilot came on board, tugboats arrived, the quay drew closer, the engines came to a halt and we made fast where a small crowd had been standing awaiting our arrival at the dockside. Even before that passengers and people had been excitedly recognising and hailing each other. I was beginning to feel lost when an elderly man from below asked whether I was Fred Plaut. Great was my relief when my identity was confirmed. With him was a young man, the son of the former family doctor Carr, at whose house at Seapoint, just below the "Lion's Head", a part of Table Mountain, I was to stay for two days before catching the train up to Johannesburg. It took nearly that long for my legs to get used to being on firm land. They were still anticipating the rolling of the ship.

Young Carr and I slept upstairs on an ample veranda, in South Africa called a *stoep*. Although it was summer now, the nights were cool and beautifully starry. I slept more soundly than I had done for weeks. Young Carr was a first generation South African and my senior as a medical student. He introduced me to the geography of the town and its peculiar relation to the Cape Point at the tip of a peninsula while the mountain divided Table Bay from False Bay. The inside of the house impressed me as darkly luxurious with its highly polished dark red "stink wood" furniture and tiled floors. The evening meal was taken in the dining room. A black manservant wearing a white uniform with a red sash across the shoulder and white gloves served. The same uniform was worn by all those who served dinner to Whites throughout South Africa. This was my introduction to the function of the "native" in the house of "Europeans", as all white persons were called. Two smaller groups of the population were the "Cape Coloureds" offspring of the mixed blood, reflecting the Cape's history. "Asiatics" consisted mainly of Indians, Malays and Chinese. The "natives" had their separate quarters at the back of the house. The Japanese were privileged not to be classed as "Asiatics", I guess because of important trade relations. South Africa exported gold and minerals, in exchange for "finished goods" mainly from Japan.

I was soon to learn more about the racial laws and social distinctions that were to prevail for all the years I lived in South Africa and for some time beyond my emigration to England. The laws that made the term "apartheid" well-known beyond the borders of Southern Africa came later. They had originated from a much earlier date, as I was to discover when I was able to get a better perspective on the matter that caused so much racial prejudice and injustice. The answer I got to my letter to the South African Embassy, London in 1964 shows the typical defence against the accusation of racism (Plate 15).

But first I had to learn how easy it is to persuade anybody who is as young and immature as I was that he is somewhat "better" or superior to others, particularly when "they" were black and "we", people like ourselves, were white Europeans; even if that meant South Africans.

A girl friend who was at home on the farm told me that it was with black people exactly like breaking in a horse, you must teach them first who is master. After that you can treat them kindly. And yet they would steal from you. "Black people know no gratitude" was a statement I often heard. But unconsciously there was fear, an awareness of being in a minority. The "lager" mentality of the *Voortrekkers*, the Africanders who pioneered the interior and the north of the land, the Transvaal, the rich gold and mineral bearing country that was discovered and developed by the white man north of the Vaal river. Had it not been for the superiority of the rifle over bows and arrows they could never have conquered the land and declared it their own. The day when the last warring Zulu king had finally been vanquished, Dingaan's Day, was still celebrated each year while I lived in South Africa.

When I first arrived in the "Union of South Africa" the country had already advanced from being a Crown Colony to having Dominion status. The Governor General representing King George V signed my commission as Lieutenant to the Defence Force in November 1939. It was at that time no lesser person than: "His Excellency the Right Honourable Sir Patrick Duncan, A Member of His Majesty's Most Honourable Privy Council, Knight Grand Cross of the Most Distinguished Order of Saint Michael and Saint George, One of His Majesty's Counsel learned in the Law, Doctor of Laws, Governor-General of the Union of South Africa". What an anachronism it all has become in my lifetime. Much later, in 1961, South Africa became a completely independent republic with English and Afrikaans as the two official languages. Since then the hateful segregation and inequality of races, apartheid, ceased and as the result of the first non-racial election in 1993 the long-term prisoner, Nelson Mandela, elected Prime Minister, instituted the Truth and Reconciliation Commission (1995). It meant that everybody who admitted to having acted cruelly against the blacks would be forgiven, if they confessed to it! A truly Christian Act of Forgiveness to the former enemies, the whites. I was moved to tears when I heard about it. Two emergent facts have become significant for me. The white missionaries had failed to make the Afrikaans and English population see in the blacks their brothers and sisters as equals. On the contrary their interpretation of the Bible was, at best, suited to protect the "natives" as one would children. Thereby the whites helped themselves to riches. At worst, they opposed attempts of emancipation with mental cruelty and physical torture. On the reverse side of this enormous step towards equality is the multiplicity of languages, eleven in all, now declared as official. In practice this means that the citizens either have to be superb linguists, or, more likely, English as the *lingua franca*. Much as happened in India, I think. Morally and for the political future I feel that more than was lost has been found. But to keep it will require unceasing effort. Instead, South Africa is experiencing a "brain-drain", which it cannot afford. By still having close relatives there I participate in all that happens.

On return from one of my frequent visits since I had left South Africa I wrote in 1964 to the Embassy in London asking for a copy of the Immorality Act since I was writing a paper on race relations. It was the year in which Nelson Mandela was imprisoned on Robben Island where he spent eighteen years of his twenty six years in prison. Nelson Mandela had been one of the leading figures of the ANC (African National Council). What I had noticed on my 1964 visit was a marked increase in anxiety and tension among the white population. One night from between ten or eleven o'clock all lights went out. Looking outside the house we noticed that the whole of the Cape peninsula was in darkness. Next morning I went out early to buy a paper to see what had happened. I met my sister-in-law on the stairs and told her. "Oh, you won't find anything about that in the papers" was the quick reply that told me more than I had known. The Act for which I sent as well as the Embassy's reply made it even clearer how "the instinct of self preservation" would have to be implemented.*

Had not Hitler in *Mein Kampf* justified his anti-Semitism in similar terms? But that is where the comparison ends. It was easy for Hitler to exterminate the Jewish minority without depriving the German people of their livelihood. On the contrary, it looked as if they could "Aryanise" with impunity all that they were told the Jewish usurpers had robbed them of. By contrast the white South African economy could not have existed without black labour. White people, "other people thousands of miles away", "best meaning, however intelligent they may be", were apparently still dense enough not to understand the important distinction between colour prejudice (good) and racialism (bad). The two should by no means be regarded as synonymous. South Africans, at least speaking for themselves, were surely actuated by the instinct of self-preservation, backed by the white man's three centuries of contact with the Bantu.

I have been fortunate indeed to survive Hitler and to live long enough to see Mandela emerge from the years of his imprisonment to become not only Prime Minister of his country but to rule with absolute fairness. It was the first of two bloodless revolutions I have been privileged to witness, the second being the fall of the Berlin wall (1989) and the reunion of East and West Germany. To have lived through and witnessed both I regard as little short of miraculous. Certainly they were the best political events during my lifetime.

* This and the following quotations are taken from the Director of Information's letter I received in answer from the South African Embassy, London, dated 12 October 1964 (see Plate 15).

5

Johannesburg in the Thirties
and Medical School

My education in matters social continued on the train journey to my destination, Johannesburg. When I looked at the table showing the train reservation, I could not find my name among the second class passengers. Someone found it for me among the first class. I connected this happy surprise with my duty call on a friend of the family the day before my departure. He was a lawyer as well as a Member of Parliament. It was my first personal encounter with the importance of knowing the right people.

There were only four bunks to the compartment instead of six, as in the second class. My fellow passengers turned out to be companions from the boat. It seemed to be customary for anybody who could possibly afford the greater comfort of the journey to the north to travel first class. It took over thirty hours. Both first and second class were for Europeans only. Blacks had to travel in separate wagons. I am not sure whether "Asiatics", mainly Indians, could have travelled second class. They, along with "Cape coloureds" were granted an in-between status on the railways and in some public places like sports grounds and racecourses. Benches in public parks were marked "Europeans only". That was the synonym for white people, who prided themselves on truly being South Africans.

The Blacks were pejoratively called "Kaffirs" particularly by the less educated Europeans. It was also widely used as a swear word. When I asked what the word meant nobody knew. I looked it up and found it had an interesting historical origin. It came from the Arabic *Caffre* meaning "infidel", or heathen; the name for all people outside the Muslim faith. The black Bantu had come from the Arab-dominated north before they, in turn, conquered the Hottentots, who had driven the previous population of Bushmen out of the Cape. So Kaffir would have made sense, if it were not used demeaningly. I also heard the name used collectively for gold mining shares. The diminutive *kaffirkje* was used by some Afrikanders when they spoke lovingly to their babies.

My fellow travellers spent most of their waking hours drinking beer and playing cards. I was fascinated by the landscape, the like of which I had not known before, the semi-desert of the Karoo, through which the train climbed its way. At de Aar, we got out. The steam engine needed water after the long uphill journey. Then on through the Orange Free State and across the Vaal River into the Transvaal to Johannesburg, where I was met at the station by the family.

The family was represented by my father's elder sister, Toni, who had emigrated to the Cape in 1902. Aunt Toni had three children, Percy and Charlie whom I mentioned earlier, and Dolly, the youngest. Uncle Bernhard founded an import business and must have done quite well. Shortly after the First World War Dolly was sent to a "finishing" establishment in Switzerland. Even without this final touch she was a lovely, intelligent person. Everybody loved her, so I had been no exception.

Dolly and Jim's house was at 33 Escombe Avenue, Park Town West, a smart suburb on the tramline to the zoo. It was situated on the slope of a rocky outcrop leading down to an exclusive golf club. The house was a bungalow, built on stilts at the lower-lying front where there was also room for the garage and the 'native quarters' for the black servants – cook, house, and garden "boys". The shopping was generally done by the housewife herself who got up early to drive to the market. The white nanny slept in the house, like the rest of the family. I was pleased with my small bedroom-cum-study situated at the back without any view because of the terraces above. There were also the three small children and a dog. Rooms were found for my mother and, temporarily, brother, who had arrived later. Like most of the houses at the time ours had a corrugated iron roof. No hailstones would go through, but on the "tin" roof they sounded like a cannonade, making conversation impossible for the duration of the downpour. Afterwards the sun would shine and the earth gave off a delicious vapour.

With exception of the bathroom facilities the house with the increased number of occupants did not seem crammed. This was probably thanks to the wide "stoeps" front and back of the house and the grounds in which it stood. The maid and the gardener, "the boy" and "the girl", lived in an outhouse next to the garage. All this was as standard as the entertainments were, mainly the Bioscope (cinema), tennis, bridge parties. My cousin aspired to more. So he played polo. A cushy life made strenuous only by having to keep up with the neighbours and if possible, be one up on them; same with the cars. Standard for the middle class were Plymouth, Dodge, "Chevies", later Chryslers.

It was not as if the family was only boringly bourgeois. Some interesting people came to the house. I remember Colonel Patterson who had commanded the Jewish Brigade in Palestine during the First World War and had the highest regard for these soldiers, more for those who came direct from Russia rather than from America. He had also written a thrilling book *The Man Eaters of Tsavo*. When the railway from Mombassa to Nairobi was being built the workers in their tents were regularly attacked at night, killed and partly devoured by lions who had developed a taste for human flesh. Several hunters tried their luck until one of them succeeded in shooting the chief murderer and was duly fêted by the surviving tribesmen.

Brother Erwin, independent as ever, earned money by being a salesman in a furniture shop and moved into a furnished flat in town. My mother, well over sixty, still worked in a sweat shop for Aunt Mali, a pretty good slave driver. Being a student I also was dependant on her paying the fees. My mother's highlight of the week was to go with me to the tearoom in the Botanical Gardens, by taking the tram down from the top of our road. My favourite cake consisted of scones and "fig-konfeit" (preserve) with whipped cream. I still had the healthy appetite of an adolescent. She enjoyed being able to "treat" me. This went on until I qualified when the hard working life of a doctor began in earnest and did not end before I was eighty-six. But in my mid-twenties it was all fun. My mother had been a splendid person who did not receive the recognition she deserved (see Chapter 2 above) – at least not from me.

It was a half-an-hour's walk from Escombe Avenue to Hospital Hill where the medical school was situated. Just above it was the "Native Hospital" for black and coloured patients with an out-patient department where on Saturday nights all available hands, including advanced medical students and dressers were kept busy sewing up the often severely bashed up scalps that resulted from drunken fights among the mine workers. More often than not the fight originated from feuds between different tribes.

Above the hospital, on top of the hill was the "Fort", used as a native prison and a source of supply of extremely cheap labour. The prisoners came in "gangs" of six to ten men together with a white warder with a 303 rifle who dozed in the shadow of a tree while they did their earthmoving labour in their own steady rhythm often in the gardens of the Europeans. This would last a day or more.

Opposite the medical school was the back entrance to the Johannesburg General Hospital. At the foot of the hill was Joubert Park, so named after the Boer War General Petrus Jacobus Joubert, a contemporary of General J.C. Smuts who at that time commanded the Afrikander forces against Britain, made the peace that was the beginning of the white-dominated South Africa first as a Dominion (1910), later as a Sovereign Republic (1961) of which Smuts was Prime Minister and Field Marshall during the Second World War. Much later, of course, in 1990 Nelson Mandela was finally released from his long imprisonment which mostly had been served on Robben Island, the South African version of "Devil's Island".

But to return to the time and place in question. Below Joubert Park on the other side of the railway lay the sports ground Wanderers, also used as a greyhound racing track. It was the last green breathing space before one came to the railway station and the city crowded with its office blocks and shops neatly laid out at right angles. Here and there some covered passages with corrugated roofs and wrought ironwork and pillars spoke of the first permanent buildings after the mining camp days.

The atmosphere of a mining dorp or "dump" as it was pejoratively called, lay heavily and feverishly over this commercial centre of a country that still lived on its mineral wealth. Not for nothing had Johannesburg been given the by-name "e-Goli", City of Gold, as the blacks called it. Other reminders were gambling and the heavy drinking of spirits. Although the liquor laws controlled the production and sale of alcohol, they were constantly being contravened. The blacks to whom no alcoholic drinks were allowed to be sold, brewed their own traditional kafir beer as they had always done in their villages. Police raids might destroy illicit breweries and stills but were powerless against the brewing that went on in the native "townships" on the outskirts of the city. Ramshackle old buses, overcrowded hence called "porcupines", because of arms, legs and heads sticking out, brought the workers from their township into town and back.

The gambling, I had been introduced to by my card-playing travelling companions on the train journey up to Johannesburg. Dice was played by blacks on the pavement. The whole adult white population seemed to dabble in shares on the stock exchange which exploded whenever prospectors discovered a new gold-bearing vein, deep underground. It collapsed again on rumours that the soil had been "salted". The gambling spirit even pervaded the students' common room in the form of card games and talk about fathers' shares. It was the second most popular gossip after bragging about sexual exploits, largely with prostitutes, who had been and were, along with publicans, the classical camp-followers of the pioneer mining days.

The yellowish-white mine dumps, refuse of the chemical refining process, lay as glaring hills around Johannesburg in the almost permanent sunshine. Until a grass was found that could grow on the stuff with soil binding effect, dust blew from the dumps on cold and dry winter days. Entertainment consisted mainly of dance-halls and the cinema. In the largest of these Archie Parkhouse appeared from below stage during the intervals to play his "Schmalz" on the "mighty Wurlitzer organ".

From the station one went down the main street, Eloff Street, to Market Street where my cousin's office was. He gave me a holiday job to encode and decode telegrams to Japanese firms with which he traded. In the evenings on the way home, there were queues of cars. Stopping at the traffic lights, black boys darted in and out, selling the main paper of the day, the *Evening Star*, containing the share prices at the time of going to press. Quick work.

I was given driving lessons as a birthday present and depended on saving pocket money and the loan of a car to take nurses out. My English improved rapidly. It was good enough to pass English language at matriculation standard, including of course English literature at the end of my first year. This was obligatory in order to proceed with one's medical studies. Afrikaans as official language would have been the alternative. But the medium of the University of the Witwatersrand, "Wits" for short, was English whereas in nearby Pretoria, the administrative capital it was Afrikaans.

There were twenty to thirty students in my year; only five of them women. The class was divided into three socially and racially distinct groups, those of English speaking stock, the Afrikanders of Dutch, Scandinavian or Huguenot origin, and Jews whose parents had emigrated mainly from Eastern Europe. This was still the case when twenty-seven years later Helen, my younger daughter, went to the University of Pretoria. Practically no mingling occurred between these distinct social groups of students. There had been none at all between their parents. Our teachers were mainly native English speakers, some of Scottish descent, the majority had qualified "overseas", a magical word in the South Africa of that time. Even today it has not lost all its halo-effect among the whites and some of the blacks. Understandably, because the country with all its indigenous problems still aspires to Western standards of civilisation based on the political principle of democracy. The historical export of Africa, gold and slaves, was still prominent. Slaves, of course, in the form of cheap and more or less forced labour, was regarded by the majority of whites as if they were the God-given order of things. The best they could do was to look after their charges, give them their best cast-offs and let them go home for holidays. The proviso was that they would never grow up into equals. Perhaps in a hundred years. They were not yet high enough up the evolutionary scale.

The Dean of the Medical School, Professor Raymond Dart was the only one to have an international reputation as anthropologist and anatomist. On arrival he received me as the first specimen from a German university to come his way. He asked whether I was of Jewish descent, alias a refugee. When I affirmed he ended the interview. Not, I thought, out of anti-Semitic feelings but because I had not come to his faculty on account of his reputation. When I told him that I had to be an in-patient for four weeks on account of my duodenal ulcer he expressed his doubts whether I was able to catch up with the curriculum as well as pass the English exam within the year. Dart never knew how much his doubts helped my determination to manage both. When after my internship I applied for a job, he gave me a glowing report.

Another memorable figure was a lecturer of Greek origin, hairy and genial by nature, Menoff by name. He lectured on surface anatomy and medical examination. The principle of "eyes first and foremost, hands last and least" was drummed in. Then came the question: "When you have used your eyes, what do you do then?" I proudly announced: "you palpitate". Lecturer and class collapsed in a gale of laughter while I blushed. The answer would of course have been "palpate", use your hands carefully. But mine was not wrong enough to be accounted for by my imperfect English. The increased heartbeat, palpitations, before the next step of examining the patient was the involuntary truth and the true cause for applause. Menoff kindly explained to me and I could then join in the laughter.

The German and English academic system of teaching at university level could not have been more different than they were in my time. The following differences may not be widely known. My main reason for mentioning these is to show that our stereotyped ideas for what is typically German, "orderly", and what English, "liberal", do not hold true when looked at in detail. Our wanting to generalise and classify is due to mankind's besetting sin, laziness of mind, rather than unbiased observations. The German notion of being a student had still something romantic about it. The responsibility of passing examinations was in my time left to the student himself with the result that one could easily become a beer-swilling eternal student (*ewiger Student*) if one's father was well enough off and willing to support one. In medicine there were only two exams, the pre-clinical and the final or *Staatsexamen*, rightly called so because it was the State itself that gave you the licence to practice as a doctor. The examinations were more oral and practical than written. In Germany it was only after the *Staatsexamen* that one required a *Doktorvater*, that is, an academically qualified tutor to supervise one's writing of an academic thesis. At a further oral examination one had to "defend" one's thesis. If successful, the applicant was given the academic title "doctor" to which the faculty was added, like MD or PhD, doctor of medicine or philosophy respectively.

At the English or English medium universities written "tests" on the subjects lectured seemed to come along every six weeks or at least once a term. A list of results together with the marks achieved by each student was displayed. "Marks" expressed percentages of perfection to tell students and teachers how well or badly we had done. There were three terms per year, not two Semester as in German-speaking universities. Students had "tutors" in most faculties who supervised one's studies. Time before finishing studies was limited. The student's responsibility for his studies was limited by the system itself. The most important part of exams consisted of written papers, set beforehand and strictly guarded by the Board of Examiners. However, a list of exam papers set in previous years was freely available and eagerly read by students. As the number of questions on subjects was not infinite, we tried to "spot" which one was likely to turn up again. We could then prepare ourselves accordingly. I can't say that it helped in the end but in our anxiety to pass and get high marks we resorted to this kind of oracle.

English university seemed like a continuation of high school, one felt more like a pupil than a student. Parliament (the "State") had devolved responsibility to a professional body, the General Medical Council to watch over the standards of all teaching institutions and licence (or unlicence) the individual practitioner. All executive power was in its hands. It still keeps a watchful eye on training, practice and ethics. Parliament, the Ministry of Health, collaborates with the GMC.

After qualifying I became a houseman (intern) at the Johannesburg General Hospital. My major interest, apart from nurses, was in objective measurements, laboratory tests, x-rays. Electrocardiography too but this was still in its infancy. No sonography yet. My first paper, written in collaboration with a laboratory colleague was about a patient suffering from a special kind of anaemia.

Shortly after that my interest changed from medicine to surgery. Here something could effectively be done. Dramatic results occurred. The patients in the wards were younger. Fewer died. There was glamour surrounding the surgeon worshipped by his team. I was allowed to play my part for minor ops at which I had previously assisted. But I knew I was not cut out for the job. My hands were not skilful enough. Gradually I became more concerned with what made a person tick, in short their psychology and its importance in sickness and health. But whatever my special interest were to be, the next step had to be getting experience in general practice by doing locums and to earn money to buy a car and to pay off the loan from Aunt Mali for my studies.

6

South Africa, Races, Locums, Quacks and a Witchdoctor

By the time I had done my year as "houseman" in medicine and surgery I was living at Aunt Mali's house. It was the base from which I did locums in the country, substituting for resident doctors who were either ill or on leave. The really incredible burden on my mind at that time was Pat in her pregnant state.

Pat had come out from England with a bunch of nursing sisters. She was six years older than I. Although there was a shortage of trained nursing staff at the time, it was an open secret that it would be easier to find a husband there than in England. Whether true or not, the belief probably dates back to the white man's pioneering days in the colonies when most of the new arrivals were men and there was a dirth of marriageable women in the country. Some early settlers had managed to get wives-to-be from their countries but many more became fathers of children by native women. In this way a whole new section of the population arose, the so called "Cape Coloureds". The laws against "miscegenation" which I shall quote later must be read against this historical background, as must be the idea that made Pat and her colleagues come out to South Africa in the thirties. Pat had been sent to look after me when I had a severe attack of measles and from that meeting our relationship had started resulting in her becoming pregnant with Geraldine.

She then went back to England to her relatives and friends awaiting my decision to marry her, "to make an honest woman of her", as the Victorians would have had it. Pat called it "to protect" her. These were the years from 1938 on to the outbreak of war. I must have hoped for a miracle to solve the problem while my suppressed guilt grew and I had not spoken to anyone about it. I felt totally alone and even enjoyed the exciting and diverting year during which I got to know the country and its population as I could not have done in a better way than acting as a locum doctor. The divided state of mind I was living in at twenty-five would surely have proved intolerable later on in life.

My jobs were seldom for more than four weeks and took me to all four provinces, mostly around the Transvaal, particularly the "Rand". Much the most interesting locums were in the country. I travelled between locums in a second-hand Chevrolet coupé with two spare wheels. They were badly needed as the earth roads were often corrugated. One had to ride over these at a certain speed so as to reduce being shaken up. Tyres did not have the strength of today's; punctures or bursts from iron nails were not infrequent. The dust cloud that followed in the wake of every car was a curse. It was best not to be overtaken. On the other hand there was very little traffic on the country roads. Gates that were used to keep the cattle on the farm to which they belonged had to be opened and shut again. But it was a wonderful silence that could "heard" when one stopped by the roadside to mend a puncture or to rest rather than fall asleep at the wheel during the heat of the day – no radios in cars yet.

An increasing hum from a long way off would announce the approach of another car. It depended on the lie of the land whether the sound came before or after the sight of the dust cloud that warned: windows up, quickly. Large herds of sheep or cattle watched over by a little black boy, a "piccaninny", with a large whip often blocked the roads.

Prieska was the name of a small-town in the Northern Cape. I arrived in the heat of the day after a long drive. Trying to find the house of the doctor I was to replace I drove to the market place. Midday, heat. Not a soul to be seen. I was fatigued and had not noticed the curbstone until I drove over it. A loud explosion; both front tyres burst. Someone came out of the garage and showed me the way after we had changed wheels. The doctor showed me over his dispensary. Most medical practices in the country did their own dispensing; the list of his regulars also gave the ingredients of their medicine. He warned me not to change the colour of their medicines as then they would do no good. My "principal", as the resident doctor was called in Prieska, whose work I was temporarily to do, had been a South African volunteer in the First World War and showed me his souvenirs, a gas mask and a haversack. The possibility of a Second World War was in the air. The nice manager of the local asbestos mine confirmed this. He made an important statement when he told me about the time he had signed on as a volunteer. "My feet were so light, I did not feel the ground I was walking on", he said. Today I wonder whether the sudden relief from responsibility for one's own life and future, the feeling of comradeship and the jubilation received from the population do not play an important role in making young men volunteer to join the army and go to war joyfully – the previous slaughter already forgotten. The death of comrades made them united in anger against the politicians who had sent them there but had themselves stayed safely at home.

Asbestos was called "garn" by the local native miners, the Afrikaans word for cotton, the fibrous threads of which it resembled. They all would eventually succumb to asbestosis of the lung. The Miners' Compensation Act could not compensate for their lost lives, it only eased the medical aid and the financial hardship of the years to follow. Asbestos was wanted because of its incombustible quality, until it was discovered that the extremely fine dust emanating even from the finished asbestos articles remained dangerous. Roofs generally and even the walls of the primitive huts I saw were made of asbestos sheets.

The doctor in Prieska also functioned as Assistant District Surgeon. When he had left I received a call to attend a post-mortem investigation at Postmasburg, nearly 200 miles to the north. The temperature was around forty degrees. No air conditioning of course. The district surgeon looked at the rope mark around the dead man's neck and said: "I know what he died of, don't you?" Great was my relief that we could leave it at that and have a cold beer instead of opening up the corpse in that stifling heat.

The distances are great in this arid and sparsely populated part. The earth road led through sheep farms of enormous acreage because the sheep had very little vegetation for their grazing. People did not think twice about driving one hundred miles, if there was a dance on a neighbouring farm. What else was there by way of entertainment? Hardly a cinema anywhere.

Alcohol was a bad antidote to boredom. So was sex. One English-speaking couple had called me out to their farm. The real reason turned out to be not the vaguely defined complaint they had given over the phone, but the husband's impotence. They were derelicts. Could I not do something to restore his potency. She was quite sober when she complained: "I played with that thing for hours, nothing happens." I got angry about their wasting my time. Still, the incident had helped me to see the danger people were in when cut off from their roots and civilisation. I was to see more of that later on among the "colonials" of East Africa.

Roughly in the same vast region of the Northern Cape, towards the Kalahari desert, lay Olifantshoek, where I also did a locum. The place was still smaller than Prieska. The police still patrolled on camel-back. The country was arid unless it had been watered like the doctor's garden. He stayed on but needed a rest because of high blood pressure. After surgery in the cool of the evening we had drinks on the stoep. A pleasant and even magical hour in the quickly fading sunlight before the stars became bright. Matron, as the head sister of a hospital is called, came to join us. Only there was no hospital, and Matron was the local midwife. Our matron, a stout figure in her fifties, was a character but not very intelligent. The stoep looked out onto the church of the "Doppers" (Baptists), an extremely conservative sect of the Dutch Reformed Church. The congregation went to Sunday church, dressed like their forebears, the Voortrekkers, or Boer pioneers of the nineteenth century. We were all sitting on the stoep as people came out after service wearing fanciful imitations of historical costumes. Matron commented that people came out of Church in the most wonderful "erections". The doctor and I rushed out not being able to stifle our laughter. Matron had obviously looked at a glossy magazine of fashion "creations" and got confused. Her limited intelligence allowed her to believe that "nothing", that is no bacteria, could survive in hot water.

From the hill behind the doctor's house one could see a low white mountain in the distance called Witsands. It was a geological phenomenon of white sand bearing minerals. When lightning struck, it would melt some of this white sand into glasslike fragile tubules. One had been given to me but I lost it again.

Natal, today "Kwazulu", is the greenest of the provinces. I enjoyed my time at a small place, not far from where "the valley of a thousand hills" offered its magnificent panorama. I learnt a few words of Zulu while I did my locum and visited some huts on horseback. The horse grazed on the doctor's meadow and was aptly called "Gashle", Zulu for gentle. Being twenty years old, it was very patient with the unpractised rider and had deserved its name.

Wild animals, mainly birds, could be seen, noticeably the officiously strutting secretary bird and the widow bird with waving long black tail-feathers, possibly so named when Victorians in mourning wore widow's weeds. Paradoxically it was the male bird that wore the "weeds". I saw a snake only once as it slithered away. In the wooded parts of the country antelopes could often be seen, especially herds of springbok which jumped as they ran in graceful waves. The black stripe on the white band along their flanks heightened this impression.

The other practice where I did a locum, also in Natal, was at Dannhauser, a small town in a coal mining district, on the railway. The doctor there was going on holiday and had wanted me to be there in good time to learn the ropes. The "ropes" were indeed unusual because my principal had built up a large native practice. As a qualified quack he no longer needed his medical knowledge but pandered entirely to the uneducated blacks who did not know about the advances in Western medicine but had apparently lost their faith in their own natural healers. The vast majority lived in townships and were detribalised people.

Anyway the doctor had built up a reputation for his correct diagnoses with the help of an intelligent and multilingual black assistant, who was the kingpin in that he mediated between the patients and his boss. There was a special wing across the courtyard where the patients and their families could stay overnight and do their own cooking. The assistant's room was next to this hostelry. He listened to their stories including of course the patient's complaint. Before they came into the consulting room he put the doctor wise. This was essential because questioning the patient closely as we do by taking a history, would have broken the magic aura which a healer needed. His diagnostic faculty must astound, even be uncanny. I found the same attitude among some of the poor white population working as unskilled European labourers on the railways. When I asked too many questions for their liking, they would say, usually in Afrikaans: "You are the doctor, you must know." Guessing right was obviously better than knowing.

In this case it worked with the help of the stethoscope which had to be put over every part of the body, particularly over the part that the doctor already knew was or was believed to be the seat of the complaint. Sometimes the patient would even get hold of the dangling stethoscope and put it on the painful spot. The examination over, the doctor would walk up and down the room for a while. The assistant might still act souffleur while the principal was deep in thought. Then came the diagnostic speech addressed to the patient and the gathered family. The words of wisdom came as close as possible to what the doctor already knew the patient's ideas were. He or she would call out in unison with the family "E-hae!", if the diagnosis together with an explanation about the cause of the illness had hit the nail on the head. This and a few questions by both patient and family and answers by the doctor ended the diagnostic part of the consultation. No further investigations were ever required. Both the doctor and his assistant would then turn to the table where all the medicaments stood around. They were alkalis for the different ailments from stomach aches to sterility, aspirin for the others. These were dispensed into large pint bottles and, most important, carefully and suitably coloured. Patients were given instructions exactly how many mouthfuls and at what time of the day the medicine was to be taken. The contents and colouring were noted by the assistant as was also the patient's address. They would need to continue the medication in which case they should enclose a postal order together with their request. The consultations were of course settled in cash.

I regret to say that I became very good at this job and even found it fun. I got on well with the assistant who told me about his personal ambition which was to study. I only contravened one of my principal's orders twice. They had been that if a European farmer would call me out for an emergency I should say that I was busy and would he phone Dr X, who lived even further away. But I went out because it sounded and turned out to be really urgent in both cases. Nevertheless the fee was paid on the spot. The mileage was later deducted from my otherwise generous salary.

Not far from Johannesburg lay Randfontein and the mine where I did a locum as an assistant medical officer. There were three of us. The team was headed by the Chief MO, a stout citizen between fifty and sixty. In the evening of the day I arrived he asked me to give an anaesthetic for an emergency appendectomy that he would conduct. All went well. He was pleased and thanked me for the anaesthetic. Overnight I had become his blue-eyed boy. I was flattered and worked hard to maintain that position. I was told that he had a fierce temper but that at the annual staff Christmas party he would sing: "Oh you great big beautiful doll" to piano accompaniment. However, I blotted my copy book completely, when the second of the medical team had fallen ill and it was uncertain whether he would be able to return to duty. The most senior of us had put the idea into my head that if I worked for two, I should be paid accordingly. This made sense and, accordingly, I asked for an interview. The chief threw a furious temper tantrum and sacked me on the spot. Afterwards it occurred to me that my colleague had made the suggestion "with malice aforethought". He feared for his succession as the Chief Medical Officer, a sinecure of a job. No matter, he had done me a good turn because I might have got stuck in a cushy and well-paid job, board and lodgings all found, and far enough from Johannesburg and the home from which I had already distanced myself.

The locum I had done for the qualified white quack made me all the more curious why the Bantu, the native blacks of Southern Africa, could fall for such deceitful practices. An obvious reason was the prestige of a white man in a white coat and adorned with stethoscope. Its magical significance was comparable with the staff and the roundish thing the witchdoctor held in the other hand, very like the sceptre and orb that signified royalty in our civilisation. My answer is that science has not totally defeated the power and influence of magic, the influence of the latter is unevenly spread over the globe, as the following interview with a witchdoctor demonstrates.

As I was too preoccupied at the time with earning a living to keep myself and family, I asked my brother Erwin, who was able to travel, to explore the practice of my opposite number in Basuto-land. The questionnaire I sent him reflects of course my own standpoint as a psychiatrist–analyst just as much as the "answers" give a clear indication of the world the witchdoctor lived in. The answers did not always meet the questions but I found it surprising how often they did and showed up the obvious and fundamental cultural differences, specifically in our approach to those who come to us for help and, consequently, the different methods of healing as well as of training our students and successors. Beneath the surface, there must also be hidden similarities. The one that strikes me most is the general quest for experts and the wish to believe in their omniscience. It flatters the expert as much as it satisfies the patient. A hidden mutuality is thus established without which the "expert" would be out of business, and those who ask for help would go on searching elsewhere – a game that has been played in different ways from the beginning of mankind and could go on forever. As I cannot improve on the documented evidence for my statement I shall here give the interview between my brother and the witchdoctor verbatim. The photo (Plate 14) my brother took speaks its own powerful language.

Report of an interrogation of a Mosuto woman witchdoctor, April 1957, in which I kept closely to my brother Erwin's manuscript.

Questions set by Dr Alfred Plaut of London.
Translator: Louisa Ntlama, school-teacher.
Witchdoctor: Matlali Ntai, aged between fifty-five and sixty-five, religion: "heathen", meaning that she had not been to a mission school.

In answer to the introductory question how she became a witchdoctor, she replied that she received her gifts from God and the spirit of dead people* which she had received through her dreams. Later she went as a pupil to another witchdoctor, who had been pointed out to her in her dreams, and studied with him for a year for the price of an ox and one pound. Her knowledge increases all the time, but through dreams only. She now has witchdoctor-students of her own, whom she examines at the end of her teaching in the following manner. They are first given a medicine which sends them to sleep. If they have absorbed her teaching, they will dream what medicine they were given and where to find these herbs in the fields, which would prove that they are now competent witchdoctors.

Question 1: *Are you interested in people's dreams?*
Answer: Yes, but, specially in my own dreams, which always come true.

Q2: *Do they come to tell you about their dreams or do you ask them?*
A: I do not ask them about their dreams, but read them from the "litaola" (witchdoctor's bones). The patients implicitly believe in the "bones" and I know they cannot be wrong, which is confirmed by my patients, when I tell them about their dreams.

Q3: *Do you think dreams have any meaning which only people like yourself can understand?*

---

* The term "God" (molimo) only came into existence with the Basuto through the teaching of the missionaries. Prior to that it had been "balimo" (plural of molimo), which meant the spirit of the dead.

A: Yes; all sickness comes through dreams, even if the sickness is brought about by the bewitchment by another person. Another witchdoctor would not interpret the "bones" in the same way as I do, as each doctor has his own special gifts and his own special set of "bones".

Q4: *Do you distinguish between different kinds of dreams, for example important dreams which concern the whole tribe, or unimportant dreams which only concern one person?*
A: Only with my own dreams; I foresee exceptional rainstorms and sometimes have dreamt of big, far-off wars, only to be told later that they had taken place. If someone consults me, I can tell them about their family and village, as well as about themselves, all – of course – from the "bones". [This question was not answered very satisfactorily.]

Q5: *Do you think the dreams of old people differ from those of young ones? If so, could you describe how?*
A: I can not answer, as I do not know.

Q6: *Do certain things which occur in dreams always have the same meaning for example the appearance of certain animals, snakes, etc.?*
A: If you dream of a snake, it means you or your wife [in case of a man] is pregnant or going to be pregnant. If you dream of a monkey, it means sickness, as a monkey is the re-incarnation of a "ntokolosi" [evil, dwarf-like spirit]. The symbols always mean the same.

Q7: *Do you look upon dreams as a means of foretelling the future?*
A: Yes, sometimes. I dreamt, for instance, of a big water-snake standing on its tail, its head like the head of a horse, its hairy tail covered with moisture and surrounded by a rainbow. Three days later a tornado struck at Thaba Bosigu [a village about 20 miles away]. While I knew that a great disaster would occur, I could not foretell exactly where it would be located ["where the snake would strike"].

Q8: *Do you think that there is a connection between dreams and disease? If you think so can you say any more about it?*
[This question was already answered in part in answer to Q3 and no further points could be elicited.]

Q9: *Do you pay attention to your own dreams?*
A: I pay attention only to my own dreams, and to my patients' dreams only in so far as I see them in the "bones" which I read for them.

Q10: *What do you think it means if people dream that they are going to die, or that somebody else is going to die?*
A: I dreamt of a man, who was very ill, that he was going to die. The same day this man woke up and was quite cured. I sometimes dream that I am going to be

ill; and invariably I will be ill then within about two days. As a precaution I take a prophylactic medicine. [Incidentally, all Basuto are great believers in "opening" medicines, which they take frequently and in large doses.]

Q11: *Do you know of any plants or medicines that make people dream certain things?*
A: Yes, I give them medicines which will make them dream whatever they wish to dream of, such as – for instance – that they are going to be rich. But I cannot make them dream of snakes [pregnancy, see Q6], only God can do that.

Q12: *Do you think there is any connection between dreams and madness?*
A: I am quite certain that there is no connection.

[PS: I tried to interview two more witchdoctors, both of them men, of whom one (ngaka Fusi; "ngaka" means witchdoctor) is widely renowned also for his success in treating mental disorders. The latter was away from his home for many weeks, when I went there, treating a patient far away in the mountains. The other witchdoctor could not keep the appointment I had arranged through the kind offices of his chief, as he had a previous engagement on that day. All these arrangements take a great deal of time and patience as the witchdoctors often live in rather inaccessible villages involving a good deal of travelling on foot or horseback, and appointments, as I said before, are not always kept.]

7
Sailing as to War,
the War Years, Victory

It came as a great relief. The family was gathered around the radio, "wireless" in those days, on the front porch of 33 Escombe Avenue, Johannesburg. We knew of course what was coming but when Chamberlain spoke the words declaring war on Nazi Germany, we all realized that we were taking part and living at a momentous moment in the history of the world.

I had been disappointed when Chamberlain came back from Munich waving the peace treaty he had obtained from Hitler and announced "Peace in our time". Only an Englishman of the old school, a Conservative prime minister like Chamberlain could have been so duped as not to see that from Hitler's point of view he was waving a piece of paper just like any other. Now, at last, the cards were on the table. Personally, I was glad of the opportunity the situation had created to volunteer for service rather than to have to buy myself into a medical practice with money I did not have or to go on doing "locums" in the country. Eighteen months of that had been enough. Not least of all, I could now grasp the opportunity to tell my mother that she was a grandmother and I had married Pat who had left her baby daughter, Geraldine, behind in England to follow later after she had married me. Our anxiety of social stigma only accounted to some extent for this crazy sequence of events that damaged the three of us. I righted it when I adopted Geraldine as her legitimate father before a magistrate in Nairobi where Geraldine now lives. Strange coincidence. Looking back I know that my fatherless state was the major psychological factor in having behaved so submissively to Pat's request to marry her. Having a father would have made me aware that as a man I also had the right to disagree with Pat's wish to "protect" her by which she meant marriage. She added the threat that if I did not, her brother in England would denounce me to the General Medical Council for having an illegitimate child and I would then lose my licence to practice. Absolute rubbish but guilt made me believe it.

This is where a father living at home would have relieved me of the burden to become a substitute husband. As it was, I continued to sleep in the double bed next to my mother after his death where I had been sleeping while he had been in the war. From this nearly incestuous relationship stemmed my overt attitude that men's task was like that of a good son to please women by being obedient to their wishes. I hid my desire to escape from this servitude, biding my time to escape, in the forlorn hope to establish my independence and identity that way. In reality, however, the pattern was repeated as two divorces and four marriages show. Of all of these my marriage to Pat was my worst mistake. She had been sexually attractive by being a no-person, proud of no more than average IQ, of being of pure English stock accompanied by the customary dose of anti-Semitism. She imitated Eastern Jewish immigrants she had seen while nursing at the London Hospital. It must be said that after I had left her she continued to look after the deserted daughters although she began to drink heavily.

Our wedding had taken place at the registry office in Simonstown, one time British naval base West of Cape Town, where the staff acted as witnesses. No family, no friends, no celebration. The trap had closed. Our second daughter was conceived at a military hospital in Kenya.

Eventually, Pat was boarded out from the South African nursing service and returned to Cape Town where Helen was born in November 1941. There we had the support of my brother Erwin. So the circumstances were better than at Geraldine's birth in England without the support of Pat's family and myself being in South Africa alone with my secret and full of anxieties. Volunteering for the South African Medical Corps had been an escape route from intolerable guilt and anxiety.

So I found myself at Durban en route to Mombassa, Kenya's major harbour. Durban was frightfully hot in February as the eight or so medical officers who had volunteered as members of the South African Army Medical Corps to go up to Kenya where war was anticipated as soon as Hitler's ally, Mussolini, would declare war and would try to invade from Abyssinia, now Ethiopia, that he had recently "conquered". We were fitted out with uniforms wearing one "pip" (star) on the shoulder badge to show our rank as second lieutenants. The *Dunera* fitted out as a troopship had spacious cabins, only two officers per cabin, a very different story from the old *Gloucester Castle* that had brought me to South Africa. There were mostly non-military passengers aboard and the atmosphere was more like a pleasure cruise. The only reminder that there was a war on was the presence of a sergeant of the marines who fired a depth-charge as practice rather than in anger when we were in the Mombassa channel. It made an incredibly loud noise, as the sea spouted. The submarine war had only just begun.

As a friendly volunteer colleague and I got aboard the *Dunera* in the February heat of Durban we met pleasant company in the form of a Chinese magician, called Chang. More important was that he was accompanied by four helping girls. Only one was chaperoned by her mother. I don't know what their ultimate destination was but Chang was the leader not only of his troupe but of several followers like myself when we went ashore at Zanzibar. His true talent showed up in the real rather than the magical world when we all went to a bazaar where everyone selected what they wanted to buy. Chang insisted that all the goods were put on one table. This was only the beginning of his bargaining technique. He began to haggle with the bazaar keeper offering a fraction of the total sum. The man threw up his hands in horror: totally out of question. Chang commanded all of us to walk out. We had not walked far before the bazaar keeper came running after us beseeching us to return. With a show of reluctance Chang agreed and we came trotting after. Needless to say our offer caused despair but was reluctantly accepted. My introduction to oriental bargaining was over.

Zanzibar seemed to live on copra as the main produce. Coconut palm trees everywhere. The places where the old leaves had been cut off served as a natural ladder to the barefooted natives who climbed up to pick the nuts. The island was apparently ruled by a Sultan but in reality from Whitehall, the Colonial Office in London. I saw His Highness, a white-bearded old man being driven to his Palace where his flag was fluttering as it also did from his ancient Rolls-Royce.

Shortly after we had re-embarked our ship had to negotiate a long channel to the harbour of Mombassa. A lascar (Indian sailor) incessantly swung a plumb line and sung the result out to the bridge. "Seven fathoms" indicated the depth of water below the ship. At long last we made fast. From there our journey went on by train to the capital, Nairobi. After some administrative delay and sorting out of our group my friend Max Jaffé, a young medical from Cape Town, and I were allotted to the Uganda Field Ambulance temporarily stationed in tents near Nanyuki, at the foot of Mount Kenya. The village was situated almost precisely on the equator. To remind customers of the fact and in confirmation of the geographical curiosity a white line was drawn obliquely across the counter of the local pub.

At that stage of waiting for the war we often drove there in our duty cars. The personnel of the field ambulance consisted of white officers and non-commissioned officers all drawn from the Ugandan Medical Service; the "other ranks" had been recruited from various Ugandan tribes. The exception was one highly intelligent tall black sergeant who bore the well sounding name Sikusoka. He had been to a mission school and spoke proper English in contrast to the pidgin-English and the language Europeans used, kitchen-Swahili.

To keep us occupied there were the daily routines, "fatigues" in military jargon. First of all the daily "sick parade", where the black personnel who were or, mostly, believed themselves to be sick stood in a queue to be examined and, rarely, exempted from duty. After a cursory examination the diagnosis and treatment was mostly "M&D", medicine and duty. Some were referred to as "lead-swingers" meaning malingerers. Every morning and evening a red-cross flag was hoisted or struck to the accompaniment of a trumpeter, a *bruji*.

But not only is the sun punctual all the year round on the equator. My commanding officer was too. Every evening at 17.45 he was pacing up and down irritably in front of the officer's mess-tent like a hungry tiger. Then at 18.00 sharp he beamed because now the gin-drinking session could begin. It lasted up to 21.00 when the cry went out to the *m'pishi* (cook) "*lette chacula*", bring the food. At 22.00 hrs bedtime. Only on special occasions would there be second drinking session. His morning drinking sessions, sunrise at 7.00, began just as punctually at 12.00. It was the self-discipline which he had learned in the Colonial Medical Service, that drew the line between a heavy drinker and an alcoholic.

The "war" in East Africa up to the point Mussolini actually entered had been a picnic. On the daily route marches the troops sang cheerily something taken over from the crack regiment of regular soldiers the KAR (King's African Rifles) or songs they had made up, a concoction of Swahili and English, like "*mboga, mboga*, (mboga = vegetables) barley soup" or something about their officers like myself who wanted to be promoted to have three stars (*nyota tatu*) on my shoulder, to be a captain, not just a lieutenant. I was nicknamed *"macho enne"*, meaning four eyes because of my glasses. Other names were *"meridadi"* (elegant) and most flattering of all *"bwana kijana"*, the young gentlemen. The black Ugandan tribes had an ever-ready sense of humour.

To keep our minds occupied Major Williams of the Ugandan Medical Service gave us proper Ki-Swahili lessons, not just kitchen-Swahili, but the proper grammatical language as it was spoken at the coast. Quite a lot of it has stuck in my mind. The assumption was that we would be there for ever.

My batman, John, had been in the First World War in South West Africa and East Africa when the British chased the elusive German General von Lettow-Vorbeck. Instead of his birthdate John knew that he was already a youngster when George V was crowned in 1910. It may well have coincided with the initiation into his tribe. He also taught me customs and local manners. To steal (*ku-iba*) for one's master was no crime. To take someone else's woman without paying for it was bad manners. The West-Africans, Nigerians, who had just arrived as a reinforcement would do that. John enacted as he spoke how it should be done. One would walk up to the father or husband of the woman, assume a respectful attitude and say which woman one wanted. The man would answer "open your purse", see how much he could ask for and haggle, if it was not enough. In the end a bargain was struck and the owner-man would say: *"chukue!"*, take (or carry) her away. That was how things were regulated in polite society. But these Nigerians were barbarians. Worse still, they had the reputation of being cannibals; one could not be sure.

Actually the Nigerians had reached a far higher standard of Western civilisation. Most of them were literate and spoke their own kind of pidgin-English. Being amused by the reputation that had preceded them they threatened the East-Africans with "I chop you small, small!" They were a wonderful bunch, humorous and of excellent physique but by no means free from superstitions. Many carried a protective charm, an amulet, around the neck. We had to censor their letters which spoke volumes about the world in which they lived. "Tell my sister to find me a nice girl, because when I get home I must be married." Or: "Tell my medicine that I have not thrown it away at all. I only left it at home so as not to lose it. If you don't tell it, my medicine will come and kill me." The "medicine" in question was the amulet.

The months during which we were later stationed in proper hutment near Nanyuki were rich in experience both of the white colonial as well as of the black population belonging to the Kikuyu tribe. I suppose the white population had their resident doctor. Until our arrival the blacks were looked after by their medicine-man. The curious came to us. We had a dentist in our unit who manufactured a denture for our driver who had more than the usual two of his front teeth missing. (Two had been ritualistically removed.) He was delighted with this gift. When we wanted to go back from the hospital to our camp three hours later, he was still admiring his teeth in the rear-mirror of the car.

Among our patients was a middle-aged male who had been gored in the chest by a rhino. The lung had of course collapsed and the cavity so left was full of pus. He had developed a pyopneumothorax (the cavity between the ribs and the lining of the collapsed lung had become filled with pus). We treated it with saline irrigations twice a day and gave sulphonamides. All the same, his survival and eventual recovery was I think mainly due to a natural high resistance to infected wounds which I also found in Africans elsewhere. When it was time to be discharged we said goodbye and he made a little speech. The highpoint of his thanks was interpreted for me. It was that when I was old I could have his testicles for my continued potency. With that he bent down, pulled up a bundle of lush grass and stuck it in my belt as a gesture of his gratitude. The best gift he could give and I could receive.

Our major adventure, a few days before Mussolini entered the War on 10 June 1940, was our attempt to climb Mount Kenya around Easter time. The officer in charge of our transport wing conspired with my friend and myself to organise it. The old boy had served in France during the First World War and was always up to such tricks. He worked out the logistics, including a lorry for porters, food and blankets. We could easily have been court-martialled, if our commanding officer from whom this was kept secret, had wanted to. He was of course furious. Mainly, I think, because he had been excluded. Our search for a local mountain guide in the Kikuyu villages had failed. The answer had been *"baridi"*, too cold. Another reply was that they would be eaten by the animals. A little more complex was the reason given that the gods who lived up there should not be disturbed. They were certainly right about it being cold as we discovered when we spent the night in a wooden hut well below the summit, at any rate at an altitude of nearly 4000 metres. The blankets we had taken were quite insufficient, we were freezing despite the wood-firing stove.

We got our first fright when the lorry had lumbered its way up to the edge of the forest past vast herds of zebra and could go no further. The driver, close on seven foot tall got out and fell flat on his face. All the way up the black soldiers, formally called "Askaris", served as porters on our illicit safari. They were carrying, as usual, all loads on their heads. They also complained of headache *kichwa uma*, literally the head is biting. Clearly, they were reluctant to proceed. The air had already got thin. Our entomologist sergeant-major knew about the various zones of vegetation we passed through, woods and bamboo forests where elephants had been. After that nothing grew but giant groundsells between the rocks reflected in the numerous small lakes. Someone had provided us with a large scale map showing where a hut was situated. We reached it after six hours climb about two hours before sunset which on the equator is as punctual as the sunrise all the year round at seven o'clock. Hence *saa moja siku* (the first hour of the day) or *usiku* (of the night). The sunrise was as beautiful as it was welcome. The view of the valleys beneath as well as the snowy top of the giant extinct volcano were magnificent. The warming rays had never been more welcome.

But, what now?

We were discussing over breakfast whether to go on to the summit or to return, as the cry went up that *watu*, people, more specifically black people, were approaching. Messengers came up sent by the commanding officer with a chit (bit of paper in Anglo-Indian) ordering us to return at once. We would have to face the music. So ended an adolescent prank. Unrecorded in military history but never to be forgotten by the participants.

The "phoney" war ended for all of us some six weeks later when Mussolini declared war. The enemy had occupied Abyssinia (Ethiopia) some four years earlier. Junkers 88 of the Italian Air Force began to fly overhead. The only fighter planes on our side were the old and slow Gloucesters, from aircraft carriers. A few months later I had my first heartening sight of the fast and agile Spitfires pirouetting on practice flights near Nairobi. Anyway, the field ambulance was off to the North to Wajir an old fortress built in the "beau geste" style of films about the foreign legion. In its gleaming white daub Wajir was situated amid the surrounding Savannah. An ideal target for Italian bombers. We pitched our tents some ten miles to the south of it, did our best to camouflage our presence and dug out our operating theatre. The first casualties began to arrive. Among them were the surviving crew of an Italian plane that had been shot down. I saw the charred remains of some of the crew. Others were not severely wounded. One of our black dressers had been to a Catholic mission school and used the Latin he had learned just as well as I did for communication with the Italian survivors.

After Wajir we moved further north towards the border of Ethiopia, to Lokitang situated in the Turkana district. The tribe was more untouched by Western civilisation than any I had met. The men walked about stark naked except that the hair on top of their heads was under a whitish cap of clay. Stuck into it was something that looked pliable like a whale bone and used for scratching underneath the clay when the lice were biting. A fairly constant occupation. The women of that tribe wore a small leather apron. When they wanted to urinate they stood still and a wet patch would appear in the sand below. This and other experiences with Africans taught me that Western civilisation proceeds slowly and unevenly. There was on the one hand the unexpected use of Latin by an African. At the other extreme was his colleague in the operating theatre who knew the name of the instruments but obviously thought that the "sterile forceps" were sufficiently protected by their name to remain sterile even after they had fallen on the floor. A different observation made me reflect on the tenacity with which a civilisation leaves its mark, for instance in the form of games. Cricket is played in all parts of the globe which had been part of the British Empire. Or again, English has become the language of North America and the *lingua franca* in countries like India and southern Africa where many native tongues are spoken.

Lawns were unthinkable in Lokitang. So cricket was out. The sun was reflected from bare rocks and temperatures of 40°C and more were not uncommon. A King's African Rifles contingent stationed there in peace-time had dug out and cemented squash courts, as if there was a need to defy the heat and sweat even more. There were roads leading to Lake Rudolf that could be seen shimmering in the sun some thirty kilometres to the west. Its waters were drinkable and rich in fish. The barren landscape on our side was empty, eerie, very sparsely populated but unforgettable. Many years later I learned that it was, according to the anthropologist Richard Leaky, the likely cradle of mankind and it was easy to believe that the place had looked exactly the same millions of years ago.

The end of my stay in Kenya came shortly after Lokitang when there were unmistakable signs of my duodenal ulcer having relapsed. It was first investigated in Nairobi where the medical board decided to admit me to a military hospital. I was put on bed-rest and a strict "Sippey" diet. When, after a few weeks of this the x-rays showed no improvement, I was sent back to South Africa.

My wife, Pat, had joined the SA nursing corps to follow me to Kenya, where she became pregnant. Now she could follow me to South Africa where shortly afterwards she gave birth in Cape Town to Helen, our second daughter. This was in November 1940.

The years spent at the psychiatric military base hospital at Potchefstroom were my apprenticeship in psychiatry. Electroconvulsive therapy and insulin-coma were work-a-day treatments. Under the eagle-eyed Doctor (now Major) Alice Cox the main thing I learned was the management of patients and staff. As in any other kind of hospital it was the teamwork of all the staff that really mattered. If all cooperated and everyone concerned had the right to air grievances at the large weekly meeting as well as at the almost daily team meetings the machinery worked efficiently and patients who had their own spokesman benefited. This concerned medical officers, nurses, male and female, the maids that did the cleaning, as well as the kitchen staff and orderlies. The negative or downside aspect of all this co-operation was the same as in every institution. It forms a microcosm, a self-contained little world. The members that belong to it gradually begin to have little regard for the world outside like adolescents who consider the parents as superfluous to the establishment of life, having "forgotten" the years of total dependence. Until the day when the apparently self-sufficient institution is called into question once more. The end of the war and demobilisation so fervently desired at the beginning now comes as a threat to the security of belonging to a group of comrades who knew very well where the next meal was coming from – to say nothing of the little bit of glory wearing a uniform with decorations and a certain small income.

While still in Cape town, on compassionate leave from Kenya, I visited Parliament which happened to be in session. It moved regularly from Pretoria to the Cape during half the year. There I saw the by now legendary Prime Minister and head of the United Party, General J. C. Smuts, who had contributed so much to getting South Africa into the war on the side of the Allies. He could go no further politically than raise an army of volunteers to be added to the small regular army officered entirely by whites. The population remained divided on the war issue and only a small majority was in favour. The debate incidentally centred around raising the pension of the "Oudstryders", the surviving fighters of the Anglo-Boer war I mentioned, Smuts sat with his head in his hands and did not say a word. The Afrikaans speakers struck me as decidedly more eloquent than the English. In retrospect I realised even more than at the time that Smuts was a phenomenon, probably the greatest man I ever got sight of. In addition to being a natural military and political leader, he made his name as a philosopher (holism) as well as a botanist with special interest in grasses. He had been a General as a Boer in the war against the British at the turn of the century, had made peace with the British (1910, at Vereeniging), and supported their government when it was threatened after the terribly costly defeat of Paschendale, helped to lift the strike of the Welsh coal miners in 1922. Obviously an arbitrator he also acted ruthlessly on occasion. Armstrong (1937) in his biography of Smuts *Grey Steel*, subtitled it *J.C. Smuts, a study in arrogance*. The people called him "slim Jannie" ("slim" Afrikaans for "foxy"). The greatness of his vision and the meanness with which he could act made him an over-life-sized human figure – strong, and full of contradictions.

Outside Parliament, in the Botanical Gardens the sun shone as usual. Soon I travelled with my wife and baby daughter up to Johannesburg. We bought a bungalow at 18 Cecil Avenue, Melrose, on a mortgage, not far from where Aunt Mali lived with my grandmother, Aunt Ella and Uncle Manfred. My house had a nice garden with a fountain in the middle. It was there that I became fond of gardening. The hard work was of course done by our servant, the "house boy" in our case. He dug a trench about five-feet deep underneath the kitchen window. We put a lot of manure in and planted sweet peas. They flowered into a beautiful well-scented hedge. My mother was full of joy and praise. Climate and soil combined produced prodigiously. The only problem, as everywhere in Africa, was water. There was never enough until there was too much of it.

Even moderately wealthy people had a house as well as a garden boy and a maid for the children as well as a cook. The wives played tennis and bridge, during the day in aid of a charity which I suppose assuaged their conscience about doing no work at all. In the evening there were mixed bridge parties. The women complained to each other about their ungrateful servants, the men talked shop and money; recurring topics of conversation. This had been the situation before the war but it did not change altogether during the war when the "wireless" reports about "our boys up north" became the main subject. In that context "boys" usually meant sons who had volunteered for service in Africa and, as the war progressed, anywhere in the world.

I was posted first to the Central Medical Establishment at Robert's Heights; Voortreekker Hoogte as it was later called when the National Party, mainly of Afrikaans origin, had taken over from Smuts' United Party. This establishment dealt with aircrew selection for the South African Air Force and also decided on the fitness or otherwise of pilots and other aircrew to return to duty after trauma or sickness. The psychological factor weighed heavily in these decisions. Having been interested in psychiatry ever since my adolescence I felt I was in the right place. We stayed in the very comfortable rondavels of the officers' mess, equipped with a swimming pool, billiard tables and tennis courts. When the King, or his representative, the Governor-General was toasted at dinner, only officers above field rank, from major up, were allowed to say "God bless him". But everybody was allowed to drink his health.

From South Africa we anxiously watched what happened up north and the progress that Rommel made from Tunisia towards Egypt where the British had their headquarters. He seemed irresistible for a time with his relatively short supply-route from Southern Italy. Sicily and other important Mediterranean islands were already in German hands. Malta, the British naval base, withstood years of bombardment. (The whole island was later awarded the George Cross.) At Tobruk British and South African units had been captured. One British general followed another at Cairo. King Faroukh of Egypt looked like an uncertain ally. Field marshals Auchinlek and Wavell had not been able to stop Rommel. More and more men and equipment were sent to Egypt. All this took time and ships. Finally Generals Alexander and Montgomery took over from their predecessors. Montgomery scored a major victory at El Alamein. In November of that year Churchill could announce to Parliament: "The bright gleam has caught the helmets of our soldiers and warmed and cheered all our hearts." From then on the Germans in North Africa and eventually in Italy were in retreat. No one would have thought at the time that it would take another two-and-a-half years before victory in Europe could be celebrated.

On the personal side, the war years were decisive for my future. From Pretoria I was posted to the military wing of the psychiatric hospital at Potchefstroom, which meant that I could only go home to Johannesburg for the weekends I was not on duty. On the bowling green of all places I met Sister Joan Evelyn Clark, my future wife and mother of my sons. What a companionable game bowls is. You can play it until a ripe old age.

Head of the military psychiatric unit was Colonel Purser from England. My immediate superior was Major Alice Cox. A remarkable personality, of Scottish decent, she was a very experienced psychiatrist and had a good head for whisky. She tried to mend my marriage to Pat, but nothing could intervene as I had gradually become aware that I had been "trapped" into my first marriage. Potchefstroom turned out to be the beginning of the end. It was a long drawn-out and agonising struggle because of the young children and my being conscience-stricken as well as very fond of my daughters, Geraldine and Helen. My divorce only came through after I had been living in England for two years where Evelyn had joined me after she in turn had been demobilised too. I had by then started my first analysis. Although I had escaped to England for the best of reasons, that is postgraduate study in psychiatry, it had also been dawning on me that I wanted to escape the dull marriage and family and professional life that would have been my lot, had I stayed. The immediate post war situation with its long and slow process of demobilisation and the return to "civvy street" also meant the next meal would not be taken in the matey carefree atmosphere of a canteen or a mess.

Life in the officers' mess had been great; we were well fed, drink and cigarettes were cheap, there was a billiard table, table tennis and, above all, the bowling green. Winter was fun on the High Veld, as that part of the Transvaal is known. Blue skies, day after day. The difference in night and day temperature was such that fountains turned on in the evenings were decorated with icicles at breakfast time. At midday we walked about in shirtsleeves. In springtime the air was scented with mimosa (more accurately wattle trees). A little later the streets were lined with jacaranda trees in incredibly violet-blue blossom. The high time of carefree Potchefstroom, interrupted only by duty visits home, was to end when shortly after VE Day, (victory in Europe, 8 May 1945) the hospital was transferred to Johannesburg. "Tara" was close enough to home to have an excuse not to live there. A decision had to be made once my demobilisation was only a matter of weeks away. I had done well enough to be granted a government loan to study psychiatry overseas, in England, because there were no facilities for postgraduate studies in that discipline in South Africa at the time. My luck was in, I was off to England. Come what may, I left wife and family. That it was for good became clear only gradually, with much heart-searching and the help of analysis and love for my wife to be, Evelyn.

8
Still Young in Post-War London,
Moving out to Jordans and back again

When I arrived in London in the late summer of 1946 there were still many buildings and houses in ruins but one could not have said that London was in ruins. Rosie, whose husband kept a bookshop in Camden Town, a friend of my wife Pat, acted as guide to many places, St Paul's Cathedral, the Tower, Westminster Abbey, the House of Commons, 10 Downing Street – all without noticeable damage. So was Harrods. Barry Sullivan of the German section, BBC, Bush House, told me that they took the German prisoners on a sight seeing trip through the undamaged parts of London of which Harrod's was a show piece. The idea was that they would write home and tell their people that the propaganda they were fed was a lie.

Rosie and I also took the little train to Kew, where London's Botanical Gardens were open to the public. That is to say the public that could afford to pay the one penny entrance fee: less than one pence by today's currency.* Rosie explained that they charged "just to keep the riff-raff out". By that she probably meant the unemployed and the working-class people. She being lower middle-class, spoke the explanation with a note of contempt in her voice. During the war when bombs and, later, rockets threatened the whole population of London regardless of class, the "classes" had been on speaking terms. Peace had hardly broken out when the pre-war snobbery returned.

Rosie took special pride in pointing-out the Belisha beacons at pedestrian crossings. They had been blinking their yellow lights for better visibility ever since Hore-Belisha as the relevant minister had introduced them in 1934. In those days the thick fog for which London was known at home and abroad had made the beacons desirable. Evelyn and I had once been caught in a specially thick fog and had to grope our way along walls and houses being lost as in a maze. When next morning the wind had cleared the sky, buses were found standing deserted at the entrances of houses. The fog had brought all traffic to a standstill. But the "pea-soupers" had been caused by industrial dirt and are now a thing of the past.

---

* The currency of the time consisted of pennies, twelve to a shilling, twenty shillings to the pound – a complicated system that was changed to the present decimal coinage in 1968 when Harold Wilson was Labour Prime Minister and told us that "the pound in your purse or pocket" had not changed in value. Fiddlesticks. Every tinkering with the currency makes the population the loser. Prices in the shops and restaurants go up; salaries do not. Same when the Deutsche Mark was changed into the Euro.

The penny I paid at Kew showed the head of George V, who was still Emperor of India and remained so until India gained independence in 1947, shortly after the war had ended and Lord Mountbatten, the last viceroy had gone home. His son, George VI, had visited Tree Tops Lodge near Nyeri in Kenya in 1952. I knew the place well from the time I had been stationed at nearby Nanyuki with the Uganda Field Ambulance. His daughter, Elizabeth II succeeded him and still is Queen at the time of writing.

In the immediate post-war London, rationing of food was still very severe as was everything else you could find in shops. People complained that it was worse than it had been during the war. Spivs (young men smartly dressed, hair brilliantined) sold silk stockings and cigarettes and other luxury goods on the black market in the streets. One had to queue for food and luxury items were mostly unattainable. Wherever there was anything to buy long queues formed. Lining, as the Americans call it, was the order of the day. Many places were still in ruins. My black and white photo (Plate 5) does not show the purplish weed, aptly called fire-weed, that flourished among ruins after the *Blitz*. The other photo I took at the time shows London at its unique best. The Thames as it passes the Palace of Westminster is authentic "liquid history" (Plate 6). No other river was historically more important going right back to Roman times. Other rivers in Europe are wider, more romantically situated, and cleaner. Lower down the river passes the docks and on to Greenwich, a naval base of world renown emphasised by the location of the zero meridian determining by plus or minus signs the comparative longitude and time all around the globe.

Other places too began to revive. I am not sure whether Speaker's Corner had been in operation throughout the war. Here anybody could practise his rhetorics on any topic and try to draw a crowd of listeners. All without special permission from the police. This kind of freedom symbolizes the reason why I have not given up my British passport. Added to that is that despite the exclusiveness, animosity, hatred even of foreigners, the public itself would intervene, if any extremist would resort to violent aggression against a "bloody foreigner".

It was fun meeting Cockneys again at East End's Petticoat Lane street market and to look for book bargains in the more intellectual market of Portobello Road, Notting Hill Gate – all so new as well as old. I felt this was where I belonged, Europe – no matter how grand the South African experience had been which I would not have liked to miss for the world – this was the nearest to being back home.

Outside theatres and cinemas, street musicians, (buskers), entertained the people who waited and waited. But they were good humoured, seemed mostly young and danced everywhere. Even at Hill End, the psychiatric hospital where I did my internship, the staff and the not-too-sick patients did the "Lambeth Walk".

I had a comfortable flat that went with the job in one of the hospital buildings. The more senior staff had even better flats and some even houses. The chronic patients worked in the vegetable gardens of the ample grounds; the produce went to the communal kitchens as well as to the medical staff's private kitchens. Cricket matches and outings were organised in summer time. The stage provided entertainment in the winter. This peaceful self-contained little world was disturbed when active treatments cured many of the more acute patients who could go home. With the advent of the National Health Service (1948), a new census of the patient population revealed that most of the others, mostly elderly patients, were "chronic" because they had nowhere to go. The hospital where they had lived for very many years was their home. Now they became the burden of the Social Service branch of the National Health Service and had to be discharged. Some of the medical staff became redundant.

It was during my residency that Evelyn, my wife to be, arrived at last from South Africa. She found a nursing job at the Maudsley hospital where she lived at the nurses' home in South London, a long way from St Albans in the North, where Hill End was situated. Visiting each other was restricted to weekends. A little later when I worked at the Neurological Hospital, Queen's Square, Evelyn worked there too and shared a flat with other staff at Mecklenburg Square, Bloomsbury, in the house where Virginia Woolf had lived and the Hogarth Press had been installed.

Evelyn and I also went to Ayot St Lawrence where we were lucky to catch a glimpse of the famous Irish writer and dramatist George Bernard Shaw walking on the veranda of his house. I had seen *The Doctor's Dilemma* and *Pygmalion* on stage. He was an old man by then, but he still wrote one last play *Buoyant Billions*. A star in his day, GBS was his own best publicist. Now he seems forgotten.

When I finished my internship we found a two-roomed, furnished flat on the ground-floor of 6 St Mark's Crescent, Regent's Park, near Primrose Hill where a cemented emplacement marked the site of an only recently removed anti-aircraft gun. Our kitchen consisted of a sliver about 80 cm wide and 2 metres long. The lavatory was communal halfway up the stairs, as was the bathroom on the second floor. But what did it matter, we were happy to be together and knew we had a future. From our bed, the only reliably warm place, we could see at the bottom of the garden the Grand Union Canal. Shire horses in the autumn mist, plodding along the towpath, dragging barges. A wonderful and mysterious picture. In the evenings we went to a life class in Chelsea or visited friends, danced and went to concerts. At a masked ball I wore a boiler suit and stuffed the arms so that it looked as if I had four. Almost a Shiva. Like the Lambeth Walk, a kind of polonaise, the Hokey-Cokey was an open dance. Pairs did not hold each other. Instead they did what they sang "You put your right leg in, you put your right leg out ... and you shake it all about" and so on referring to all the mobile parts of your body. Never tired, never a dull moment. The gas or electric fires barely glimmered – that too did not matter. Such was our home when I absolved my scholarship at the Child Guidance Training Centre, went to "Lola" for analysis and attended seminars. It was during that time, in January 1949, that my divorce in Johannesburg came through and we got married at a Registry Office from Cosmo's house in St Peter's Square, Hammersmith. Cosmo was Evelyn's uncle, a painter like his father, James Clark, and a one-time war artist. Both he and his wife, Jean, were most kind to the young couple. Many splendid Christmas dinners, until Cosmo suddenly collapsed and died in the street.

It was not long before we could move into a much better flat at Park Crescent, where there were lawn tennis courts for us tenants in a secluded private park. All housing was cheap in those post-war years and the flat was good and large enough for two. But it was high up to the third floor in the old Regency house. Anthracite for our stove in the large living room is heavy stuff to be carried up from the cellar. When Adrian arrived in 1952 we had our first "au-pair" help from a Swiss girl, Doris. She moved out with us to Jordans, Buckinghamshire, because, beautiful as it was for a childless young couple, this was no place to bring children up. Commuting had begun and was to last twenty-six years. First by car. But uncertain and difficult road conditions especially in bad weather and increasingly heavy traffic made me feel tired before I even saw my first patient at eight. Evelyn needed the car for shopping. Frequent evening professional meetings went on until late so I stayed over in my consulting room at Devonshire Place. Strictly not allowed except in war time. But who cared? For early breakfast I drove down to Lyon's Corner House at Piccadilly which was fun. At that hour the ladies of Soho had congregated there after the night's work. The punters, as their clients were called, presumably had breakfast at home, having had "a late night at the office". The chatter was amusing as well as instructive as I saw my fellow men through different eyes.

Then came the Festival of Britain (1951) on the South Bank of the river with the building of concert halls and theatres. It has been described as a tonic to the nation. It was needed and it worked. A sculpture exhibition had opened before in Battersea Park (Plate 8). The four statues I photographed (Plate 7) as "displaced persons" who had been in protective custody during the war went back to the roof of the Nash terraces, Regent's Park, where they belonged. Slowly, year by year, the country came to life again and we helped by being young and "with it".

Had the twenty-six years of commuting on British railways been a waste of time? When there was no hitch, but there often was, each journey took forty minutes and it certainly added up to quite a lot of time. Had I lived closer to or even above the consulting room, could the time have been better spent than in travelling between Seer Green and Jordans, Buckinghamshire, and Marylebone Station? Marylebone – still with Victorian red-bricked station hall, a real gem of contemporary architecture. A film maker found it authentic enough to use for a scene showing British troops departing en route to South Africa during the Anglo-Boer war.

A quick journey by car in the mornings when Evelyn ran me to our station that consisted of no more than two platforms, a shed and a bridge. She took me back to the house and a warm meal, often late, the children already asleep. Once arrived at Marylebone, a brisk walk to the consulting room. The sons had called the one I had at home for Saturday mornings the "insulting room". If the train had been late, there was a competitive race for the taxi. Unfortunately, I could not always stop the receptionist from entertaining the patients in the waiting room, since he was of the firm opinion that they liked it, which may have been true of the upstairs dentist's patients. Evenings saw the process in reverse, times depending on the combination of my private and the railways' timetable.

Coming back to the question whether the time of commuting could have been better spent. It depends on what "better" means. If I think of the time I did not give to my wife and family, the answer would seem a straightforward "yes". For my own selfish ego it could not have been better. I liked listening to the gossip on the train and sometimes took part. Everyday things, weather, a child sick at home, a new car, politics, hotting up at election time. Football and cricket, of course. Anything slightly malicious spoken *sotto voce*; the whole compartment silent, ears aflap. Some of my fellow travellers were also interesting people. The Foreign Office and the BBC were represented, so was the stage. Everyone felt free to dip their nose into whatever they pleased, the gossip, the paper, a book, their notes. As I write I think that today the laptops would be much in evidence. Business. Don't waste a moment. But at the not so hectic hours when I usually travelled, early and late, the company was less ambitious; so were the trains. The race done, they now stopped conscientiously at every station and took their time. I tried to read.

Watching us five or six, men as a rule, in the compartment of the old rolling stock, badly heated and smoky, the shaky windows to be pulled up or let down on leather straps. Definitely up before a tunnel, smoke and soot from the steam engines that still drew the trains in the early days of my commuting; smoke also in the compartment from the pipes of some travellers. "No Smoking" compartments were as rare then as they are now customary. Of course, I remember some fellow travellers in more detail. A stocky, ruddy-faced Irishman who had been to sea, full of yarns of faraway places. He believed in the miracles of his Catholic faith and knew more about roses than I did. Denis, that remarkable linguist who had been taken prisoner when his aircraft was shot down over Germany. He wore the bowler hat as part of the standard outfit of the Foreign Office staff in Whitehall. One day as we passed the engine, the driver wanted to know whether Denis' father had also been just as tall which Denis confirmed. Turning to his mate, the stoker said: "What did I tell you? You can't make rats out of mice." Cockney biology on a steam-engine.

All the people and observations don't say much about the inner journeys that took place while commuting. It gave me the leisure to contemplate the coming day's timetable. Or, should I have to buy anything for lunch. Sandwiches, sometimes from home, a tin of soup from the supermarket, milk for the coffee. Who would be the first patient, would they be waiting as I came in, meet me on the doorstep, be late? Who it was I usually knew not so much by the name written in my diary as by the anticipation in my stomach. What preparations for the evening meetings; would they be boring or stimulating, who would be the awkward customer? Anyone to have dinner with beforehand? When tired, just staring out of the window, watch the ugly grey houses, little patches of garden, blackslated roofs, tall orange chimney pots, all flying by like snatches of a recurrent dream. Depressing when not in sunshine. Less so the few fields and woods that turned up more often as the train left London further behind. Soon they too would be buried under stone. Most of the year it was dark on the way back and I read while my thoughts anticipated the situation I would find at home. Would the children be in bed? Had they watched television for hours, having done their homework in minutes? What's for dinner or were we going out? And on to all the domestic matters that cover and threaten the emotional network of family life until something happens that helps to distinguish again between the important and the trivial. Pity we only learn from blows. Valuing the everyday routines seems to be beyond human capacity unless it is newly lit up after the darkness of some preceding illness or disaster. Ours came with the drowning of the baby daughter and my wife's subsequent depression.

Susi, our miniature poodle when the boys were little and after her demise, Nina, a golden labrador were the loving and much beloved pets around which we all met. What with Evelyn at home, the children at school, myself in London most of the week and often writing papers when at home, the dogs helped to keep us all together. A loving common interest. Of course, in the summer we drove out and walked through the woods at Burnham Beeches or in the Thames Valley, where school friends lived. Other friends gladly took over our affectionate Nina when after Evelyn's death I sold the house and the sons, now grown up, moved into separate London quarters. By then I had begun to practice from my flat in Montague Street.

But I had not got over Evelyn's death and the loss of a family home. Unable to mourn, I tried to escape into manic behaviour, including another marriage which quickly proved disastrous. As an analyst, I should have known that some losses are forever. Instead, I cunningly kept from my analyst at the time that I had already "been up to the town hall" as she later put it, meaning the Registry Office to give notice of an impending marriage. But knowing and behaving accordingly are often quite separate things.

When I came over from Berlin on a visit to England my son Adrian has often driven me to Jordans to have a look at the former home. Much like visiting a cemetery. But we also called on old friends in the village.

The Society of Friends

My comments on the Quaker community or the Society of Friends at Jordans do not strictly belong here but I cannot find a better place for mentioning it. The people who belonged to it were our neighbours and formed the greater part of the original Jordans population. When we left after Evelyn's death of cancer in 1976, the core and founders of that community were outnumbered by families from outside like ourselves whose breadwinners were commuters, mainly to London. The "Friends" had welcomed us newcomers and I have remained impressed by their remarkable tolerance and humanity which is a hallmark of their religion. Remarkably, they were even tolerant towards their own kind. While other people would enjoy malicious gossip the most they would indulge in would be to refer to any black sheep as "poor old" so-and-so. Wherever in the world help was needed they would do their best to send supplies, an ambulance, helpful and skilled volunteers. Instead of buying luxuries they would spend money on special experiences, no tourism and five-star hotels. In saying this I am aware that many Quakers were well-heeled and knew the value of money very well but did not show it. I am including my knowledge of psychoanalytic terms like reaction formation, repression and all the other technical terms which indicate that something of the opposite kind is going on beneath the glowing surface of "do-gooders". But the surface can also be true and above all, effective. Why not leave it at that for once? Surely the quality of mercy is sparse enough in a world filled with human greed and intelligent cut-throats. In analytic jargon that quality would be called reparation, thereby giving aggression and destructivity prime of place. The greater the evidence for the rightness of that assumption the more welcome an oasis like the Quakers' communities in this world. I attended "Meetings" at the seventeenth-century-built meeting house on Sunday mornings and liked it much better than the Church of England services held by a muscular Christian vicar at nearby Seer Green.

Meeting consisted of the Elders sitting on a raised platform, the congregation on wooden benches below. Bare walls, no music, no singing. To mark the beginning and end the Elders shook hands. There was silence and, I assume, contemplation. Then, when anyone was moved to speak they stood up and did so. Maybe it was an incident that had struck them during the week. In any case, it would not be commented on by the others who listened to it. Then silence again until another Friend spoke. There was neither an intentional continuity nor discontinuity between the content of what they felt urged to say. Was this a watered-down dis-emotionalised English version of what I had read about the "Shakers" and similar sects in the United States? Anyway, I afterwards felt that there was an inner cohesion among the members and "attenders" like myself. The prevailing spirit was one of tolerance, neighbourliness and friendship.

9

On Training
within a Human Context

Training to Become a Psychiatrist

The relative length of this chapter indicates that training does not end with an examination and a diploma. It will not stop before I have seen my last patient. Training in any subject cannot be free from political influences. Here I tell my story.

When I was at school we all had to say what we wanted to become. That was at the age of sixteen or seventeen. A couple of years earlier I had wanted to become a journalist. I had met one at a seaside resort who had long conversations with a psychiatrist. The two let me trot along with them on their walks. I listened eagerly. As I liked writing essays, I thought I could write for a newspaper. But then I discovered that reporting was not the same thing and that I was not as curious about the news of the world, as I had been about the discoveries of the world in my childhood. They seemed somehow connected with getting to know why we behaved and lived in our daily lives as we did.

But I must first say how it all started. No doubt, the early death of my father and my mother's clinging on to me for consolation influenced my choice to free myself of these fetters by knowing more about the workings of the mind and to get beyond being tied to its sicknesses. I had suspected an incurable depressive illness in my maternal grand-mother. So everything pointed in the direction of making for psychiatry via studying medicine after I finished school.

The names I mention in this chapter will only be of interest to a few colleagues. Their counterparts can be found in the history of most institutions, whether of education and training, of commerce or industry and in politics. Because of this similarity I thought of my story as a paradigm for humans working together and against each other.

Shortly after my arrival in England I attended, as planned, the foremost psychiatric teaching hospital, the Maudsley, where I had been accepted for the first post-war course in preparation for the Diploma in Psychological Medicine (DPM). Aubrey Lewis was professor. His wide knowledge of literature was not confined to psychiatry. When a friend and colleague, R. F. Hobson, "Bob", was reading *St John of the Cross*, Aubrey casually picked up the book and expressed his surprise that Bob was reading that particular translation from the Spanish rather than another that, Aubrey said, was much better. His knowledge of literature, classic and professional, seemed encyclopaedic. It was difficult to take notes during his lectures because he read them out monotonously at breakneck speed without looking up once at his listeners. It started as abruptly as it finished.

He might just as well have recorded his lecture. But if it had been we would have missed the Aubrey phenomenon. He had been particularly keen to collect on his staff prominent members of each category out of the whole wide range of the healing professions related to psychiatry. His collection of representative personalities, as a kind of Noah's ark was unique.

In England staff and students refer to their professors by the first name. When Aubrey interviewed me he was very pleasant. He knew of course all the German publications of my psychiatrist cousin Paul Plaut. After I had passed the DPM he offered me a job on his junior staff. I never knew whether he was offended when I declined on the grounds that I was more interested in what the Tavistock clinic had to offer. The "Tavi", short for "The Tavistock Clinic and Institute for Human Relations", was and still is as well known for its psychotherapeutic approach to the patient as the Maudsley is for its neuro-psychological research, pharmacological and physical treatment. Both have widened their scope considerably since.

The other remarkable figure was Emanuel Miller, father of the playwright and theatre director Jonathan Miller. He was a pleasure to listen to with his lively style and quotations from English literature. Comparing Freud's with Jung's analytic concepts he quoted from John Gay's *The Beggar's Opera*: "How happy I could be with either were t'other dear charmer away!" Miller's lectures were the ideal antidote to Aubrey's for whom we might as well not have been present – or so it seemed.

Neurological lecture demonstrations were held at Maida Vale Hospital; lecture demonstrations on mental defect at St Ebba's, Epsom. All this was part of the 29th Course of Instruction for a Diploma in Psychological Medicine. So was Professor Hans Eysenck, who was then already, and increasingly so later, hammering away at psychoanalysis when he gave his lectures on psychology. Denis Hill gave lectures on the electro-encephalogram. He later became Aubrey's successor and my chief at the Middlesex Hospital. My practical experience at the South African Base Mental Hospital and at the Central Medical Establishment for the Air Force and, now in England, at Hill End psychiatric hospital were essential preliminaries. After the Diploma I became "clerk" to Purdon-Martin at the famous Queen's Square Hospital for neurology. The precision with which lesions in the central nervous system could be localised was as admirable, the inability to do much about it regrettable.

So with all the travelling, personal analysis as well as training in child psychiatry on a bursary, seeing Evelyn and getting married to her I was kept fully occupied. None of this quite numbed the pain of missing my daughters Geraldine and Helen. Being young and enthusiastic living on a demobilisation grant from the South African Government there seemed plenty of energy left for exploring London and the home counties. Some photographs bear witness to these wonderful post-war years when so much was in ruins but the spirit of rebirth was in the air.

The division within the psychiatric profession affected me and my training as it did many of my contemporaries. We had to decide in which direction we wanted to go. Only a few kept a foot on both sides of the fence. Aubrey Lewis in his officially non-partisan comprehensive way lectured that in the history of schizophrenia the fortunes had swayed preferences between the physical and psychological methods of treatment. He added that at the time the psychological approach seemed to be gaining ground. Intensive, "direct" analytically-orientated therapy for psychotic patients was about to arrive from the United States. But soon the fortunes were to sway in the opposite direction. Emphasis on the pharmacological approach has remained the order of the day. Electro-shock and insulin-coma treatment were "in" in 1946 and for some years to come. I practised both as a junior doctor at Hill End Hospital in St Albans and even wrote a paper on the negative psychological effects of the former. Without anticonvulsive and anaesthetic premedication it was horrifying to the patient and not much less so to the staff. We were convinced of the benefit to the patient whose dearest wish was to get away. One was continuously waylaid by patients who asked "when can I go home?" Escape from these overpowering methods was more important to them than even the prospect of cure. I could see the patient's point of view and wrote my first psychotherapeutic paper which John Rickmann published in the *British Journal of Medical Psychology* "Some Psychological Observations on ECT" (1948). But it took quite a long time to sink into the heads of the permanently resident staff who had found a sinecure in the old-fashioned mental hospitals and now with its active, "modern" treatments found themselves more than ever justified in leading cushy lives. The social order and hierarchies had spelt security. Now it was threatened. How many wards could be closed? How about the redundant staff? Would they have somewhere to go? I observed the same in the army before demobilisation, when the same anxiety about the future was felt. Even hospitals become "self-supporting", little empires of administration rather more than instruments for the purpose for which they had been created. Administration was rightly lampooned by Parkinson with his laws. For instance: Work expands with the time available for it. Also: Expenditure rises to meet income. Or: You must always have at least two assistants. If you only have one, some envious people will hint that you may be dispensable.

How I Became a Psychoanalyst ("Jungian")

When I asked a medical colleague at the military hospital in South Africa, a much respected physician and very bright, what he thought of having analysis, his reply was: "It will give you a lot of knowledge that won't make you any happier." Looking back over some fifty years I can see what he meant and that he had a point. If the pursuit of happiness is regarded as the aim and object of life, knowledge, especially knowledge of one's own psyche, cannot have the aim of establishing happiness. Freud's psychoanalysis teaches that the pleasure principle is opposed to the truth enshrined in the reality principle. Art, Religion and Philosophy ("Weltanschauung") are illusory. Psychoanalysis must be a science. The proof? Unpalatable. Nevertheless often beneficial.

Unhappiness has no vote; but paradoxically it may become grounds for secret happiness. As in the course of an analysis increased self-knowledge is an inevitable by-product, so a feeling of superiority over less aware fellow beings may remain at the end. However, most people believe that they know themselves already, therefore more "insight" as the only aim is not marketable. But curiosity is on our side. If the Greeks thought that self-knowledge was the most difficult knowledge to acquire, how exciting would it be to experience the superiority that self-discovery would bring me in due course. Would curiosity kill the cat, or give it new life. In retrospect I can say without any doubt that my curiosity was rewarded. Some new perspectives have been found which strengthened me. I felt less guilty for having left wife and children.

Besides, even in those days I thought that happiness was at best a fleeting state. But, why not go for it whenever possible, knowing that it will be lost almost as soon as found. Yet I wondered how anybody could not want to know about themselves; in fact I questioned how one could live without trying to discover whether happiness means anything other than momentary fulfilment of an appetite including the thirst for knowledge. Longing as I was for such moments, I knew that I could not lead a life in pursuit of "happiness" as a permanent state. It would never be enough for me. I went to England with the intention that analysis should become part of my further training. Soon after I had started on my first analysis, I knew that I wanted to become an analyst. I began by using my psychiatric knowledge in order to show my analyst, Lola Paulsen, how mistaken all her utterances and interpretations were. Her splendid survival convinced me of the viability of what she stood for.

I must first relate how I got to Lola, who was at that time a very junior Jungian analyst. Colonel Purser, then my commanding officer in South Africa had given me a letter of recommendation to a colleague who lived in Thayer Street, just off Marylebone High Street, London, a neighbourhood that became like a second home during my praxis years, 1951 to 1976. He advised me to see John Rickmann, one of the better-known psychoanalysts living and practising in nearby Baker Street. Rickmann sitting opposite me focussed his eyes on the middle of my forehead from which I concluded that he regarded our interview as the potential beginning of an analysis. This would have been in accordance with Freud's "well-polished mirror" role of the analyst who himself remained unseen. I should not be able to guess what went on in his mind while I talked about myself. I had to admit that I did not have the money to pay for a high frequency analysis, the only true psychoanalysis there was, and is still, believed to be. He immediately relaxed and was very kind and mentioned that the Jungians saw their patients only twice a week and advised me to see Michael Fordham. Fordham's spacious consulting room was situated on the first floor in St Catherine's Precinct, near the Danish Church on the East side of Regent's Park, an elegant address. All went well again until we came to discuss fees. He thought that Lola Paulsen might have a vacancy at a fee I could afford twice a week. Years later when "Michael" had become a friend and weekend neighbour at Jordans he apologised for not having taken me on himself. Lola had at the time been in analysis with him. More about Michael later.

"Lola", as she was known from the start, lived in a very modest flat near

Swiss Cottage, a neighbourhood which at that time had not yet become fashionable for analysts to live or practice in. Her waiting room was the kitchen from which one had a splendid view of the bathroom where the washing was hanging up. The living room doubled as consulting room. It had a colourful wall-hanging of a Buddha sitting cross-legged, wearing a robe and a nirvana smile. This adorned the place above the bed that was my couch. That is where and how it all began. As Lola's circumstances changed for the better she moved from place to place, five times during my nine years I was in my first analysis with her. Later there was a proper couch and the Buddha had vanished. But not so the atmosphere of familiarity. We became colleagues when I qualified after five years and friends afterwards. She never was reticent about her personal life. I did not follow her example but even up to this day ex-patients who became colleagues and former supervisees are among my best friends. An occurrence, by the way, that was quite common and almost inevitable in the early days as the history of the circle of loyal men around Freud shows. Looking back from today's point of view over the intervening fifty-four years it is easy to be scornful of the ways the very small institutes were run and the ways analysts practised and behaved with some familiarity towards their patients. But that would mean to ignore the growth and evolution, as well as the institutionalisation that had to take place as the numbers grew. To this day cliqueyness constantly threatens to invade the democratic structures of administration.

The Society of Analytical Psychology (SAP) had been founded only eight months before I came to London towards the end of 1946. Being young at the time I thought they had been sitting there for ages. According to the Articles and Memoranda of the Society of Analytical Psychology there had been seven founders, four men and three women. They became of necessity our training analysts and supervisors. Michael Fordham was the real founder. His wife, Frieda, became an analyst later but in 1945 it was still possible to sign the foundation document as "Married Woman" in the place where the others had given their profession. It has never happened that the wife of a leading analyst has failed the qualifying examination at any institute of training throughout the world. I only know of one case where the husband of a woman analyst was adopted into the profession. He also had none of the professional qualifications that were required of others.

Obviously an institute of training must be an organisation of people who have sound reasons to feel themselves qualified to teach. In that way they also hand on a traditional body of knowledge. But the teachers and their offspring also have a group-coherence that offers mutual support like a religious community does. The similarity may be there at the beginning when any deviation from the group belief or faith is treated as heresy. Gradually, as the group grows and factions and divisions arise in the group so the tolerance of differences is put to the test. Where there was unanimity in the veneration of the founder there are now feuds. Is any deviant, any new or even original thinker or, on the contrary, any "fundamentalist" to be banned from the community that has grown and evolved? Or is the spirit of the community of professional analysts strong enough to bear differences, irreconcilable though they appear? If yes, the individual members, no matter which faction they may feel themselves drawn to, will feel themselves strengthened both in the loneliness of their work as well as in a world outside that is not always in sympathy with the work psychotherapists try to do. As Winnicott put it when calling his paper: "On being alone with the patient".

The office and meeting room were situated at St John's Wood at the house of Fordham's friends; the honorary secretary was an impoverished ex-patient of Fordham's, soon to be replaced by an elderly spinster an ex-secretary of Rudyard Kipling's to whom she had been devoted, as she became to Fordham. There was an all-round family atmosphere. At the Annual General Meeting there was a buffet and drinks, the membership danced (to gramophone records) after all the business had been dealt with in one hour. I was one of the "children", the first generation of trainees; we were five in all. The Institute of Psychoanalysis in New Cavendish Street was already twenty-two years old at that time. It had been founded by Ernest Jones, one of the wearers of the "seven rings" given by Freud to his six "bodyguards", *Leibwächter*, as he called them. He, of course, was the first and last source of knowledge, the alpha and omega. They constituted the "Secret Committee" dating from 1916 following on to Jung's defection. For many years during which I sat on and soon chaired SAP committees, what "The Institute", meaning the Institute of Psychoanalysis did was a model for our administrative and policy decisions. But no symbols of unswerving loyalty like the seven rings could have been handed out. For one thing we did not anticipate a hostile reception, for another we were divided from the start. I also noticed that the persons closest to Freud had been like a band of brothers, whereas in the circle closest to Jung women were in the majority. The difference seemed only partly due to a cultural development during twenty-five years. I thought it said something about the psychology of the two pioneers. Freud was bent on being "scientific". Jung's psyche was feminine, the anima, the other great concept, the self, was, if anything, bisexual.

Institutes and Power Struggles

The division noticeable among our founder members was between those who came from the Continent and/or had had close contact with or had even been analysands of Jung. They were mainly German refugees about ten years older than myself. The other was the London contingent around Michael Fordham who was as much a leader as Ernest Jones had been twenty-two years earlier when he founded the Institute of Psychoanalysis. Many years later, the division led to an open split between Michael Fordham and Gerhard Adler, who was proud to be a pupil of Jung's. In the end he hived off and founded the Association of Jungian Analysts (AJA). All this is well known to older members, but it is not well recorded and therefore unknown to the present generation. Loyalty was something Jung officially abhorred. His: "I'm the only Jungian" is frequently quoted. Everyone should become his- or her-self. Yet he was just as susceptible as the next person to admiration, especially from influential or attractive people. Tolerance of criticism was neither his nor Freud's strong suit.

My becoming an analyst at the same time as training as a psychiatrist involved different kinds of conflict. We were just a handful of first generation trainees. Our beginnings and the development of our new institute were closely intermingled. But whether members or trainees, all of us were newcomers who had to find their way. What went on between our elders and betters both at committee meetings and in their personal lives was as important to us as what they had to teach. We were as curious as children are about the sexual life of their parents. Fundamentally, this human curiosity has not changed despite the increasing membership, committees, office bearers and the caution to preserve the blank screen or "well polished mirror" onto which the analysand should be free to project his own unconscious images and fantasies. Analytical emphasis has changed from a one-person analysis where the analyst is in the detective role to (at least) two persons both being involved in a process of relationship, the "transference". However, the progress has been accompanied by a noticeable change from a family-atmosphere to the comparatively rigid dealings as between civil servants and members of the public, applied here to the relation between training analysts and the applicants for training. Increasing membership requires more and more definite pre-training qualifications. Administration of training programmes and larger housing, all require more money. Trainees today are as keen as we were to acquire the tools of the trade and to pass the initiation rites in order to become fully-fledged and earning analysts. The priority of lessening the burden of time and money spent during five and usually more years of training has not been complemented. But today's trainees are more aware that their contributions are needed to keep the whole institutional machinery going. Their voice and criticisms of the training programmes are taken notice of because of late the number of suitable applicants for training has dropped.

Just as important as the official workings of the institute and the conduct of its members is the friendly spirit that prevails in the small informal discussion groups of members as well as of trainees. Depending on the personality and seniority of the participants the training analysts were called "the inner circle" by the juniors. I have come to regard what happens there as a kind of barometer that helps to predict the climate (cyclical) and the weather (variable) of the whole institution. The atmosphere in all the small professional groups I ever attended was supportive and helpful. The same cannot be said of the large official meetings where party politics and rivalries often masquerade as favourable results of "scientific" importance. When taken together the two kinds of meetings among colleagues gave me a stereoscopic picture of analysis as a political movement, a small world within the larger one of psychoanalysis, and the still larger one of psychotherapy as practised in different countries by social and political differently-oriented groups.

In the post-war years and as a newly arrived guest and potential colleague I was also allowed to attend a circle of psychoanalysts, all male and mainly Viennese or German refugees. One evening the topic was sexual perversions. The verdict that summed it all up was that mankind was "a terrible kind of vermin" ("*ein schreckliches Gewürm*"). It gave me a clue to the realistic but joyless view that informed psychoanalysis. Many years later I was invited as a child psychiatrist to attend discussion evenings at Anna Freud's house at Mansfield Gardens, now the Freud museum. There was a friendly hospitable atmosphere, heightened by Paula the maid and her traditional Viennese *Apfelstrudel*. I could not help noticing that doctors who held a position in the National Health Service were specially welcome. The prestige of the guests played an important role.

The "vermin" view was in stark contrast to the viewpoint of the Jungian groups that I first got to know. Here the manifestations of "the Unconscious" were being celebrated as if they were the revelations of a deity. The focus was on archetypal dreams reflecting the collective unconscious. Of course, mythology was much in evidence as were also its manifestations in the arts and literature that spoke louder to me as I grew older. Other than in dreams the archetypal imagery and collective unconscious could be discovered in various phenomena, notably in mantic methods such as astrology and chirology; also in the visions of saints and psychotics but also in our interpretations of stage dramas like Beckett's early plays.

Far Eastern religious practices were regarded sources of unconscious wisdom such as the mantras of yoga and the illuminating simplicities of Zen Buddhism. Eugen Herrigal's book *Zen and the Art of Archery* popularised the basic notion. The Master could hit the bull's eye of the target even in the dark by means of an inner concentration and one-ness reminiscent of mysticism. Also, much in fashion was a Chinese oracle (the I-Ching). It was regarded as a mysterious source of wisdom that spoke to the questioner's condition. Seen psychologically, the questioner communicated with his unknown self by the random throwing of coins with a question he wanted to have an answer to in mind. I have often been surprised how appropriate and balanced the answers appear to the questioner. In 1951 I thought I had done quite well until I received my income tax demand. I asked the I-Ching "Must I return to South Africa to earn a living?" The judgement was "It does not further one to go anywhere" and: "one should submit to the bad time and remain quiet". A heady wine it was that presented itself in the form of an answer that turned out to be surprisingly apt.

In the same vein, *Jung's Synchronicity – An Acausal Connecting Principle* appeared in English in 1955. It meant that Jung linked different physical and psychological events not by the principle of cause and effect but by a common root, namely "meaningful coincidence". A well-known example: Two people walking together in the street talk of a third, their mutual acquaintance. Then, suddenly and unexpectedly that person comes walking along towards them. The two say, "how strange, we were just talking about you", or, if they are on familiar terms, they might say "talk of the devil". They leave unsaid: "and there he appears", which is based on an old superstition. Jung's clinical example is that of a patient telling him a dream of an Egyptian scarab, when another beetle, the nearest European relative, knocks against the window pane. Conclusion: The realm we call the unconscious possesses something like magnetic attraction. We cannot explain or analyse the phenomena by cause and effect reasoning. It strikes us as eerie. Giving these phenomena a name, synchronicity draws attention to this power. Although nearly everybody can quote an example of a similar occurrence in their own lives the importance of the unconscious in our mental life thereby gains a significance which one could not have realised before.

However, by emphasising the importance of happenings that are inexplicable by everyday causes has bequeathed us some problems. Just because these phenomena can connect without a rational link they seduce one to give up reasoned thinking about an ordinary connection. From then on "meaning" carries that burden. I have heard it said "what does the unconscious have in mind?", as if the unconscious had a mind of its own. And the danger of that attitude is not that "meaning" is attributed by an interpreter but that different interpreters are free to interpret differently. In other words, it all becomes hermeneutics without a counterpole in natural science. And a treatment that is not explicable in scientific terms is an abomination in our time. If it were tolerated, then, analysts would have to demonstrate the curative effect of their method and defend its superiority vis-à-vis the more "rational", easily explicable and quicker "cures". If they cannot demonstrate that, their livelihood is in danger. Small wonder that one hears far less about synchronicity as evidence of the powerful effect of the unconscious on our lives. There remain at least two further problems. One is that of all the possible interpretations of unconscious phenomena, dreams first and foremost, Jung's must be demonstrated to be the most convincing. This implies that the signs and language of unconscious meaning are capable of becoming conscious but can be read and interpreted differently to the patient by individual practitioners of Jung's analytical psychology. It is a problem that also besets Freudian psychoanalysis now more than ever. During his active life Jung's pupils and followers tried in vain to settle arguments between themselves by saying "Jung" or, familiarly, "CG* told me", relying on the "ipse dixit" of the master. Freudians had that difficulty too. What Freud had said and written came from the most "unimpeachable source" as one follower put it. No further discussion needed.

A technical problem that Jung left is how to apply his theory of the collective unconscious in everyday practice. He deliberately left no method or technique, no tools of the trade. Instead there was on one side the limitless field of the unconscious and its transformation into the better definable and more controllable dimensions of language and other expressions such as paintings, music and dance. Although he introduced active imagination** to the analytic repertoire, he maintained "Every psychotherapist has his own method – he himself *is* that method". It calls to mind Marshall McLuhan's slogans. The better known: "The medium is the message" – I read that it is the use of words, be they technical terms or metaphors as interpretations, that expresses the method which analysis uses. But even more so, "The medium needs the message", meaning that the analyst's personality, the medium, requires a method, a theory of meaning or

---

* Carl Gustav.
** Comparable to Winnicott's 'squiggle' in the psychotherapy of children.

philosophy to put across in his work with patients. To do this without becoming an educator is an art.

Power Struggles and Politics

I want to take a closer look at a struggle I took part in. My institute, the SAP London, followed Fordham's lead. It meant the demystification of the unconscious as a quasi God-given entity by taking over some of the detailed psychoanalytic methods. Most noticeable among these was the patient lying on the couch that Freud had taken over from hypnosis, rather than sitting in a chair opposite the analyst as was Jung's practice. In addition, the frequency with which the patient was seen was stepped up. Twice a week had been customary when I began analysis. Later it became three – preferably four – times, again following the psychoanalysts' lead. The theoretical reason for this change was a far more personal interpretation of the transference, one that emphasised the projection onto and even into the analyst of parent figures in relation to the patient's fantasies, feelings and behaviour rather than the conscious narrative. Personal history was seen to repeat itself in the present transference situation. For example the late arrival of the patient at his session as an expression of his/her feelings towards the analyst is closer to Freud's than Jung's way. I more than once "forgot" my analytic session altogether. It was not due to the traffic, nor the alarm clock.

Back to my main argument that every institute of teaching and training, no matter what subject or where, also has its individual political climate and history, often unwritten. It soon becomes evident to the new trainees who, like it or not, become involved because their training analyst and teachers belong to one faction or another of their institute. I call it the "party political climate". It is not exclusively due to different kinds of interpretation of the founder's writings nor that of subsequent generations. Much depends on the personality of the interpreter. Like all people, analysts can be categorised into more or less active or passive, extraverted or introverted, types. These attributes don't do justice to an assessment of their professional skill. We are in a region where craftsmanship and personality are inextricably mixed with the currents of political necessities and the ambitions of individuals.

In addition, there are the wider "outer" politics reflecting the socio-economical circumstances of the country and its government's attitude toward the helping professions all of which influence the trainee's career. It is only at the birth of a new institute that there is the unanimity and the fresh breath of a new found common interest. Youthful enthusiasm rules the day. The small band of founders is like a friendly, mutually supportive family. But soon the realities of competition, differences in viewpoint, alliances or personal antipathies and intolerance begin to dominate theory rather more than practice. Analysts are of course no more immune to human frailties than the rest of mankind. I have time and again been surprised how my colleagues and I fall into the trap of partisanship. As a new trainee one has initially no choice but to follow one's teacher; first one's training analyst, later the most influential dominating personalities of the institution. Officially, as always, the latter is ruled by committees and majority decisions. But there is also lobbying for the sake of personal ambition.

Long ago, I had been deeply involved in the event at the time when the first big feud occurred when a power struggle broke out between Fordham and E. A. Bennet. Bennet had won the Military Cross as a major in the First World War. He had been close to Jung who stayed at his house when he came to London to give lectures at the Tavistock. Accordingly Bennet felt quite happy to entitle his book: *What Jung Really Said.* The Tavistock lectures given and recorded in 1935 were published by Bennet in 1968.* The title alone indicates that he was convinced that he knew what Jung really said with a further hint that others had distorted the truth that had come to the author straight from the horse's mouth. At any rate Bennet held a powerful position as lecturer at the Maudsley and was regarded by the establishment as the authority on Jung. I sat in on his outpatient clinic in Marylebone Lane and was a guest at meetings attended by doctors, mainly in psychiatric practice, at his beautiful consulting room in Harley Street with a Wedgwood ceiling.

The struggle for dominance had been brewing for some time. Bennet had not been a founder member although he would have been an obvious person to ask. Now he was attracting young psychiatrists into his circle. His standing was such that they might well have regarded it as an easier road to becoming a "Jungian analyst" than the detailed and long and expensive training programme of the newly established Jung institute, the SAP. Bennet was summoned to appear before the Council by Fordham as chairman and Robert Moody, his one time ally. Trainees, like myself, were allowed to be in the audience. Bennet had sent me a patient when I first started to practise. Comparing notes with other new-starters in private practice we found that when Bennet sent us patients, they were not only suitable for analysis but could also afford our fee. This was not the case with patients sent by other senior colleagues. Now Bennet was accused of persuading disaffected trainees to come to him as teacher and training analyst all in one. It was only then that he noticed the seriousness of the situation. He was sitting in a chair by himself, confronted by a bench of at least six senior members. Angrily he asked: "What is this, some star-chamber court?" Bennet was referring to English history. This court became proverbial as an arbitrary and aggressive tribunal. The meeting ended with Bennet leaving the Society. Years later Fordham asked him to re-join which he did, although I never saw him at our meetings again.

The next row was big enough to shake the foundations. It was between the faction that was directly under the influence of Jung and the Zürich institute and those close to Fordham who was the protagonist and founder of the SAP, London. Not all their differences could be attributed to rivalry and power struggle. The conservative faction (Zürich) under Gerhard Adler had a legitimate grouse. Those in charge of our administration (London) did not direct trainees to

---

* The title was *Analytical Psychology. Its Theory and Practice.* C.G. Jung was named as author.

them. The training programme contained few of their contributions. It was also true that more and more psychoanalytic (Freudian) concepts and methods were taken over: the patient lying on the couch instead of sitting in the chair opposite as was Jung's practice; being seen three if not four times a week instead of once or twice; transference interpretation on the "I–you" instead of on the mythological and archetypal level. All these standardised traditional procedures have become more flexible in time.

But the Fordham faction of which I was one was more numerous, younger and predominantly English. The "Continent", Germany and Switzerland in this instance, meant "airy-fairy", poetic, rather than pragmatic. The discussions grew acrimonious and the Adler-Zürich section eventually hived off. A few years earlier at the Institute of Psychoanalysis a comparable split had been patched up. The opponents had been Anna Freud and Melanie Klein. The ripples resulting from these explosive forces are still clearly recognisable at international congresses. But their common interest was and is survival. Therefore the tension between the branches of analysis bid fair to keep us alive and united with the help of large roof organisations with registered members. On the level of foreign politics, the lurking threat comes from health insurance systems whose primary concern is to keep costs down. Taking it all in all there is now a degree of insecurity in the profession comparable to that of over a hundred years ago when Freud collected his first patients and followers. If the spark and enthusiasm were as powerful now as it was then, practitioners of analytical therapies would fight politically and cultivate public relations for the sake of their survival.

"Family Feuds"

Unfortunately equality of status, some common ideas and purpose that had united the families were not enough to guarantee a peaceful co-existence for ever. Ours was another case of some being "more equal than others" (just as it was in George Orwell's *Animal Farm*). They adopted tactics against those who merely thought they were equal. Just like before the outbreak of a war, the important first step is to find allies. And so it came about that opposing factions were established both claiming greater authenticity and invoked the ancestor's blessing, Jung's or Freud's as the case might be. The others were regarded as usurpers. As with political parties the democratic way to power is to gain it by gathering as many adherents as possible, the largest clan. In training institutes like mine it means collecting pupils, by becoming a lecturer, training analyst and supervisor of young colleagues whose loyalty can be counted on when it comes to voting at meetings on controversial matters. And so step by step empires were built as disunity and feuds broke out between the chief contestants and their followers. When the trend continued, as it did in our case, a split of the original institution occurred. The outvoted minority with its leader, hived off and founded a new institute. This happened three times in London, so we now have four Jungian institutes. Either the tendency stops or a new unification must occur, if a common enemy or an emergency situation arises from outside. An example would be if the State as the ultimate authority that grants licences and supervises practice to "protect the public", introduces new legislation that curbs the growth of institutes, say by overloading practitioners with office work and making the job financially less and less rewarding so that nobody wants to enter the profession. All of this is actually happening in our time in the healing professions, probably because another emergency, like the State's threats of bankruptcy, dictates that the tap be turned off, starting with the not immediately productive departments like the arts, health and education.

Pay Masters and their Influence

The method of payment and the actual height of fees and the average yearly income of analysts have not been published in any of the professional literature that I read. It is as if it were "not quite nice" to mention such matters. The subject is simply swept under the carpet even more so than the purely human relationship that is not based on the projection or our images like those of parents or of heroes or demons but on the perception of the other's reality as an ordinary human being. This establishes itself in the course of the years that psychoanalysis usually takes, judging by my own analyses. I have come to this conclusion not purely on the basis of my own analyses – experienced colleagues felt as I did. Although I regard transference as an invaluable tool in the analytic process, it certainly requires a nice distinction from a relationship in the social sense. The quality of relationship, in plain words the liking or disliking of each other, is left out in case reports. And yet it plays a part in the patient's future well-being. Hard as it is to assess quantitatively, the indefinable dimensions of relationship cannot be irrelevant. For example a colleague of mine went as a patient to an analyst of excellent repute. When she got into his consulting room he said that the post had just arrived. If she did not mind, he would just open it. I think that this kind of treatment anticipates that there must be a "I doctor, you patient" relationship that prevents the spontaneous and individual development of a transference.

In addition to the social injustice of analysis for those who can pay, a further negative side of direct payment is that it increases competition for the high fee-paying patient, the most senior longest established analyst who have published most, have the greatest influence at their institutes, attract most trainees, have the largest "family" of followers and can reward their pupils by sending them patients who are financially not strong enough to pay the senior and presumably best analyst. This is a pattern that exists in various ways in other professions and in commercial enterprises.

For as long as pressures from outside the analytic professions were minimal, that is for as long as psychotherapy was virtually synonymous with analysis, strife and competition were limited to the main "schools", as Freudians and Jungians, there was no threat to their existence and growth. True, the medical profession did not like the "unscientific" mumbo-jumbo going on which interfered with their monopoly over the body and soul of the patient, with the possible exception of the clergy's domain. The claim was justified in the case of the old family doctors, those general practitioners who knew the whole background of each individual under their care. If they did not know it in analytic depth, they knew them in the gene. Had they not seen each individual into the world and helped the parents of many of them on their way out? But society has changed especially in terms of the patients' mobility and the proportion of the population living in the conurbation of large towns has increased and remains on the move. The doctors do not know many of the patients before they come to the surgery or when an emergency arises. Psychologists, no longer confined to schools, prisons or selection boards, become frequently "clinical". Now there is an ever-increasing competition between psychiatrists and other psychotherapists, let alone between the clergy and the other soul specialists. I witnessed the power struggle in the teaching or "university" hospitals. Jockeying for the top administrative positions was a relatively benign form of power struggle. The medicals there, especially the neurologists have the edge over the other professionals in that they can maintain that the psyche depends on the brain's functioning. So it must have taken a lot of manoeuvring to get the person with all-round qualifications, like being a psychiatrist-neurologist-psychoanalyst into the top places of administration. Success would be complete if that person had also undergone a successful analysis him/herself. But that desirable number of qualifications did not reckon with the complexity of an ever-increasing number of other psychotherapies which does not recognise the importance of the unconscious mind in the motivation and mental health of the patient. Cognitive therapies, like behaviour therapy and their concepts are easier to grasp by common sense alone. They may even claim to know the unconscious too, but do not realise that this is a contradiction in itself. Even if their quick cures do not last, in the short run it looks as if time and money could be saved that way. Research rather than arguments will show who in the long run achieves what.

I have gone into some specialised details about the course of my training. It did not run smoothly, nor was it confined to the subject-matter. The personalities of my teachers and their hierarchies, in brief the human side in combination with the structure of organisations, have taught me another aspect of life. I assume that this is not so very different in other kinds of training and other kinds of institutions.

10

How My Practice Has Evolved
and Some General Reflections
on Analysis as Therapy

The evolution of my practice reflects a mixture of general trends within the profession as well as of my own personal development. The one cannot be separated from the other. To appreciate how this came about I have to sketch in the background.

At the beginning I encountered the strict followers, not to say disciples, of Jung in London with their worship of the wisdom of *the unconscious* in its various manifestations as described in the previous chapter "On Training within a Human Context". At the same time there could be no doubt that the fairly recently (1946) founded Jungian Society of Analytical Psychology took many cues from the neighbouring Psychoanalytic Institute, twenty-two years older. The cues were not confined to administrative and training methods but included psychoanalytic techniques. Most important of these was the analysis of transference as a projection onto the analyst of the patient's parental figures from early childhood on. Consequently, after having qualified for only two years, I divided all the members and trainees, some thirty to forty people at the time, into "Transference groups" of five to six members who discussed and tried to analyse their relationship to each other in transference terms. (Fourteen of these sessions are recorded in James Astor's book.*) The combination of psychoanalytic techniques and Jungian concepts, such as archetypes, meaning here repeated patterns of behaviour including mythological themes as guidelines, have shaped my practice ever since. More recent additions (see "Meeting Famous Colleagues and Other Notable Figures") and, of late, my interest in the socio-cultural environment have influenced my practice. But the over-riding task has remained throughout: how to combine the fellow feeling for the patient as the other suffering human being to be listened to with the professional point of view, to be transmitted by dialogue.

If the evolution of analytical practice over half a century demonstrates anything, it is that the theory and practice of analysis not only changes in time but also that it is at no time the same for everybody and everywhere. The lack of uniformity poses the basic question what analysis is, how it is practised and how it works. I have described some of the ingredients and perspectives in my book *Analysis Analysed* (1995). Writing more personally, I find that the individuality

---

* James Astor (1995). *Michael Fordham. Innovations in Analytical Psychology.* London / New York: Routledge.

of each patient and analyst accounts for the unrepeatability of a mutual experience. This puts psychoanalysis outside the range of natural science with statistics as evidence. Unless of course one takes systematised qualitative and developing knowledge as criteria. The practice of analysis seems to me closer to an art. Its various theories could qualify analysis as a linking science, one that facilitates the relation to and between other humanities, such as psychology, history and sociology, showing ways each can learn from the other. A cross-fertilisation takes place that can only be seen in retrospect. Today we speak of the Middle Ages as the "Dark Ages" or of the rediscovery of natural science as the "Renaissance" and the "Age of Enlightenment". For want of a better name I regard the present era as "post-analytic" in which such a linking science would be a post-modern concept.

The general background does not free me from the need to identify myself. If I look at the constant flow of journal articles and books I can see that there is a frantic search for a definition among my colleagues. Not many of the diverse writings by practising analysts are overtly addressed to this basic task. On the contrary, it seems to be avoided, except that indirectly each one of the multitude of books and papers all gathered under umbrellas such as "Clinical Communications", "Theory and Technique", "Research", "History" can be seen as small particular contributions to the larger question of what analysis is and what it can and cannot do. The classical answer or, better, hope is that it can cure, meaning that the complaint with which the patient came has disappeared or, more likely, become irrelevant. That answer is not only dubious, it also raises a whole swarm of new questions which, again, elude statistics.

The question which must be answered first is, how do we know what happened. Clearly, the testimony of some enthusiastic or disappointed former patients or analysts will not do. Likewise, if as usual, the connection between what seems to have happened in the course of an analysis and the outcome is made by the only witness who is also the reporting analyst. Nor does the judgement of several qualified observers of tape or video recordings help. It only multiplies the difficulty of assessing what really happened. The procedure itself with its confidentiality is further impeded and influenced by being watched through a one-way mirror. There is no getting around the problem in this way because analysis is completely lacking in the quality that the natural sciences thrive on: objective, quantifiable measurement and, as mentioned, repeatability, because each case report bears the unique features of the mixed product, namely of the analytical couple. For want of these we take like a duck to water to comparisons with other patients, metaphors and analogies with anatomy, neurophysiology, psychology and physics. I only know of one brave attempt where analyst and patient wrote notes on each session and published these together (Yalom: *Every Day gets a Little Closer*); a procedure that is nevertheless bound to disturb the free-floating attention demanded by Freud.

There is no fundamental difference between Freud's early comparison of analysis with a surgical operation and later analogies such as laser beams and chaos theory, and a whole host of physical predecessors. Each one has had its adherents at the time who wrote plausible papers. After initial enthusiasm sceptical readers like myself recognise every time that analysis has its own indefinable essence and limitations. Nowadays not a few of us flirt with cognitive psychology: let us have something solid and quantifiable seems to be an ever recurring cry. Something that would convince the public and, above all, the insurance companies.

For me analysis is in the main the art of interpretation known as hermeneutics, such as is required for the "understanding" of a myth like that of Oedipus or the biblical Tower of Babel and the confusion of the tongues, *provided* the metaphor is applicable to the patient. Nevertheless each case can be used by the analyst/researcher to index and categorise patients. If the analytical climate is right the myth and the personal fiction woven around it make sense and so alleviate the isolation of suffering. Also the analytical couple can refer back to it when the theme is repeated in the course of a lifetime or an analysis, as it usually is. Out of a chaotic accumulation of narrated events, dreams and fantasies, sense can thus be made with the help of mythology as the key. I had known about this for many years before I could apply my understanding not only by empathic interpretations but by waiting for the patient to discover the not so obvious causes of suffering and its potential significance almost unaided. I had to have a key or guideline in order to be able to wait or be the obstetrician to the patient's discovery.

Patients, I found, do in their own way and time quite often tumble to the meaning of their irrationality or "non-sense". But I doubt whether they could have done so without my presence. Transference of thought, para-psychology? Maybe. Anyway, the analytic process takes longer than mere talking-explaining-teaching. I am convinced that the effect of self-discovery lasts longer, but our paymasters, insurance companies more so than privately paying patients, impatiently demand quick results.

Meanwhile economy-minded administrators try to bring order to bear into this psychoanalytic, apparently mysterious and therefore suspect and unscientific, method of psychotherapy. They introduce more legislation in paragraphs and issue forms to be completed, all designed to control the procedure and measure the time and cost of both short and long term results. Evidence, please! The sum-total is expected to express the efficacy of cure in terms of time and money. All this goes under the laudable cover of "protecting the public" against hocus-pocus. But I suspect that there is a deep-seated distrust of anything "unscientific", dependant on nothing more than "opinion", unfounded belief. Much like a heresy at the time when the church was the ultimate authority and judge in all matters, only that instead of the "public" the "souls" of the faithful had to be protected against heresies. Science has taken over as the ultimate authority. Instead of the clergy, our administrators keep a watchful eye on the Nation's well-being and the established values of the whole civilised world. To this end they demand "evidence-based" psychotherapy-analysis as of all other psychotherapeutic methods. Excellent. The question only remains: How is the evidence to be collected, if not by the personal belief and the attitude of the collectors? These are the true sources of all reports that purport to reflect the state of art in which I am involved.

Analysts knowing that their own reports cannot objectively reflect what they are doing will nevertheless toe the line which necessarily involves spending more time in completing reports and filling in forms, not only about patients but also showing what they are doing to keep their skill up-to-date. They quite rightly take steps of their own accord to inform the public by lectures, brochures and other publicity, like appearing on television. But so far nothing has lifted the aura of mystification that still surrounds our image. The difficulty is easily understood, if one considers how reluctant people are to accept the notion that no-one has ready access to that powerful but immeasurable large part of the mind referred to as the unconscious. Nobody likes the suggestion that they don't know themselves, nor that what they don't know is not in keeping with the image they have of themselves. In this situation I like to quote Herman Melville who in contrast to our measuring administrators wrote "It's not down on any map; true places never are."

However, I think there is one map of a "real place" and that is the labyrinth. It has a very ancient history and is open to many interpretations. The labyrinth is of mythological significance as in the story of King Minos and the bull. It has also been found in churches like the Cathedral of Chartres. I wrote a chapter about its psychological interpretations in my book *Analysis Analysed*. All that matters here is that it is an "inner" map, therefore "real" in the sense that Melville in *Moby Dick* means. In my view it is a map of space and rhythm, of danger and getting lost, requiring both courage and help to find the way out again.

To give credit to the external and historical discovery and mapping of our world, free of gaps filled in by fantasy, we have to remember that it took courage and enterprise over thousands of years.

To be tolerant of an extraverted view one has to recall that it took centuries before even quite learned people could accept that the soul was not located in any particular organ. I am also mindful that "true places" can easily tip over into utopias and that without an organic substratum there is no life. I have paid attention to the importance of ordinary maps. On the other hand analysts must focus on the unconscious of their patients and their own. For that reason they are, ever since Freud advised it, duty bound to undergo periodical re-analysis, much like Catholic priests have to go to confession. Unlike priests, analysts are never granted absolution by their colleagues. Self-knowledge is expected to temper their omnipotence with humility. It does not always work for long.

The shift from the relative freedom and popularity of analysis in the fifties and sixties of the past century to a state and insurance companies controlled profession in Germany and similarly in most other countries goes to show that the way practice evolves is not altogether the private business of the individual analyst. It runs parallel with the general social and political climate of the country where it is practised. An analyst is further influenced by his own health, family, relationships, maturity and age.

Having practiced in London for forty years, I came to Berlin in 1986. I therefore had the unique advantage of being able to compare the influence of the two relevant social and political systems. My observations in both countries confirm the importance of the financial aspect on the practice of analysis. I mention it here because I have not seen any publications on the subject, perhaps because it is "not quite nice". Money has however played an important part in my life and in the life of almost all patients I have analysed and that of most colleagues with whom I have been on friendly terms.

The British National Insurance, to which everybody has to belong, does not recognise analysis as therapy, whereas the German *Krankenkassen* does and therefore pays for it. This major political difference has many detailed consequences on the way analysis is practised, some of which are relevant here. Others I mention may be of general interest only because they make reference to the taboo subject *money* essential. It plays an important role in almost everybody's life, naturally also in mine. Happily it has never been a guideline for me, rather something incidental. However, I took notice of money as a dimension of reality which refused to be ignored.

I had to pay for my own analyses. Although every analyst knows that an analysis by any other name is still an analysis, a training analysis in Germany is regarded as educational and not as therapy, therefore analysts-to-be have to pay out of their own pockets. And yet, if an applicant had a previous analysis for therapeutic reasons, it does not count towards the hours required by regulation for a training analysis. It is the most essential part of training and therefore of becoming eligible for membership of a recognised institute. This rule has been decisive when I became a Jungian instead of a Freudian psychoanalyst. The requisite money counts in Germany just as much as it did in England. My institute in London gives loans to selected trainees just as it treats selected patients at a nominal fee. I am proud of these exceptions in a capitalistic system.

My knowledge of the differences is derived from close contact with colleagues and medical practitioners in Germany over the last sixteen years. They are paid according to a point system, in fact for piece work. The more they do, the more they earn. Result: they are tempted to do (investigate, treat, prescribe) more than strictly necessary, until the insurance companies complain that there is no more money and the payment per point earned has to be lowered. The "privately insured" charge and pay out more per point than low-earners, who are naturally less welcome, that is they may have to wait longer before being taken on. But this is not nearly as bad as being on the waiting list in the UK's National Health Service. In fairness I have to add that once patients are taken on, be it for a surgical operation or analytic psychotherapy, the low income group gets the same treatment as "private" patients do. The influence of the insurer on the practice consists in all cases mainly in "the presence of the third", the influential insurance company, which not only gives permission to treat but also decides for how long, there being a maximum of hours granted. Not surprisingly written reports to me as supervisor of analysts-in-training begin with the number of hours of the session that was discussed showing how much of the granted treatment time had been used up.

In contrast to the strict administrative but open to all patients, irrespective of income, in Germany the "free practice" UK represents a completely capitalistic system as it also does in France and the USA. Treatment is based on an unwritten but understood contract between analyst and patient. It is not the business of national or private insurance to determine for how long it may go on, nor is the frequency of sessions per week. Of late the State and the General Medical Council of Britain have taken on a supervisory role, again to "protect the public". I assume against all practitioners who may not be qualified or do not take steps to keep up-to-date.

The institutes of training are themselves hierarchically organised and advise on technical details. That is to say the senior analysts at the top demand the highest fees on the assumption that they are the most experienced, therefore the best. The analyst-in-training or junior in the profession depends on getting referred those patients that their seniors don't want, be it because they are unpromising or extraordinarily difficult cases or, usually, have very little money. It takes time and cultivation of relationships to the people at the top as well as all legitimate means, like giving lectures and writing publications in order to become known. But with perseverance most juniors end up as reasonably well earning seniors.

This was the situation when I started fifty years ago and according to a much younger colleague it has not changed essentially. On the other hand analysts in England are relatively free and can have their practice anywhere they like. If there are a hundred obstetricians in Harley Street the patient has free choice. No one else has the right to tell them where they are permitted to have their practice. In Germany the administration determines how many psychotherapists and other medical practitioners are permitted for each district.

To sum up: analysts in Germany are relatively secure as regards earning a living. So far there have always been more than enough patients to go round. But the profession is subject to officialdom telling it what it may do. In England analysts at the beginning of their careers have to tighten their belts and must look out for a steady job to supplement their income. They have to take what comes but they are free to practice as they please as long as they keep to the ethics and standards of their profession.

So much for the all-pervading influence of administration and social structure, as the limiting and containing factor of intrinsic and personal development to which I shall now return.

When I came to London at first I had been bowled over by all the predictive, teleological soothsaying aspects that were then widespread in the Jungian circle, especially in one close to Zürich, as mentioned previously in "On Training within a Human Context". Here was the complete opposite of the active interventions of surgery. The "Jungian" patient at the time had nothing more important to do than to find out what type he belonged to, under what astrological aspects he was born hence what the omniscient unconscious had in store. The patient could help by writing down their dreams and take these to the analytic session. There they were told how to confront the archetypes which, amalgamated with the ego, formed complexes in their as yet unaccepted, unintegrated relation to the conscious life. The analyst's job was comparable to that of a guide and educator, a kind of Hermes in Wonderland. His orientation was given by mythological themes of which there were many more than Freud's implications of the Oedipus story as told by Sophocles. The Jungian analyst's role was also in keeping with the archetype of "the wounded healer". My first analyst certainly did nothing to hide her wounds, rather the opposite. I have not followed her example in this respect, because I felt at the time that the analyst's personal story distracted from my own. She was in many ways an admirable person, who might well have benefited from working analytically with me but it was *my* analysis that counted and I who paid for it. I have tried to stick to that in my practice, although it cannot be helped that over all the years that analysis often takes the patient gets to know details of the analyst's life, nor that the two meet incidentally at a concert or, predictably, at the institute of training, should the patient also want to become an analyst like I did. In spite of all precautions, the patient's antennae are in due course sure to pick up my feelings about them which were mostly in response to what they felt about me. Technically known as counter-transference.

Soon after the initial tuning-in phase I joined the sceptics of the Zürich school in London led by Michael Fordham. Jung had remained a genius for me. His book *Modern Man in Search of Soul* had impressed me when I first read it while I was still in South Africa. But I could not put up with all of the mumbo-jumbo he seemed to inspire in many of his pupils and followers. For the actual tools of analysing we had no other available than educating the patient by means of interpreting his dreams as manifestations of archetypal themes reflected in his own narrative. Personal difficulties, especially in relationships were explained on the basis of differences in Jung's typology, extravert-introvert and so on. There were quite a few other archetypes to choose from, for instance the ever-recurring role of the leading lady in a man's life, the "anima". Or, confronted with his failings the patient was told about his/her "shadow", the archetype representing everything one did not want to be and therefore tried to attribute, project, onto the other. This armamentarium was limited and in my view often more educational than analytical. That is to say that it put bits together (synthesis) before they had been taken fully apart and examined in detail. Our approach also did not cover the events that could be observed directly in the here and now of the consulting room between the you and I of patient and analyst in the course of their dialogue. Details remain more convincing to me than the general archetype for the understanding of events in the patient's life in its continuity from childhood to the present. Differently put, it is not the archetype of the "Great Mother", but *your* mother and *your* personal relationship to her and her successors who incarnate the "anima" in a man's life and as such influence his relationship to other women right up to the present. This is reflected in the transference. The same applies of course to girls and women in their relation to the father and to the present carriers of their "animus".

Starting with the general concept archetype and drawing conclusions from its configurations about the details later characterises the Jungian approach. In our day and age with its Western society's emphasis on the individual and personal achievements the importance of the individual, his successes, failures, relation-ships is stressed. In analysis the "inter"-personal and "inter-subjective" reactions have at present taken priority at the expense of what is "intra", the private inner world of the individual as portrayed in his fantasies which largely determine attitudes and behaviour. In our civilisation the collective "we", like we in *our* family, *our* village or street has lost out to the importance of the "I". Obviously there is a place and a time for both. But nobody has so far succeeded in combining the two, the first person singular and plural, in a generally accepted theory. In practice I have had both in mind. An extreme illustration of combining the two could be taken from the case of a psychotic patient who threw a stone through my window because of a fantasy he had that I wanted to shut him out. He was acting out the "intra-psychic" factor.

Most of us first trainees and subsequent generations of analysts found that we had to borrow tools from Freudian psychoanalysis. Jung had never denied the relevance of a Freudian approach but stressed the importance of the analyst's personality which Freud does not. No wonder that the Zurich hard-liners made "London" out to be heretics, traitors of their beloved "CG". The gap remains and shows up to this day in various Jungian institutes of training and at international congresses. I became one of the moderate heretics using the couch in most cases, interpreting the transference in personal terms, seeing patients three to four times per week while keeping mythological motifs at the back of my mind.

My analytic evolution did not stop there, neither did the psychoanalytic development on both Jungian and Freudian sides of the official fence, that becomes noticeable on occasions when flags of allegiance are waved at large meetings. Closer direct contact between individual colleagues from our different institutions shows that in practice the similarities outweigh the differences by far. After all we see the same kind of patients and have the same aim, namely that by enlarging the horizons of self-knowledge we can help them to become themselves and to accept what cannot be changed, to enjoy better relationships and ease some of their complaints and suffering, even if we cannot cure it. A slight shift in the focus or perspective and attitude towards everyday matters and specially heavy blows can already help to a more contented and fulfilled life. However much I was fascinated by the different approaches to a variety of patients the events in my own life, family and friends were a constant reminder of the common ground between my patients and myself. Here I am thinking of real blows like my drowned daughter and my wife's untimely death, events that had to be suffered and made me equal to all mankind.

But that does not mean that translation and interpretation of symbols from one language and one culture into another is a matter that allows us to ignore worlds of difference. If, for instance, a dreamer in Africa where snakes are common dreams about a snake, it has to be differently interpreted than a dream-snake that turns up in, say, Finland. Or again, Jung's interpretation of an Eastern text, "The Secret of the Golden Flower", a "golden" flower does not automatically mean that any yellow flower that is used as a herbal remedy in any other part of the world is also "golden" simply on the grounds of the unconscious being a "collective" entity. Similarly, a phrase that has metaphoric significance in the mother tongue of one dreamer cannot be understood by an analyst unfamiliar with that language. The same with quotations from the classics of literature, poetry and proverbs or nursery rhymes. Of usual unacknowledged significance is the religious and political background of each partner of the analytic couple.

The collective unconscious lacks a skilled translator. The native cultural, social and political background of both patient and analyst have influenced my practice. Even if the primary needs and hopes of all mankind are the same, I had to learn that there are subtle distinctions in daily usage as well as in the symbolic language of individuals which deserve the analyst's close attention. I have to admit another selective factor in my practice. It has not developed in that my analytic work has remained privately paid for, even after I settled in Germany, where as mentioned, the insurance companies pay for analysis. But I hated their interference and all the paper work demanded. True, that even in Germany the privately insured or better insured patients may receive a subtle preference at the start. But the system on the whole is socially just and selection according to income is virtually non-existent. In fairness to myself I must add that the majority of my fee-paying patients were far from wealthy but they all could afford to run a car.

Qualified professionals are on a refresher course in the form of analytic supervision, deductible from income-tax just as keeping up-to-date by weekend workshops is, whereas the analysis of other persons is therapy, recognised as treatment. Everyone in the profession is aware that the supervision of a qualified analyst involves analysis. Analysis by whatever special name or category remains still analysis. The fundamental principle of bringing the unknown, the blind spot, the unconscious, in relation to the analyst and nearer to awareness is something that has to be taken into account in all our dealings. It remains a way of becoming who one truly is. The techniques of bringing it about are subject to variation and depend on what special theory or pluralistic view is adopted. This applies just as much to training analysis as to supervision. Both remain the most important part of a training and ought to be repeated at intervals during the professional life of any analyst.

Towards the end of my evolution as an analyst, during the last fifteen years in Germany I was in the privileged position of analysing colleagues who had not been in practice for as long as I. This advantage was partly offset by two disadvantages. Although colleagues as patients needed no introductory phase on the other hand they know too much. Or, which amounts to the same, believe they do. They offer not only the narrative of their daily lives, their "reality", but include the cause and meaning of problems, not only their own but also those of persons close to them. They believe they know their 'unconscious' which by definition nobody can. There can only be hints, such as "slips" of the tongue and dreams, about the hidden meaning about which one's colleagues can make more shrewd guesses than other patients. In this way they are able to anticipate my interpretations and interventions such as insisting on greater or reduced frequency of sessions. The temptation to analyse themselves in my presence remains very strong. It is a professional deformation to believe that one knows as much about oneself as one's colleague-analyst-therapist does. I have been no different from these difficult colleague-patients and only the capacity to be surprised about my ignorance of myself and my endlessly repeated patterns of behaviour has saved me. My patients and colleagues, just like my own analysts, became aware of the contradictions in my character earlier than I did. To assume one knows one's unconscious is like assuming that in the dreamlessness of sleep one is aware of who and where one is. A lesson that needs to be repeated at regular intervals. For analysts that means periodically for as long as they practice.

To return to German, the language of my childhood and of the last seventeen years of practice. My "mother-tongue" is not the language of my four children and their offspring, nor the language in which my own analyses were conducted, nor, of course, the language in which I talked to my late wife and to my friends in London. For forty years I practised in England, sat on committees and wrote many professional papers. The split language is relevant to my general problem of identity. The switching from an involuntary, internal translation from one language to another and back can lead to a "confusion of the tongues", by speaking German and thinking, counting, dreaming and swearing in English. I dealt with the problem by putting relatively less stress on the patient's narrative and more on the voice, the nature of speech, gestures and silences, breathing and general "body language", including, of course, my own. I found this helpful for a primary understanding between two people that could be put into words later on.

When I started I wrote detailed notes after each session although I rarely looked at these notes. At first it seemed terribly important to get everything down. Later I saw the importance of such notes mainly as an off-loading without which I could not go on to the next patient. Later still, I began to wonder whether the written summary mixed with my own affective reactions and ideas were necessary for keeping in touch or whether they might lead to a publication as a clinical study. All such publications reveal the therapist's self-interest and pre-occupation. The patient as co-author never appears, he or she is merely quoted. This implies that patients have the right to complain, if they have not given their written consent *after* reading the analyst's description and before their case is published. After several years have passed they might still change their minds and complain about their having been wrongly quoted. Even written permission for publication does not prevent resentment long after the event.

We, the patient and I, are the actors in an on-going drama but who or what is the real playwright? While the present rules of co-operation may be ethically unobjectionable, I feel uneasy, whether publication does harm to the unselfcon-scious spontaneity required by the climate of equality in which the analytical process has room to unfold. A good rule used to be not to publish until the analysis in question had been finished. Another old motto says: No research without therapy, no therapy without research. However in practice I found that I have frequently departed from these ideals.

Taking an overview

Revolutionary as psychoanalysis was at the start, analytic practice has become a mirror of the society that my patients and I live in, the professional politics and financial structure included. We cannot expect our revolution to continue. The fuel has run out. We have acquiesced, become *petit bourgeois*. The realities of money and administrative curbs now take precedence over sparkling fresh ideas.

The evolution of my practice made me realise once again that the mental life of the individual and that of the community are indivisible. It has opened my eyes to the importance of the wider context of analysis which I had ignored up to the time of 1986, the year I came to Berlin, although it had stared me in the face in London already. With the help of a discussion group of colleagues I am trying to look very carefully into the special circumstances just as much as into the predominating theoretical viewpoints which influence everyone's analytical practice. Human beings with their concerns remain the same, however much our perspectives and the terms we use change like the fashions.

The fall of the Berlin Wall in 1989 has been a classical example of the influence of socio-cultural circumstances on the profession of psychoanalysis when the patient came over from the eastern zone. In a paper I wrote on "Cultural Influences on Analysis" I emphasised the social aspect of analysis because I think it had not been paid sufficient attention to. Now it seems right to add that I hope no patient has noticed this specific interest of mine, because each individual has meant just that to me and as such is unique. The way my practice has evolved has run parallel to what was going on around me both in professional and social circles as well as my personal life. My migration from London to Berlin first and foremost. At the central point has been a mixture of concerns. What and how much did the patient need, how much money and social stability did I need to keep fully alive. This was just as important as the mixture of theoretical considerations that attracted me to the profession most and, consequently, worked best in my hands. Jung is believed to have said that it is not what you know but who you are that matters. He had a point. The manifold aspects of analysis I described remain finally unanswered but still play a part in my way of thinking professionally and are inseparable from my personal life, even if I can't always see it that way.

In a later paper "An Undivided World Includes the Shadow" I set out from the assumption that we behave and analyse in accordance with the gods we actually worship. I arrived at the conclusion that we divide the world when we presuppose that the opposite qualities which inform our sensuous perceptions seem "real" rather than remember that they are a model for our orientation. The split is perpetuated by dividing the image of an all powerful god-head, e.g. into God and Satan, Christ and Antichrist. Instead of such dualism I propose a comprehensive "*Weltanschauung*" whereby Evil becomes an aspect of God. I try to do away with the opposites and replace this concept with that of the paradox, giving examples from personal experience. Without Hitler and the wars I would not have become for better and worse the person I am.

Creativity has become a sort of Holy Grail. While I acknowledge the need to have ideals such as this, I also point out their enormous destructive potentials as when new weapons of mass destruction and faster delivery systems are convented. Are creativity and destructivity emanations of the same unknowable ultimate truth? What criteria do we have for creativity? Is creativity, like individuality, the whited sepulchre of our civilisation? Do we not create Evil too? Such "philosophical" questions belong to thinking about analysis and being an analyst as much as an ordinary human being. Freud once called analysis "weltliche Seelsorge".

11
Meeting Famous Colleagues
and Other Notable Figures

I think of my encounters with some colleagues as important events in my life. Their names are known beyond the narrow confines of the helping professions. They gave directions to a form of psychotherapy that dominated the century that has just passed, known as psychoanalysis, analytical psychology or, broadly, analytical psychotherapy and still more loosely, hence often wrongly, "analysis". Nearly all my professional life has been devoted to it. The realisation that with two exceptions they are all gone is the price I pay as survivor. If I call the following personalities "colleagues", I am not exactly modest. They were pioneers in opening the field in which hacks like myself ploughed. I shall return to that point. I nevertheless address them as colleagues because that was how they referred to me, with the exception of Mrs Klein whom I did not know well.

I first met **Carl Gustav Jung**, "CG" as he was referred to by those close to him, at his home in Küssnacht in May 1952 when he was nearly seventy-seven and I was thirty-nine. My then analyst, Gerhard Adler, had written to Jung and consequently a meeting had been arranged. I was very excited as I sat in the waiting room late that morning when his secretary came to call me. Jung began the interview by saying in German: "Ach, das ist der Plautus" referring to the Roman playwright Maccius Plautus. He then asked about my family and told me about his, presumably to put me at ease. In the same vein he continued to tell me about people who came to see him as if they were to meet some guru or demi-God. He would then tell them that he was on the reserve list of the Swiss army and that his wife bought her vegetables at the grocery shop they had passed on the way to his house. He succeeded in calming me down.

Having gained confidence and being seated in the chair opposite his by the window I did what I had intended to do and told him about a dream I had had twice in the same night, once in English and again in German. That visibly impressed him and he repeated "First in everyday language and then in your mother tongue." He continued by comparing transference dreams with projectiles that hit you and emphasised his words by prodding his finger at my chest. My dream had spoken very clearly about a danger analysts, here myself, are in of becoming inflated. He added: "and then they become like jealous gods and can't talk to their colleagues anymore". "You may think", Jung continued, "that you know all about projections but when you sit alone at night and ponder the day's work, the devil comes and taps you on the shoulder and says 'Didn't you do that well?' Then you know you are suffering from an inflation." And so in a very kind, acceptable way Jung had interpreted my dream for which I felt grateful.

Next I questioned him about his recently coined term "synchronicity". I asked, provocatively as I later realised, whether synchronicity was an archetype. He doubted that but added perhaps one could evoke synchronicity. Jung illustrated this by referring to a native of Africa who was shocked when Jung had mentioned the word for ghost, in case the very mention might make the ghost appear.

And so the conversation turned to Africa and our mutual experience of East Africa. He likened the patriarchal attitude of the Boers in South Africa toward the blacks to that of the Southern farmers in the States. Investigating negro mental patients he had come across an old nanny who said to him: "I have got God right inside me, here. He tells me things, sometimes serious, sometimes funny." Quoting her, Jung thumped my chest again, as if to drive the point home.

Somehow the conversation turned to his past relationship with Freud. Jung mentioned how on their journey to America they analysed each other's dreams. Freud himself had, of course, never been analysed and had what Jung called a painful affliction. When it came to an "extremely personal thing" in one of Freud's dreams Jung told him that he would do well to talk to somebody about it. Freud replied that he could not risk losing his authority. Turning to me Jung said: "At that moment he had lost it already." I had heard this story before.

When his secretary came in after about an hour I prepared to go but Jung pressed me down in my chair and again put me at ease by looking at the cigarillo I had been smoking, while he had been smoking his pipe. He said that he sometimes smoked that kind of tobacco too and then resumed the conversation about the religious view of a negro nanny by saying that he was a dualist, a Manichaen (meaning briefly that God and the Devil are both co-existing and eternal principles). For him God was not the *summum bonum*, the ultimate good.

The other stories were also familiar anecdotes but to hear him recounting these stories made me feel as if I had never heard or read them before. I had put him in the storytelling mood just like the professional fairy-tale tellers I had heard; one was in America in the mountains of New Mexico, the other in the market place of Marrakesh. Obviously I am an easily captivated audience. The contact was maintained as he told me about the case of a clergyman who had come to consult him. "One of these princes", as Jung described him, who had expressed his contempt for alcoholics and had come across one of these creatures lying dirty and dead-drunk in the gutter. Jung had retorted: "that man is your brother".

Jung was also quite inclined to have digs at people. "Medical people and theologians can't think." About Laurens van der Post who had written extensively about Southern Africa he said: "He knows about it." And then, with a conspiratorial smile: "But he thinks he knows it all." As I left he told me that I was in a very advantageous position meaning that I was at home in German and English and trained in medicine and analysis.

By now it was lunch time. I had been there for two hours and was completely carried away by Jung's personality, charm and interest he had shown me. Frieda Fordham, who was staying as Mrs Jung's guest at the house, told me afterwards that Jung had seemed stimulated by the interview and quoted him as saying that I had a religious problem. Religion as well as Africa had certainly been major points. He was right but I failed to see how he arrived at that diagnosis.

I left the house feeling in a euphoric mood. Sitting in brilliant sunshine on the terrace of a lakeside restaurant I made detailed notes on the interview of which this is the gist. I felt as if I had been shown a great honour. A friend and colleague went for an interview with the great man a few months later. He had asked Jung how it felt to be so old whereupon Jung seemed to have lost his temper completely and shouted at him that he was not a bloody American who had to remain forever youthful. Obviously, we had met two different Jungs. I believe that both were real.

It is strange how both **Freud** as well as Jung, convinced as they were of the importance of their discoveries of layers of the unconscious mind and their methods of bringing these into the light of consciousness, would have welcomed affirmation in organic medicine. Freud in his earlier days had hoped to find this in his "project" which Ernest Jones had persuaded him to give up. Jung apparently still hoped to find evidence of the mandala in the midbrain. I corresponded with him about this as something like a mandala had appeared to an epileptic patient on electric stimulation of one of the side lobes, the temporal, of the brain. When I pointed this out to him, there was no further reply. The letters have remained unpublished although I had offered them for publication to Gerhard Adler, the editor of the Jung letters. I donated the originals to the archives of the town of Zurich* and kept photocopies. Although I regard Jung as a genius in his field whom I am glad to have met, my admiration does not extend into the field of human relationships.

I met W. R. Bion before I met D. W. Winnicott. They were contemporaries, born within one year of each other, the greatest analytical minds after the pioneers in the twentieth century in London and the whole world of psychoanalysis. Melanie Klein was the controversial figure, with whom they were both professionally joined by way of the object relations theory. Bion and Winnicott were in many ways complete opposites. Bion, it was agreed among colleagues, was as difficult to meet as Winnicott was easy. At least on the surface. I have been lucky to get to know both of them a little more than superficially.

Two events had marked **Wilfred Bion** for life. One was his birth as the son of a British civil servant in India. This meant having had an Indian nurse or ayah and being sent to boarding school in England at eight. He never returned. The other was his experience as a tank officer in the First World War. As an analyst I am careful to avoid the word "split" in my description, because it is commonly associated with schizophrenia. But I certainly gained the impression of there being two Bions. Together they meant that I had met a unique personality, perhaps a genius, but certainly one who could and would not "fit in", having a mind all of his own. I think it was his pointedly anti-conventional and uncompromising manner that made him appear unapproachable.

---

* Wissenschaftshistorische Sammlungen der ETH-Bibliothek Zürich.

I was in the first psychoanalytic group Bion led after the war. He had come from the Intelligence Corps of the Army in the Second World War and had been on the selection board as Senior Psychiatrist of the War Office. He was a fairly tall, well-built man with a big, bald head, wearing dark-rimmed spectacles.

We were six to eight people in this first group, all students, more men than women, eager to learn about groups. Our group met once a week for two hours, starting punctually without Bion who would come in half an hour later as unobtrusively as his large figure would permit. Sitting there, Buddha like, the expression on his face impenetrable, he would take a pinch of snuff. We continued talking about whatever our topic had been, the men, as usual, talking more and trying to impress the women. Taking apparently no notice of the content of our discussion, Bion gave an interpretation. What he said seemed quite unrelated to our subject. Instead it had probably something to do with what "the group" was up to. His reference was remote and I never understood him and doubt whether the others did. There did not seem to be a meeting point between what we had been talking about and his interpretation. Much later, in the second volume of his autobiography, I was amused to read that Bion expressed himself very similarly about Melanie Klein's interpretations during his analysis with her. His focal interest in groups was the group mentality, that is to say the subject that the group was discussing was not what he chimed in with. He knew that his interpretations of the mental process were unwelcome just as humanity was hostile to learning. As the group expected someone to be the leader, so it resented his implicit refusal like a "community" – as if an attack was made "upon its religious beliefs".

It was an altogether different Bion whom I consulted about how to continue my studies when I had to choose between the Maudsley Hospital's mainly psychiatric and the Tavistock's mainly psychotherapeutic approach to the patient. He could not have been more considerate and warm-hearted. As I left he remarked that in this job one remained a student all one's life. Bion's modesty and social shyness were characteristics one could not easily overlook, particularly evident in his *All My Sins Remembered* where I felt he overdid his modesty a little. In fact I failed to discover what his sins had been, unless one counts self-effacement as a sin. In addition the self-portrait is one of a man extremely sensitive to slights. Consequently, his remarks about those who had hurt him were rather biting.

I remained full of admiration for this multi-talented man. His psychoanalytic writings were highly original and indicated how to make and record exact analytic observations on patients and on the communications between man, the animal and man, the tool maker and thinker, the mystic and the civil servant or the "Establishment" of which his father had been an exponent. Wilfred Bion hated conventional religion. At least that is the conclusion which I drew from his mocking imitation of family-prayers beginning with "Our Father" as "Arf-Arfer".

Looking at his biography and letters to wife and family, the artist also manifests himself in his humorous drawings and excellent paintings. It was his courage, however, that won him the Distinguished Service Order, "to cover my cowardice", as he characteristically put it, during the First World War. There was further his athletic prowess that got him into Oxford and medical school. When he had said that he wanted to study medicine in order to become a psychoanalyst it had nearly cost him the opportunity to get into University College Hospital, London.

Of all the psychoanalysts of the past century, barring Freud, **Winnicott** has remained the best known and the most frequently quoted. Deservedly so, because he combined the gift of an original mind with that of a superb communicator. Strangely enough much less has been written about Winnicott the man than about his achievements. He was like a sprite who could suddenly appear, gain everyone's liking and disappear again. I have only two very personal impressions of him. One was a throw-away remark in reply to a cheeky question about *his* mother after a seminar. He replied: "My mother? Well, yes I had one that's all I can say." This answer spoke volumes to me. Illegible, of course, but not unguessable. All psycho-people have personal reasons that led to their coming to the job. When he gave a series of seminars to a "master class" of which I was a member he brought sherry and glasses for us. He introduced an especially interesting case with his original insight and flattered us: "You are all doing exactly the same, I don't know why I am telling you." I once glanced at the draft of a paper he had read and there on the margin of a sentence was written the word "buffoon" to remind him that the sentence had to be spoken in a clowning way. He could certainly act as well as draw and play. The diagnostic-therapeutic tool he invented and used, mainly when seeing children, he called "the Squiggle game". It consisted of the child and himself, spontaneously and alternately drawing some lines or dots on the same paper, each reacting to the other. An unspoken dialogue developed which he was afterwards able to interpret and record in words.

His ruthless struggle against compliance with the environment, as Adam Phillips calls it in his book on Winnicott, was epitomised when he said in a seminar that a schizophrenic who lies in bed sucking his thumb was, for him, healthier [whole] than one who with the help of medication goes to work like an automaton. This outlook was, if anything, even more radical than Bion's vis-à-vis the Establishment. This break with convention had been the spark that launched psychoanalysis at its birth. Without it analysis becomes just one of the many psychotherapies that can be taught and administered like any other craft. I fear this is happening today and could imagine that the practice of "analysis" can soon be left to computer programmers; just as chess is already.

It is impossible to limit Winnicott's importance to one sentence. I think of him as an artist free even of the convention that made his colleagues at the time cite Freud as if he were the *fons et origo* of all psychoanalytic truth for ever. In fact Winnicott's major contribution consisted of a frank departure from Freud by granting and valuing an area equal in importance to the opposites of "illusion" and "reality". This intermediate area of the psyche playing, art, religion and philosophy, Freud had dealt with as unscientific illusions. Winnicott gave it a legitimate role to play in human existence. Analysts will know that I am now referring to Winnicott's transitional phenomena. "DWW", as his names were familiarly abbreviated, was not only a truly free thinker but also a paediatrician and an intellectual heavyweight, who was never "heavy", as some of his books written for the family as well as the general reader convincingly show. In his review of Jung's *Memories, Dreams, and Reflections* he showed great insight and fairness. He even referred to me as a Jungian analyst in *Playing and Reality* at a time (1971) when Jung seemed to be a proscribed name among psychoanalysts.

My closest contact with Winnicott was over a sick relative of mine who came to him for help but lived some distance away making the usual frequency of analytic sessions impossible. He therefore corresponded with me to keep in touch. His notes and observations showed that in his outlook he remained a thorough-going, convinced Freudian psychoanalyst. Reading through his notes years later and comparing them with my own, I realised that the difference was as great as listening to a concert pianist and an amateur piano player.

In case my description sounds idealistic, I would add that "DWW" could also sting. As somebody rightly remarked, he had an imp.

Balint also became a household name in the profession as well as among medical practitioners, as the founder of the "Balint groups". Not that Balint made his name as a group-therapist. But his idea was that some of the psychoanalytic principles and methods, above all to listen carefully and with empathy to what the patients had to say about their complaint, was applicable to general practice and added to the interest of the doctor to the benefit of patients. Their thoughts and feelings, as well as the effect their complaint had on persons nearest to them were often just as significant as the physical and medical aspect itself.

I met Michael Balint and his wife Enid when we were neighbours in Regent's Park, London. We had met before at the Medical Section of the British Psychological Society, which had been captured and dominated by psychoanalysts much to the annoyance of the academic psychologists. For a few years the section became the meeting place of analysts and psychotherapists of all denominations, Jungians included. There even appeared a *Journal of Medical Psychology.* When Balint became chairman, I was his secretary.

Balint's accent left one in no doubt about his Hungarian origins. Obviously a man of extraordinary intelligence, he had added a PhD and an MSc to his MD. Although he was, like Winnicott, a good Freudian, he was far from toeing the party line and replaced Freud's "incestuous" striving with his "harmonious interpenetrating mix-up" as the love desire of all mankind. He could sum up long theoretical diatribes in just one pithy sentence. Stockily built and extremely short sighted, he could be very kind as well as satyrical. I remember a saying which he translated from the Hungarian. "If you have a friend, you never need to worry about having an enemy." Much of his resigned attitude to the ambivalences of life being what it was, was expressed in that single sentence.

Many years after his death his wife, Enid, became my third analyst. We had both loved Michael. Her new husband seemed to know and resent this common bond. That was the likely reason why my analysis with her came to grief in the end. Her seeing me once for a session, sitting together on a couch in a public room of her husband's club, had not helped. Nor had the neighbouring rooms which my daughter Geraldine and Enid occupied at the same time at the same nursing home. Her husband, it transpired, accused me of spying on her.

Michael Fordham was far and away the most eminent among the leading Jungians in London. Even among the Freudians, sworn as they seemed at the time never to quote or mention Jung, Fordham was respected. Not only because of his intelligent understanding of psychoanalysis but also because he took up the cudgels on Jung's behalf in public, while other colleagues stuck to their self-sufficient in-groups.

A long friendship developed between Michael Fordham and myself during the twenty-six years we were neighbours in Jordans and had many stimulating discussions over the weekends. Joe Wheelwright, whom I shall soon present, observed with acerbity but not without some justification that our professional society, the SAP, was run from Jordans. I saw Michael not only as a very good and fertile mind but as a type of Englishman proud of his land-owning ancestry. Far from being bigoted he had something patriarchal, shading off to being authoritarian about him. When I contradicted him, he would continue to argue. Always listening to others, he would not, in Army slang, "pull rank", that is gain advantage by using his seniority. He was older by nine years and very pragmatic, inclined to call philosophising continentals as talking "piffle" (hot air). Fordham's greatness as a human being showed when he had, in his own words, been "very nasty" to his great opponent at our institute, Gerhard Adler. He told me that later he put his arm around Gerhard's shoulder and said that we all loved him very much. This was apparently well received as just the right sort of balm.

Gerhard Adler, a German-Jewish immigrant and former teacher had been an analysand of Jung's and had become, like so many others, an admirer and outstanding follower who published three books. I got to know Gerhard as his analysand for not much more than three months when I broke the analysis off. At that time the Society in London still followed Zürich's rule that every trainee had to have been to an analyst of the opposite sex of the first training analyst. So Gerhard became my lot after Lola. Another common view among analysts was that an analysand's judgement carried no weight because it was biased on account of the transference or resistance or any other technical term that amounted to saying that he or she was an unreliable witness. Traces of this attitude are still noticeable to this day. There is, as usual, some truth behind this opinion but truth or not, I could not get on with this self-loving man. In nearly every session, he talked about his rich and gifted patients who gave him magnificent presents. The implication I felt was that I was poor and insignificant. On the other hand, he had brought about that I could meet Jung. Yet he sold me some books which he had in duplicate. The lesson was finally driven home when on one occasion our session was interrupted by a telephone call. He answered it and sent me to the waiting room while he talked for twenty minutes. Realising that perhaps his behaviour had been wrong, he tried to appease me by offering me coffee. I drank the coffee and never returned. It was some years later that Adler split off from Fordham and our Society. But the splitting process continued and there are now four institutes of Jungian training in London. All that is history. Today the question is how much more propagation of analysts of all shades can the market take? I am glad not to have to answer that question nor the more fundamental one whether there will still be a market.

By far the best known personality among my colleagues was **Fritz Perls**, whom I had met at the military hospital. He too was a German refugee and had written *Ego, Hunger and Aggression*, a title that was also self-descriptive. Fritz became the founder of the Esselen community, where he developed a style of active group therapy, far removed from psychoanalytical principles. At the hospital he gave demonstrations for our benefit which was a foretaste of the Californian mode. Every one of his sessions began with his putting his cigarettes and matches on the chair next to his, saying: "The tools of my trade. First of all I please myself." He gave an unprepared demonstration of this principle, when during his first session after lunch, a colleague knocked on his door with an urgent message. No reply. On entering he found Fritz snoring in his chair, with a folded newspaper over his face and the patient lying awake on the couch. Fritz awoke and grasped at once what had happened. With admirable presence of mind he whispered to my colleague: "Shshsh, I am teaching the patient how to relax!" Small wonder he went down so well in California.

Louis Zinkin was a less well-known but nevertheless important figure within the Society in which we both had been trainees. I was said to resemble him at a younger age. When he died, Helga and I remained close friends with his widow, Hindle, who was also a colleague. I can do no better to describe my relationship to both than by adding an abbreviated contribution to Louis' memorial service at the Guildhall School of Music, a fitting place for he had been a gifted pianist.

My first recollection goes back to 1964 when I was in charge of Child Guidance at the Middlesex Hospital and thought of leaving. I had already come across Louis in connection with his training to become an analyst and thought that he might be interested to take over my job. He gave me a lift back to my consulting room in is little MG, in English racing green, a sports car of which he was very proud. He drove with gusto. Alas, that pleasure was not to last. His failing eyesight forced him to give up driving altogether.

It was about that time that Louis and Hindle became my neighbours at Devonshire Place. They moved into No.10 where I had previously had my consulting room on the first floor before moving to the ground floor at No.11. I think we were more conscious of our being on different sides of the garden wall than we actually let each other know. But when they had got the place straight after their move Louis and Hindle asked me over. Later they came to see us at Jordans. I recall that Louis was always happier if one came to see him rather than the other way round. He seemed happy as a giver rather than accepting anything. There was an exception to this when I visited him after his eye operations which I had been glad to do.

Among the vivid snapshots which I hold dear was a marriage crisis in my own life with my wife Helen which Louis and Hindle were unfairly forced to take sides in. They were obviously quite unprepared for it and were quite shocked. Persons other than Louis and Hindle might have been angry and stayed away. Not they. Instead they offered help by remaining friends with Helen, my third wife and myself. My debt of gratitude increased immeasurably. When, years later they acted as witnesses at Helga's and my wedding, they even offered their beautiful home at Painswick for our reception.

Perhaps I have said enough to convey that Louis' sudden death has left a large gap in my life as, I am sure, it has in the lives of his many friends. By now I have repeatedly said "Louis and Hindle". As in any long-lasting marriage that has truly survived one had come to regard them as an interdependent, inseparable duality. Few of us can know what death must in such a case mean to the surviving partner. I am grateful to have known and loved this couple. Hindle very bravely made a new life for herself and fought cancer over many years until she too succumbed.

Among the Jungian analysts who had both trained in Zürich and therefore met Jung and his entourage where the two American medicals, **Joe Wheelwright** and Joe Henderson, known as "The two Joes". They became the pioneer founders of the institute at San Francisco, today the "Society of Jungian Analysts of Northern California". The two were totally different in other respects. Wheelwright was a restlessly active extrovert, physically a tall man with wide shoulders, not stout, a connoisseur of good wine and food and a great entertainer in whose company one felt in a buoyant mood. If there were several tables in a restaurant, his was the one where the laughter came from. He loved London where he had studied medicine. He had also played the saxophone in a jazz band in the twenties. I liked him, as I believe, everybody did. But I would never have gone to him for analysis. My expectation that he would give priority to information about himself, was apparently not unfounded.

Joe Henderson was and still is an exact opposite. An introvert of slender build, he was a scholar who published books and gave interesting lectures on recondite subjects. Meeting him, I felt he was also a good listener. He is also remarkable as a survivor. In 2003 he celebrated his hundredth birthday.

Hans Dieckmann is the founder of the Berlin Institute of Analytical Psychology, part of the larger Institut für Psychotherapie, the other consisting of the Freudian wing. It is rare if not unique, that one finds both under one roof, and sharing some of the administration and lecturing programme and occasionally even supervisors. "Hannes" is a war veteran who has seen service on the German-Russian front. We have been friends for the last thirty years – still are, and still sharing our losses and complaints while enjoying coffee and cake together.

Vera Bührmann was our pioneer-analyst-anthropologist in South Africa where she was born and so were her parents. The family had originally emigrated from Germany. Her home language was Afrikaans but she was thoroughly bilingual. Her best known book is *Living in Two Worlds*. Subtitle: *Communication between a white healer* [Vera] *and her black counterparts.* Vera has been a great friend and a good hostess to me. I had got to know her while she was an analyst-in-training in London and our communication never stopped although her knowledge of South Africa and its people was, of course, so much better than mine. A person whose very presence was heart-warming, one could not only discuss but also argue with her. Passionately dedicated to her special interest and love of indigenous culture, she could listen to the other person's (my) point of view. I found this combination rare. But then those who were privileged to know her realised Vera was a very special person.

Naturally, many leading personalities in analytical psychology came from Switzerland. I call these the "true" Jungians, if they were his immediate offspring and I am sure they would have raised no objection. I do so in spite of Jung's probably anecdotal, but often cited statement, that *he* was the only Jungian. The appellation as such would be a theoretical contradiction of Jung's major aim. He called the completed development of the individual personality, "individuation". I have never seen it in reality. Nobody can be so individual as not to depend on and be influenced by being in a relationship with at least one person under ever varying circumstances. My scepticism is supported by observations I made on the occasion of my visit to Zürich. Two of the true Jungians were affected by "gesture identifications". When it occurs in small children psychoanalysts refer to kitchen-mimicry. It is an apt term for the involuntary imitation of their mother being busy cooking or other preparations for a meal. In this case it was the speech, the laughter, the way of pipe-smoking of their master that "the only Jungians" had acquired involuntarily. I was not the only "grandson" to make this observation.

Marie Louise von Franz was a PhD and a highly intelligent woman; a good lecturer who researched for Jung and wrote something in collaboration with him but also wrote her own book and many journal contributions. Her identification with him was given away by her laughing and moving like him. She was never seen without her dog which, by contrast, behaved in his own doggy way. She founded the Research Institute for Analytical Psychology including its Journal having cast off from the existing institute which did not follow Jung's views closely enough for her liking. It is still going strong. I quite liked her without feeling warmly for this creative personality.

C. A. Meier ("Freddy") had been a medical before undergoing an analysis with Jung. He drove up to Küssnacht for his analysis for an astonishing number of years even after he had become professor at the technical college, the position he took over from Jung. He had also taken over the exact mannerisms with which Jung smoked his pipe. He drove very fast and his relation to his wife was locally compared with that between Zeus and Hera, meaning that he was always gadding and travelling about while she stayed loyally at home. An archetypal couple.

Heinrich Fierz was already approaching fifty when Toni Frey introduced us. He was a psychiatrist, the head of an institution; of spare build and an aesthetic man. There was something aristocratic about him when he told me that in every generation of the Fierzes there was one eminent figure. In his it was his brother, Marcus, a mathematician who had helped Jung to bring some statistical evidence to bear on Synchronicity. Jung never ceased to look for "hard" support for his concepts in physics or mathematics. Freud had given up his comparable "project" at Jones' advice. Heinrich was a well-read and educated man. His Jungian leanings were towards mantic (soothsaying) methods particularly numerology. He gave numbers to every letter of my three first names and my surname and then went into complex calculations that in the end enabled him to tell me something about myself. It did not impress me at the time and I have forgotten what it was.

Last but not least, **Jolande Jacobi**, a voluble and cheeky Jewish Hungarian, a roundish woman of uncertain age. She had even dared to tell Jung a few home truths, as she only too readily admitted to me. When I saw her she talked at full tilt, mainly about herself and her heroic deeds, for instance how she braved the Nazis to rescue her husband. The students at the Jung institute at their annual fête stage a little play. The sketch I was told about showed a student-to-be doing the rounds of analysts before deciding on the right one for their training. Each analyst this student saw closed the interview with: "Whatever you decide, don't go to Jolande."

Other notable representatives of the next generation were my late and very old friend Toni Frey and the prolific writer and traveller Mario Jacobi. Toni with his degree in philosophy and dry sense of humour, always supported by his wife, Rita, was a special warm-hearted and passionate person. It is heart-warming to know her making a life for herself after Toni had died after seemingly endless suffering following operations for a stricture of the oesophagus. Their hospitality at the time when I had been a frequent visitor and lecturer at the Zürich institute was unforgettable.

Nor are the Jungians short of new stars. There are a good many. If I only mention two it is because I did not get to know the others at close quarters. Others rose like meteors but disappeared without trace. Among those whose place is surely among the "stars" is my best friend, "Andrew", as Professor **Andrew Samuels** is known all over the world. The world has to be taken literally. From his native Liverpool to almost all European capitals, to America, North and South, to South Africa, Australia and Japan, wherever analytical psychology has been heard of, Andrew has given lectures. He is known as the author of seven books, many translated into several languages. He is the father of by now three children, and professor in analytical psychology at the University of Essex, visiting professor at Goldsmith College, University of London. I don't want to go on, no one can doubt Andrew's star qualities, as author, speaker and tutor. He has been my friend for nearly thirty years, from shortly after the time he had been in supervision with me, and just before he wrote his first book *The Post-Jungians* that established his claim to fame, to the present day. After discussions with Andrew no matter whether personal or professional even now mainly over the telephone I always feel better. We trust each other.

The only thing Andrew is not applies to his co-professor at Essex also a friend, **Renos Papadopoulos**, whom I first met at Cape Town where he was lecturer in psychology. He acquired his doctorate there after he had emigrated to London. Renos is a linguist. Speaking not only Greek, Italian and English, he knows Serbo-Croat and has turned his knowledge of that language to good account during the critical years, not just lecturing but actually helping the victims of persecution. He is also a religious man, much more as a practising Greek Catholic than Andrew is as a Jew.

There are many other leading figures, several of them known to me, in England and other countries, notably the US. I hope to be forgiven as if I don't mention them as part of my biography it is because they were not part of my "family".

I too have been a leading figure in my society not only as one-time chair of committees but more particularly as editor of our journal, the *Journal of Analytical Psychology*. I well remember the little launching party of the Journal when my copy of Vol. I No.1 was signed by the editor, Michael Fordham and the four assistant editors: Gerhard Adler, John Layard, Robert Moody and Leopold Stein, whose ranks I joined three years later when I had become a frequent contributor.

After a contested election, I took over editorship from Michael Fordham who had been editor for the first fifteen years. That was in July 1971. I had been closely associated with the affairs of the Journal from its inception and had picked up many useful tips from Michael over the weekends at Jordans. He had quoted a professional editor to the effect that the trouble with editing was the authors. But by and large I found this not to be the case and enjoyed meeting the authors at least on paper, many of whom I had not known before. The job entailed keeping abreast of the literature, meeting the printer and other people in the publishing world and going to some social functions which I would otherwise not have attended. So, editorship proved to be an eye-opener.

I continued until the January issue 1977, when the time seemed to have come to change the Journal from a half-yearly into a quarterly publication, there being sufficient demand on our space. My wife Evelyn had just died and that was the reason why I asked the Council for help with the increased work which editorship of a quarterly would entail and Judith Hutsback was elected co-editor from April of that year. I think we got on well together for the next two years when I asked Judith to take over sole editorship. She proved to be an extremely capable successor.

Like all editors right up to quite recently, I relied heavily on our invaluable Journal secretary James Seddon, one time observer in the RAF who in his unobtrusive way did a superb job. The Journal and all who were associated with it owe him a lasting debt of gratitude. James and I managed to get the circulation up to a figure that, to my knowledge has only recently been surpassed. It is a matter of some pride to us all, that over the forty years of its existence, the Journal has gone and is still going from strength to strength under various editors in London and the US.

"Miss Freud" and Melanie Klein

That is how Anna Freud, Sigmund's daughter and close associate was generally referred to by her followers. I had read her *The Ego and the Mechanisms of Defence* when I was first introduced to her because of my position being in charge of the Child Guidance Clinic at the Middlesex Hospital. The book mentioned was a translation of her original German edition published in 1936. In psychoanalytic theory as well as in Jung's analytic psychology the Ego plays an important part and is regarded as a very vulnerable entity from early childhood on. No wonder then that it needs "defences". "Mechanism" is however a typically psychoanalytic term and incompatible with Jung's humane attitude and my own view of the psyche which is conceived as too pliable a concept to be regulated by mechanisms like an engine. Nevertheless when I looked at her chapter "Identification with the Aggressor" I realised again how apt this term is not only in the case of children, especially boys, who in their play so often pretend that they are the dangerous bully of whom others, or the therapist, have to be afraid. It helps them, temporarily, to deny at once their own anxiety and to deny their guilt about having injured others; that "other" had always attacked first. President G. W. Bush's self-righteousness which determined him to smash up Iraq bears the features of "Identification with the Aggressor", the wicked Saddam. Not having found so far Osama bin Laden, the person who is suspected of having been behind the atrocious attacks against the US and the original personification of Evil, Saddam had to do.

I have already mentioned Anna Freud in the chapter on training. Here is more about her as the person I met. Anna's leading of the discussion of our cases was always helpful. She did not speak with the "having to be right" assurance with which many of her colleagues spoke. Anna was persuasive and had her father's rhetorical gift and wit to give long vivid lectures with hardly any written notes. After a lecture I attended that had been about a child, a former patient, there was as usual a discussion. Someone got up and said we had heard a lot about the child's relation to her mother but nothing about the father. There was some truth in it. But it brought the house down when Anna began her reply with "I have never [before] been accused of leaving out the father."

Her famous antagonist at the Psychoanalytic Institute was Melanie Klein. I heard her speak while she was wearing a wide brimmed hat but did not get to know her personally as she seemed constantly surrounded by a bodyguard of young people, mainly men. She spoke and lectured with the self-assurance which to this day characterises her followers. A split of the institute as the result of the years of "controversial discussions" between the leading ladies and their factions was narrowly prevented by Sylvia Payne, my predecessor at the consulting room at 11 Devonshire Place, a generous and diplomatic lady who later was ennobled as Dame Sylvia Payne. As for Melanie's practice and more doubtful theories, these were based on extreme but nevertheless original ideas about human aggression and destructive fantasies based on envy and jealousy from birth on. In that she was more extreme than Freud and even her own analyst, Karl Abraham of Berlin but her statements have stood the test of time. The Kleinians are still a strong direction within the mainstream of psychoanalysis. Both Winnicott and Bion have been influenced by Melanie Klein who at one time had been their analyst. Once again I felt how important family relations were in the profession and probably elsewhere. The persons I described had got to what they became under their own steam.

12
Hobbies, Old Maps, Gardening and Painting

It all started when shortly after my arrival in England during the immediate post-war period I looked into the window of a suburban antique shop and saw a framed map. It caught my eye because of its unusual design. It looked like a scroll with continuous bands running up and down the page. On close inspection it showed the highway from London to Portsmouth. Each band was decorated with a windrose that gave the direction in which the road was running on that section; bits of landscape, place names etc. were marked for better orientation, as was also the time it took by horse and coach to get from one place to another. I noticed in particular that the present South London Vauxhall had started life as "fox hole". Eventually I could not withstand the attraction of Ogilby's eighteenth century map any longer and bought it for the considerable sum of ten shillings (fifty pence in today's currency). A price I had to think about every time I passed the shop window and also in between.

The map remained a solitary piece among my decorative valuables. It remained so for at least twenty years when the business of establishing myself and family needed all my attention. But the hook had stuck fast until the pull began to draw me to the then predominating specialist book and antique map shop close to my consulting room in Devonshire Place, "Francis Edwards", established at 38 Marylebone High Street. I had to pass it frequently until one day I needed no further excuse to gaze into the window of what was a unique shop, the only old one in London originally designed as a bookshop. So in I went.

Some while passed before I met Mr Tooley who became an eminent figure in the map world, commercial as well as academic, editor of *The Map Collectors' Circle*, author of several distinguished books. I was of full admiration for his sales technique. He showed one a map, explained its origin and merits and mentioned the price. After that he left one standing leaving it to the appeal of the map to do the rest while he was busying himself elsewhere waiting for the customer to come to him having been hooked. No bargaining. His attitude to the sale was "take it or leave it". I took it and bought my second map for £17, again quite a bit of money even if money had devalued a lot during the intervening twenty years. But I was now earning, no longer mainly living on a government grant. The map is still a prized item in what remains of my collection after I sold most of it before I moved to Berlin. Regretfully. But leaving my house meant less wall space for the display of framed maps. The map came from the 1513 edition of Ptolemy, the Alexandrian mathematician and astronomer, whose geographical tables were rediscovered in the fifteenth century. His original maps are lost and all Renaissance editions are reconstructions from the author's written tables. Mine came from the Strasburg edition (1513) and showed a section of the North African coastline and part of the Mediterranean. In his Geography, Ptolemy had divided the then known world into twenty-seven tables which were marked with a grid, giving longitude, latitude and climates as well as the distances of the sun at midday in terms of hours from the equator. All this amazing mathematical achievement had been lost while mediaeval map makers depicted their highly entertaining but nevertheless mainly confabulated geography. I have often wondered whether W. R. Bion knew about Ptolemy's work when he invented a grid with the help of which the theoretical assumptions and interpretations behind the psychoanalytical observations could be located and "mapped". But he does not mention Claudius Ptolemy among the references from outside the analytic field.

Today I only possess one other map that, like the first Ptolemy, is based on a grid but is also a hybrid in that it also shows mediaeval features, based on legendary Roman origin, like the monocular human being in the middle of the roughly-outlined African continent. It is about forty years older and also a woodcut edited at Basle, in Sebastian Münster's atlas, the *Cosmographia*.

Nearly all the maps one sees in specialist or antique shops come out of atlases or books. There are several reasons for that. One is that antique atlases are far too expensive for most individual collectors to buy, so they rightly go to the national libraries or museums where they are expertly preserved. The other is that the maps cannot be displayed when bound in an atlas. Dealers buy up atlases and break them up into separate maps stating that the atlas was defective. Single maps from favourite areas are then much more readily sold to collectors like myself. Such maps are highly decorative as well as historically informative. This is a unique way of making one aware how long it took man to discover his world. The history of discovery was what had interested me already as an adolescent.

All "map-nuts" like myself have their speciality by which they are sometimes introduced after their names when map collectors, dealers and academics meet. I became "Plaut – Paradise". Mine was Paradise because its existence on a map had been sufficient evidence of its reality. International congresses and fairs gave me the opportunity to meet interesting professionals, librarians and academics and all kind of amateur collectors. What is it that determines an amateur collector's favourite area? In the case of a national library it is of course pre-determined. The Library of Congress for example after some twenty years of negotiation acquired the first known map of America. It is of enormous size, requiring twelve strips of woodcut put together. The map is the only surviving print, the year 1507, the author's famous name is Waldseemüller. It had been in private possession, law had protected it from export. Then, as a gesture of German–American friendship, the law was lifted and a sales figure could eventually be agreed upon. Statesmanship and money celebrated a happy union in the place where it belonged.

The amateur collector is free to express his individual choice but is limited by the pocket. Nationality and birthplace of the map maker are of some importance here as well, so are favourite holiday areas. The whole world or continents are hot favourites. But there are many others like the collector's birthplace. Not being able to afford world maps I finally chose maps of Paradise as my area because it is a Utopia as well as mythological and can therefore only be projected to anywhere as long as it is "in the East" according to Biblical source. There must also be four rivers meeting at or issuing from the place. I read around the subject until I was able to write about it myself. My "General Gordon's Paradise", more about him later, appeared in the magazine *Encounter* (June–July 1982). I was also asked to contribute the section on fantasy maps in a lexicon of the history of geography, and was elected a Fellow of the Royal Geographical Society.

For fifteen years I actively pursued cartobibliography until I left England in 1986. Was pursued by it would be nearer the truth. To my knowledge it did not interfere with my professional work but I had a conscience about it possibly having had a detrimental effect on family life and finances. There was a lighter side to this. Whenever I was caught unpacking a map from the trunk of the car and the family noticed that there was something secretive going on they asked me about it. My standard reply was that the parcelled up map was "something I had picked up very cheaply, a long time ago". Of course, the opposite was the case. But the transparent excuse became a standing in-joke. All this was a long time ago at the high point of my life.

I asked myself what it is that makes a person collect old maps. They are in the first place images and men are drawn to visual images much more so than most women. The vast majority of painters are men and I do not think that this is because of the late advent of feminism. Buyers of pornography are almost exclusively men. But the magnet of a possible sexual component can also act as a catalyst for acquaintance and serious study. Old maps with their distinctive outline are often distorted geographically which makes them all the more interesting, whether the mis-shape is due to ignorance filled in by fantasy or merely due to the difficulty of getting the globe projected onto the flat surface. For closer acquaintance with a map one has to know something about the historical and political context of the epoch and the intention of the maker. Further study leads one to get to know not only the map makers and their patrons, but also the techniques of printing and lettering, the composition of the colour, whether contemporary or recently added. What colours were available when the map was printed? Were the conventions that the sea was blue and the country green? Knowledge is further required about the paper and watermarks. The condition the map is in, its importance in terms of progressive knowledge or the opposite; its scarcity on the market at any given time and the fashion among collectors. All these go to determine the market price. But in the end the collectability is largely determined by the sheer decorative beauty of the map that attracts an average amateur like myself who sees the map he always wanted in a shop window and can hardly wait to buy it.

Maps in shop windows are usually well known and not rare. If they were, the price would be accordingly high. All antique maps for sale fluctuate depending on the market but in time they become, like other antiques, more expensive.

Other characteristics also help to date a map and the nationality of the maker. Is north at the top or is it as in older and rarer maps east (Paradise), or south or, rarely, west? Are the mountains drawn as chains or mole hills, are the oceans left blank or indicated as parallel striped, stippled or wavy lines? What flags, emblems, coats of arms are shown? So many details to study. My remarks concern mainly world maps and maps of continents and whole countries. Witness the framed maps on the walls of homes. If the attraction got seriously bad and there was enough in the kitty, I would even attend sales at Sotheby's where the competition from the professionals usually acted as a deterrent. Once I was lucky and sold a map for £4000 which I had bought from a bookshop in Italy for £800. And yet I found it hard to let the map go.

But in spite of all the explanations given and my no longer collecting, the magic of maps still works. Whenever I see one out of the corner of my eye in a shop window or on the wall of a hotel or public building I make for it and establish whether it is genuine or a modern copy. Then I look to find out the maker, date and colouring. It has become irrepressible as a drive, like hunger or sex.

Paradise, as a personal choice among many possible "locations" is one of the utopias and as such of particular psychological interest. Once a place is located, "earthed" so to speak, it gains credibility and is believed to be true and correct to an astonishing extent. At a time when the scriptures alone represented indubitable knowledge the additional authority of a map showing the earthly Paradise was established forever. We can convince ourselves of it being real by putting any fantasy place on the map, however wish-fulfilling it may be in reality. Pride of place among the utopias go to the earthly Paradise. The Bible tells us that it is in the east. But east of where?

Localisation represented still carries convincing power. Even psychoanalytic theorists use location in a hypothetical space, the aim being to orientate themselves and their colleagues. I read about a Japanese con-man who had a less harmless intent when he invented an island republic in the Southern Pacific which was a tax-heaven. He was issuing expensive passports to this "paradise" to which investors could shift their ill-gotten gains. I do not know whether anyone was duped but the issuer of passports accompanied his brochure by a map showing the locality. The con-man certainly knew how to convince his would-be victims.

The convincing power of maps is best illustrated by the historically classical example of California shown as an island. Eyewitnesses had testified sometime early in the seventeenth century that they had circumnavigated California which made it into an island. This happened at a time when the Dutch rivalled Spain for supremacy at sea and as a colonial power. The report may have been accompanied by a map which fell into Dutch hands. They were indubitably the foremost map makers in Europe at the time, who had then showed California as an island. For over one hundred years this held sway among map makers as if it were gospel.

The various mixtures of fact and fantasy attracted my interest professionally and my hobby drew me into the same twilight region. Surely the last person in history to "discover" the true site of Paradise was the British General Charles George Gordon (1833–1885). He was stationed at the god-forsaken military post of the garrison at Mauritius, meant to guard the sea route to India. Maybe he was bored at the time when he put various clues together. Always a keen Bible reader now passages in Genesis suddenly gained for him a new significance. His main evidence stemmed from the Bible and his belief in the sinfulness of man. At any rate he came to the conclusion that Paradise had been situated in the Seychelles. He constructed a map accordingly. In the localisation of Eden on a map Gordon had had many predecessors going back as far as the sixth century. But none had given the various textural and geographical evidence as precisely as Gordon. After he had been slain at Khartoum he became a hero in England. His courage, or rather fearlessness (not the same thing!) was well known. The Seychelles lay on the way to India. There was the fruit of a palm tree, the Coco de Mer, resembling a woman's pudenda. Gordon photographed it. There was further a snake. All the geographical "evidence" was in keeping with his interpretation of Genesis. Furthermore he wrote: "Milton wonderfully works it into my ideas", and quoted lines from *Paradise Lost*. Gordon was now completely convinced. I do not know whether he was able to convince anybody else.

More than a few people believed Gordon was a little mad. He certainly had no capacity for symbolic understanding. It had to be reality or nothing. As a Royal Engineer he had been very inventive and could draw maps. I think my psychiatric chief would have referred to him as "a tame schizophrenic". As a personality Gordon was anything but tame, rather the opposite, being of fiery temperament. The only woman in his life he was close to was his sister. The War Office surely found him awkward despite his great merits. His brother Henry published Charlie Gordon's journals including details of the "discovery" of Paradise. The last biography about him was published in 1993. My professional interest as a psychiatrist and the map hobby met in this historical figure.

In the outhouse I had built for table-tennis and a general play area I set up a trestle table for framing the most decorative maps I had collected over the years. I had learned the craft by watching the artisans at nearby High Wycombe, a centre for furniture making. Of course, I never reached their professional standards. But a few of the maps I framed have survived for forty years and are decorating the walls of my home in Berlin. The parting from many valuable framed maps when I left England in 1986 was painful. It still is.

The garden at Old Ways, Jordans, Bucks, was a great source of satisfaction to me in spite of all the work it meant. Many a summer weekend was spent working in it and my wife, Evelyn, and Adrian too took turns to cut the ample lawns when rain had made them grow or my work prevented me from doing it. The younger, David, usually managed to escape. He often could not be found either when visitors came. I must admit that I joined him once in hiding when such an unexpected intrusion occurred. But I believe that none of us four could have imagined our house and home without the sizeable garden, its roses, lawns, orchard, vegetable patch and play area with outhouse. I also loved the smell of compost and well-rotted manure, as all gardeners will appreciate.

It was our neighbour Frieda Fordham, an impassionate gardener with plenty of experience, and the help of a gardener from whom I learned a lot. To this day I remember that *Philadelphu* means lilac, *Syringa* is jasmine, and *Laburnum* is Latin for the tree that in Germany is aptly named *Goldregen* (golden rain). All the first blossoming trees are varieties of *Prunus*. It is spring again as I write this. Roses that bloom later may go by many names, particularly the modern spectacular hybrid-teas. New varieties and names are added yearly. Then there are the floribunda type of roses like the white "iceberg". The old-fashioned and most highly scented but sparse by blooming Bourbon roses are rarely seen at a florist's. Latin botanical names are still in use in nursery catalogues. For instance the *Cornus*, which turns sealing-wax red in winter, also goes by the humble name of dogwood.

The all-round most-valued piece of the garden was the mighty oak tree that marked the boundary between our garden and the neighbour's field. It had been estimated to be four hundred years old. Evelyn in her resourcefulness had slung ropes over it and constructed a swing for our sons, Adrian and David (Plate 11). Underneath it they waged their post-Second World War battles and died their heroic deaths before fighting on. In the autumn its leaves were gathered to make leaf-mould, the remainder used for setting the fallen twigs and branches alight to make bonfires and bake potatoes in the hot ashes.

Roses were my favourite that I wanted to get to know all about. I knew something about the growers and breeders and the prizes they had won at horticultural shows. My enthusiasm had begun with a tragedy, the death of our three-months-old girl, Yvonne. I shall come to that disastrous day. I drained and hacked up the cement that had formed the pond in which she drowned. Then I filled it with the best earth and added bone meal and other nutrients before planting roses in the area that had been her watery grave, only a few steps away from the entrance of our house.

Even now, over fifty years later, I have delayed writing about the disaster that had befallen us one Wednesday afternoon while I was doing my session at the Child Guidance Clinic. The secretary interrupted my working with a child. I was urgently wanted on the phone. In the corridor she told me that it was our doctor with some bad news. He tactfully introduced it and ended with the words "we could not save her" while the secretary took care of my patient and his mother. I left and drove as quickly as I could to the corner where Evelyn was waiting with a neighbour. I remember that I had prayed not to let me commit suicide or kill anyone by reckless driving.

A couple of days later, it had been the fifteenth of May, the pink, double-flouring Japanese cherry strewed the ground with its blossoms. I read a Japanese verse: "Although on the sign is written: 'Do not pick the blossom!' it's no use against the wind that cannot read." Evelyn never forgave herself for having left off the brake of the pram. The slope of the ground and the wind had done the rest. A few weeks later we had to go through an inquest.

Gardening is not all beer and skittles. There are nearly as many blights and pests as there are scents and colours and a lot of time and money needs to be spent on fighting pest and prevention, on weeding and nourishing the soil. But taking it all in all, I agree with another saying, also from the Far East: "If you want to enjoy yourself for a few hours, take a bottle of wine; if you want to have fun for a year, take a wife. But if you want to have pleasure all your life, take a garden."

Gardeners, professional gardeners, that help the owner not only with labour but with their know-how were already becoming scarce and expensive. I remember two, both were characters. One was Irish. I enjoyed his lilt as well as phrases like a plant was "going home", meaning it was dying. The other was a sturdy son of the English soil. His hands were what fascinated me. It looked as if they were hardly moving yet the work they were doing, like cutting roses back or grafting a tree for hybridisation, was fast and sure. They were just like the hands of an extraordinarily skilful surgeon I had once assisted. He tied off four or five spurting arteries in the time I clamped one. They were like the hands of a magician whose "quickness of the hand deceives the eye".

The best thing about gardening, even if it was something monotonous like cutting the lawns, was the doing something, moving about using one's hands, and seeing the results of one's labour. All that in stark contrast to sitting in the analyst's chair for eight to ten hours, five days a week and often a couple of hours on Saturday mornings as well. What a wonderful antidote gardening, enjoying the country side and walking the dog, our golden retriever Nina, across the fields. Perhaps I owe my longevity partly to those twenty-six years in the countryside at Jordans.

Nostalgia overcomes me when I think of the prime of my life and the person I shared it with, Evelyn. At such moments I feel particularly lucky to have my sons with their own recollections and my daughters who came from Africa to visit us when we lived at Jordans. I had lived as if there was no tomorrow. Time went by unnoticed. My wife was much more conscious of time. She once told me that I had reached my peak. The proximity of her death, although she could not have known about it then, may nevertheless have sharpened her sense of time.

When I come to think of it, I believe that women in general are more time conscious than men. Biology, the onset, duration and end of menstruation, pregnancy and the menopause contribute to this strong feminine awareness of time. Men are better at estimating distances. I know that my disabled back has limited my walking without a break for five hundred metres at best. When I ask Helga or any woman of my acquaintance how far she thinks it is to a certain shop the answer will be in form of the minutes it takes her to get there. Mine is the number of metres I can walk. But professional runners, male or female think of distances, of course, as measured in metres.

When I began to reduce my practice about three years ago I decided to attend an art class. Until then I had drawn at odd times most of my life more often than I had painted. The time had come to do it more systematically when I saw an advertisement at the physiotherapist's. One of the partnership turned out to be the wife of my future teacher. The reason for attending at their studio was an arthritic condition. As usual, a chain of unfortunate events that led to something positive.

When I started to go to Andreas' Thursday evening classes not far from where I live there were five other pupils, almost always all middle-aged women, their particular style already set. The atmosphere was pleasant, friendly, supportive even when critical. There was light music and Andreas turned out to be a wonderful teacher because he did not teach but let us get on with it. First drawing objects, later painting. That is how it was for me. Those who were not newcomers like myself were already into colour. Somehow black and white – pencil, graphite, Indian ink, charcoal – has remained my favourite (see Plate 17).

Although Andreas did not teach, he made suggestions how to improve and express more effectively when one wanted to get to but lacked the technical know-how. He knew what each one of us intended but did not have the craftsmanship to express. At the beginning I drew by making little fussy strokes. I learnt to simplify and to get away from attempts to imitate.

This lasted until I had an operation on my spine. I did not recover without a hitch and was in different hospitals and a rehabilitation centre for two-and-a-half months. All were far away from where I live. So it was quite an undertaking for Helga and my friends to come and visit me. Although I was well looked after by the staff, I often felt lonely. So I made a drawing of the way I had begun to feel after a while – in need of comforting.

For anyone interested I summed up what I learned about drawing:

- It requires daily practice. Even a little is better than nothing.

- Vary the pressure on your pencil or whatever to make the line look alive.

- Observe what you want to draw first for a long time and from different angles before starting. If it is an object, take it into your hands. Anyway, get the feel of it, not just the outline.

- Take the space around the object into consideration.

- Draw more the image you now have internalised rather than try to make a photographic copy. Time for corrections later on, when you look at it, or the next morning.

- Don't draw without putting love into each stroke.

13

Reflecting on
Various Kinds of Love

Reflections and Confessions

This chapter, more than any other, is full of *"obiter dicta"*, personal and non-authoritative comments. Some will sound like generalisations. They are a cover for autobiographical revelations. The only real people mentioned are wives and children.

Nearly everybody seems to know what love means, yet nobody can find the ultimate definition. All are agreed that it is a most important driving force and an indispensable ingredient of feeling fully alive. In these reflections I consider two ways of approach that precede the complex, varied and ever mysterious phenomenon of love that never ceases to puzzle and arouse us humans.

The most mystifying aspect of the love remains the relationship between it and sexuality. It resembles the distinction between being in love and to love with all the tolerance, devotion and lastingness that the latter implies. Love then ranges from apparently purely instinctual gratification, "making love", from the fulfilment of an appetite to the selfless adoration the Greeks called agape. Sex as a one-night-stand is not all that different from self-gratification. Somebody even coined the phrase that intercourse was a poor substitute for masturbation. Masturbation leaves more room for fantasy.

It is different when it is "the first time". No matter how successful or disappointing, it is an anxious situation that is rarely forgotten and just as rarely pure bliss. Even though it may be followed by a sense of achievement, a signal that the border between childhood and adulthood has been crossed, a border that normally separates generations more distinctly than any other single act including leaving home. At the other end of the spectrum is the love that puts the well-being and pleasure of the other before one's own but satisfies at the same time one's own need to be loved.

By writing "normally" I am excluding child abuse, especially incest. But I include incest in a wider sense. When, for instance, the age gap between the older (usually male) and younger partner is, say thirty or more years, self-righteous people, analysts included, say indignantly: "she has married her father". But the incestuous aspect of a couple, heterosexual or homosexual, need not be all that obvious. The question only is: What is a couple? The word usually indicates a couple of lovers or a married or life-long partnership. I go further than that and apply "couple" to any twosome (dyadic) relationship in which both feel in close contact. I am particularly thinking of the nursing couple or the analytic couple. By using "contact", "relationship" and "close", I do not mean that these words apply only to prolonged togetherness nor to it being overtly sexual. It could be the feeling of contact at first sight that may or may not last. Nor need this contact be the beginning of love in any of its varieties. It does concern the impression a personality makes, whether this is by direct meeting or indirectly by way of the media. Let us suppose then that there is an immediate and positive impression of the other. What do we mean though, when an actress or actor is said to be "loved" by the public. In such cases "love" is no more than a cover term for a mixture of admiration, devotion, worship. Is it love? The actress may give us pleasure and our pleasure is hers. But is she concerned about our well-being after the show under different circumstances?

When a word has so many facets and seems to work on so many levels of feeling one begins to suspect that it is meaningless unless confined by circumstance and context. Without that it is used like the Joker in a game of cards which has the meaning the player wants it to have, "neither more nor less", as Humpty Dumpty said in Lewis Caroll's *Through the Looking-Glass.*

Therefore, instead of searching for any general definition I limit myself to distinguish between two basic categories of the positive attracting force that makes itself felt between human beings. Several existing categories of love are in common use, like mother-love, puppy-love, transference love or mature love. I include all of these when I make the following basic distinction between two kinds of attraction. One would be by similarity or fitting in with the image one has of oneself in relation to the other. In fact the fit can seem so close that I prefer the word "kindred", indicating a degree of being related, like members of the same family. If physical appearances do not confirm this, there remains a kinship in spirit. I am trying to define one of the primary attracting forces by "likeness" or "sameness" which may proceed to actually liking or even loving the other person when one gets to know them better, whether of the same or opposite sex does not matter here. Occasionally the being alike can cause hatred as well. After all one does not always love oneself when the surface of the ideal self-image is scratched.

Of course, once the relationship progresses or, analytically seen, "regresses" to being "in love" all kinds of "sameness" such as having the same thought at the same time, become everyday events. A couple in the state of being so synchromeshed suns itself in samenesses.

The opposite kind of primary attracting force is at work when the other to all appearances is totally different, strange in manner and appearance, racially, socially and culturally. Yet the very difference arouses such curiosity that it demands and promises an exciting exploration. "How is it possible that someone can be so different from me? I must find out", is the challenge that emanates from the otherness of a stranger. This kind of attraction, of wanting to find out, is close to what Melanie Klein called the "epistemepholic instinct" when she gave the term to the enormous curiosity of young children.

Of course we know that the first kind of attraction, sameness, will, given time and patience end in the second and that on further exploration the second kind of attraction, "otherness", must eventually lead to the recognition of having all basic needs in common. Failing this realisation, the end of the couple's mutual exploration is in sight. The "sameness" couple, on the other hand, will be getting bored by constant agreements and must pick quarrels to survive.

I have generalised here about two primary varieties of attraction that may lead to two persons loving each other whether briefly or permanently. It is my own curiosity about this most elusive power we call love, that makes me want to research the origins of this mysterious force. I cannot accept that it is in any event nothing but a "sublimation" of sex. Its manifold appearances and endings do not do justice to such a simplification. Realising as I do that our fear of loneliness and reluctance to face a radical change has a no less important part to play in seeking and maintaining relationships, I have nevertheless dwelt on and distinguished between these two kinds primary attraction. What I described as opposite qualities of primary attraction by "sameness" and "otherness" is not confined to meeting someone from inside or outside the family. But I apply it to blood relations as well, particularly so in the case of one's own parents or children and accept that my psychological-social observations go well with what I recently read from the side of biological geneticists.

Four examples

Of all the people I know, my own four children are the most likely to forgive me if I use my relationship to them to illustrate the primary categories of approaches of love. The subject has cropped up in conversations with many parents. Often they brought up the differences, in the way they felt about their children, spontaneously at the Child Guidance Clinic. Therefore, what I have to say about my four is not just confined to a tiny non-representative empirical sample.

The differences were there from birth on and coincided more or less with their smell and physical features. The appearances may change and the parental feeling need not be lasting. Also, the children themselves may feel quite differently about our kinship. After all they are and become more and more individuals in their own right.

Geraldine is my eldest daughter. Her kind of beauty and body build clearly did not come from me or my family. Nor did she resemble her mother but her looks and gifts came presumably from the maternal side. Owing to the unusual circumstances that surrounded her birth and the first years of her life, I did not meet her until she was two-and-a-half. But it was love at first sight and my recognition was based on our being different yet related, strangers impelled to explore and get to know each other. Although frustrated, the fascination lasted, the exploration of "otherness" never ceased.

It was quite different with Helen, three years younger, where it was obvious from birth that she resembled me, and even more my mother. Same coloured eyes and hair. More introvert than her sister, more like me. This too did not change. Later in life we often argued but were always on the same wavelength. Deep feelings, not always shown. If upset, we both react with our bowels. I regard the common weak spot, the bodily kind of reaction to emotional turmoil as a sure sign of "sameness".

Adrian, born in London 1952, is thirteen years younger than his half-sisters in South Africa. It was during one of the best times of my life. I recognised our otherness right away. It showed in his being and remaining blond and blue-eyed. He takes not so much after his mother as after one of her brothers. All our lives we explored our being different and became very good friends by getting to know our otherness so extremely well that it has become a sameness, in the sense of putting oneself effortlessly in the other's shoes. He knows me better than I know him. Being extrovert he makes social contacts very easily. His own kind of weaknesses and suffering makes him different from me. We can help each other out.

David, the younger son and I have much in common. My recognising this again dates back from birth, although dark eyes and hair could be a feature he shares with his mother, Evelyn, and myself. Our shunning parties, being essentially very private persons who feel easily intruded upon are common characteristics. So is our strong interest in art and literature. Compared with him I have been able to overcome social shyness. We both make few but lasting friendships.

"Using your children as examples is all very well", I can hear someone say, "but how can you compare loving your children with the erotic love you feel for other grown ups?" Well, I think that the patience, tolerance and concern required for the real thing are mere words until you can see the lovable and infuriating child in the grown up person of your choice. Until that time arrives you are likely to have loved your image of the other person.

The difference in the primary quality of attraction does not need to be lasting, nor need it be mutual. Psychoanalysts would all too easily call the sameness kind of attraction "incestuous". The second kind would then become a heterophilia and as such a defence against the primary incestuous tendency. Or, again, they might refer to "sameness" as "identification" or a self-loving projection of "idealisation". Otherness would then become "dis-identification". None of these terms take into account that genetic factors contribute to whether the one or other kind of approach predominates. I regard this factor as at least as potent in the bodily as well as in the psychic similarities and differences. Even more so than the psychological events and influences after birth. Just as "genetic" as the chromosomes which determine the sex of the embryo. But if my two pairs of daughters and sons and my primary approach to loving them is anything to go by, their being either male or female has been irrelevant. I have to be so explicit because psychoanalysis overemphasises the psychodynamics of incest, its taboos and conflicts in human relations. Nevertheless, that daughters want to marry their fathers, and sons their mothers, and say so when they are small children is common enough to be smiled at by adults. But if the frustrated childhood wish lasts and becomes abhorrent, they may take refuge into homosexuality of the open or covert kind. Even this plausible explanation does not exclude a combination of biological and psychological factors. If I take the incidence of practiced hetero- and homosexuality as criterion for "otherness" and "sameness" of love, otherness as primary attracting force is the more frequent. During adolescence the issue is often in the balance. It reminds me of my own youth.

Taking primary attraction on the homosexual but non-genital-sexual level, I recall my meeting with Jung as an example. This attraction was on the level of sameness which he promoted by comparing the supposed origin of my family name of his ancestry, as I described earlier ("Meeting Famous Colleagues and Other Notable Figures"). Later I discovered the otherness in our attitudes to work. While he worked from the general (archetypal) to the particular application to the individual patient, I worked from the particular, unique case and kept a look out for the general lines that made up the pattern of behaviour.

Much later when I wrote about two basic differences of primary attracting forces in love I decided to include as an example my feeling of sameness at first blush that changed afterwards into the feeling and knowing about our otherness. It also became obvious that there was more than one Jung. Quite the most dark suspicion I harbour is that one aspect of the many facets was opportunistic, cultivating anything and anyone that could further his cause. A human failing, but not easy to accept in a person one thinks of as "great".

Love without sex?

The commonest example of overtly asexual love is friendship, requiring as it does the same tolerance and patient cultivation as marriage. Occasional thunderstorms are needed to clear the air. An equivalent of sexual intercourse? Transformations from having been lovers to becoming friends are a rare achievement. I can only speak of one successful experience and I doubt whether there are many. Much more often former sexual relationships that were also loving at the time ended in superficiality or never meeting again. My good friend and former lover Monica Furlong has died recently. She had been a great person, acknowledged as a leader in her chosen field, Christian religion, and a writer by her precarious profession. For me she is still alive in my thoughts and feelings, especially when I need solace or simply kindness to myself. Of course she could not help. But her wisdom allowed her to look at my problems impartially. Her answer was much in the same vein as Jung's: don't attempt to solve a conflict. If you leave it in suspension, a solution will come of its own accord. All this sounds like the eulogism of an obituary. But I had said the same to her before and again when she was dying slowly of cancer. Monica had been eighteen years younger than I.

From this single success I can draw no other conclusion than that it is rare that a sexual love relationship can become a non-sexual friendship. That is when both partners are single or only one is married. I observe it more frequently when both have remarried and then become friendly, perhaps with children of their own or of former marriages.

I know of a third form of primary attraction which is to one's own image. This is either literally, or as in the mirror image of puberty like Narcissus saw in the pond. Or in the later sublimations in narcissism, as Freud called it. Sexual intercourse with other persons in that case does not alter the basic lack of relationship between individual "others". Here both forms of primary attraction are rolled into one and can last a life time. In my experience it is not at all rare, even quite common among artists and analysts. Do I belong there? I would not like to but others must judge. Certainly, nobody would write their own biography without some degree of self-love. Without it I could not have recovered from any love-affair that broke up.

Sex without love?

Everybody will agree that sex is a most powerful, even awesome drive, next only to hunger. Although it seems so clearly definable, I believe it is no less complex than love and depends just as much on the circumstances and accompanying fantasies. If we were to accept biology, the reproductive instinct, is at the root of all sexuality all other phenomena are mere ramifications and deviations. But we are then at a loss to explain homosexuality and a whole host of sexual practices that are not confined to the genital organs. According to Freud the sexuality located in other "erogenous" zones starts in early childhood, called "pre-genital" or "infantile" sexuality. When predominating in the adult these are referred to as deviations or perversions. Here I confine myself to my own development and that of many adults I have known and regarded as "normal" including some anxiety in matters of genital sex. I would even say that some degree of anxiety such as caused by secrecy heightens the excitement and its subsequent discharge. The same applies as to "stolen fruit", said to be the sweetest. Put another way, a hard-boiled attitude to sex trivialises it and lessens the enjoyment. The potentialities of an enriching experience that lasts beyond the act are correspondingly reduced. The same is true when, as often happens in marriage, sex becomes a programmed routine.

But that means taking a too depreciative view of routines, as if all our routines like sleeping, eating, excreting and intercourse were always and only necessities and could not under certain circumstances become emotionally or ritualistically endowed and so add to the enjoyment and become a celebration of life lost, restored, renewed. Sex on New Year's Eve is special. So it is on other anniversaries. As with love, the circumstances and context determine the value given to sex at a given time but also the sadness, as when sex is shallow or one-sided, without love. Here the comparison with love has its limits. One is set by the more easily definable physiological events that accompany the success of sexual intimacy and by the common sensual borders it has with the aesthetic and spiritual spheres. Shape, size, colour and smell of the whole person as well as the specific sexual organs contribute to verify a pre-existing image or fantasy. An image that remains to be confirmed, refuted or renewed by the naked truth of the partner, revealed under the conditions of arousal and subsequently by mutual relief from sexual tension. Feelings of love or hatred and aggression are now on a hair-trigger set to break through the expected repose. The limits of wanting to really get to know the other as someone quite separate and independent of oneself make themselves felt after post-orgasmic relaxation. Later comes doubt whether the event has changed anything fundamental.

Supposing there had been no such spontaneous release by what is after all the highly valued climax of intercourse regardless of the "technique" by which it has been reached. Something I learned relatively late in life is that most men respond differently from women to sexual arousal and orgasm. I probably had an inkling about that difference earlier on. Why had I preferred not to know? Because thinking in terms of sameness is easier than accepting the reality of otherness.

The reason for not wanting to know is vanity combined with self-doubt. Vanity because I believed in my youth like many young men do that the number of "conquests" is more important than the quality of one intimate relationship that could become binding. Although this is what I longed for, the aura and mystique that surrounds "love" intimidated me like many other youngsters. Hence the endless jokes meant to trivialise sexual encounters as a fraught situation. I thought that love meant "forever" and that you would have to marry any girl you had made "love" to. It was much easier to accept the myth that numbers mattered. These, in turn, would depend on the frequency of orgasms one could achieve and give one's partner at the time. It was the prerequisite to being regarded as a "real" or "he-man", as my American friends called it seventy years ago. The word has been replaced by "macho"; with the advent of feminism it has acquired a derogatory meaning. But the myth has not altogether vanished. Where it persists, it blinds the sexes to there being real differences between the arousal of sexual feelings in men and women and also that they are not "all the same". What makes any generalisation about sex by itself wrong is that gender* is more important than anatomy. In other words there are women who respond sexually more like men and there are men who have a lot of attributes that are commonly believed to be female. The proof of this, if there can be any, I regard as the always present degree of bisexuality. It makes for good sexual partners. More than a little would lead to a split and become not bi- but homosexuality. Here too I speak from the personal experience of one short marriage, when my wife turned out to be predominantly lesbian. That I married her at all points to a homosexual side in my psyche.

The myth of the singular importance of penetration and orgasms has persisted in the form of sex as a therapy, a cure for all ills. Where rifts between couples originate on altogether different, usually psychological levels, the attempted sex-cure is likely to make matters worse in the long run. What I just wrote is based on my experience with patients. What I am about to say is based on personal experience. The intimacy of the subject is such that personal details must remain discreet, hence the generalisation.

---

*I take gender to mean the conformity with the specific female or male behaviour that is regarded as typical at a given time or epoch independent of anatomical sex. To what extent the gender behaviour is determined by genes or brought about by identification with one or other parent is not my concern here. "Gender" enables me to distinguish between two major modes of sexual reaction, one that I would associate (without regarding it as causative) with male or female physiology. I do not think of it as unusual, if a man's sexuality should correspond to the female gender or a woman's sexuality resemble more closely the pointed type of reaction I regard as male.

An undeniable difference between the sexes shows up in the preferred fantasies. Pornography is a prime example as it is big business and an almost one hundred per cent male domain that breaks through taboos and censorship by the display of sexual parts in states of excitation. Women's sexual fantasies, as far as I know, are more comprehensive and embrace the whole person who is the desired and desirous partner. The "whole object" is nearer to love than the genital parts as objects of desire.

However the appreciation of difference in the sexual arousal of men and women and consequently of orgasm is partly supported by the differences in anatomy and physiology. The difficulty men have in appreciating the difference is not only their conceit. Surely the pointedness of male arousal easily persuades them that in women the corresponding maximal point of stimulation (the clitoris) must necessarily be the point of release by orgasm. A simultaneous orgasm is the most highly valued, because the differences are forgotten for the moment. But this does not happen all that often in couples of long-standing, when the newness has worn off and the "otherness" has become undeniable but is difficult to bear.

That the regions of sexual arousal in the woman are much more widely spread than the "push-button" functioning of man is well enough known but easily disregarded by men when in the heat of battle they are determined to cause evidence of orgasm in their female partners as clear as their own ejaculation.

What I have got to know is that nothing stops learning about the link between love and sex more effectively than to think that one knows already because of much "experience". I have used widely known aspects of sex in order to emphasise some that I think of as not being taken care of by everybody. They are the importance of gender and of fantasy which applies particularly to couples of long standing. Second, the predominant importance of the context, both when love, sex and the relation between the two is considered. "Context" covers things as different as hotel beds and meeting again after prolonged absence or estrangement. I have omitted the cultural context as an influence on the consequences of intercourse. Stringency, "no sex before marriage", or its opposite permissiveness of the upbringing would determine the difficulty or ease with which taboos are broken and discoveries made, depending also on individual characteristics. I have also left out the spiritual and religious potentialities of sex as they are probably closer to esoteric creeds and to some Eastern religions. For Western religions sexual arousal is still incompatible with a religious frame of mind. However, comparable links can be found in our culture, when, for instance, Heinrich Böll in *Letters to a Young Catholic* writes: "It is impossible for me to despise what is erroneously called physical love; it is the substance of a sacrament ... there is no such thing as purely physical or purely spiritual love, both contain an element of the other, even if only a small one" (my translation). And Nietzsche in *Beyond Good and Evil* touches on the same connection between sex and spirituality when he writes: "The degree and kind of a man's sexuality reaches up to the topmost summit of his spirit" (my translation).

A specifically Jungian thought has impressed me as it refers to love as a symbol. Jung refers to sexual love as mankind's symbolic striving for wholeness and uses Plato's image of the original man as a completely round being with four arms and four legs. The gods became jealous of this powerful Titan and cut it in half, one half male, the other female. The two have been striving to unite ever since, hoping to re-establish their original oneness. Pleasure bent, love-making couples are of course not the least bit interested in such deeper significance. What they do know about is the loss of all egoistic control and the thrill that accompanies orgasm. I think that this is the ultimate reason for the jealousy, not only of the gods but of all who feel themselves excluded from that omnipotent and magic moment of forgetfulness. A taste of Nirvana? Rather lofty. Easier to let oneself know about a taste of honey.

"Love Affairs"

Yes, I had. Not many. But always shattering in the end. For which I am grateful. Only two were extra-marital and important. Regrets? Yes, some. The joy of discovery of one another, not just pleasures of sex, but of having got to know, having had at least a glimpse of the truly other person, their past and present life and sorrows. The confidence of intimacy outweighed my guilt and the pain of also hurting one another as well as our legitimate partners. So, on balance, I feel grateful for having known the heights of being fully alive on every level at the right time, or just in time. This includes the shamefulness of lies. If I had my time over, and despite knowing all the suffering that followed, I would do the same again. "Love affairs" have not been trifling matters in my life. Memories come back from time to time. They are precious souvenirs, not trifles. My wives generously forgave me in time. We all returned to our daily lives and chores.

Only when shaken by something unexpected, such as a severe illness or accident and death, are "the doors of perception" opened and we can distinguish clearly between the price of potatoes and the heights and depths of being loved or forsaken. At those times the routines can gain a new significance, if they are invested with the awe of a ritual. I light a candle at such moments as well as when I hear of the death of anyone I have known well. It helps me to mourn the end of a life cycle and to celebrate the hope of renewal in the face of my approaching death. As for the rest, the ending of a love relationship means that everyone in his sadness must in their solitude find that touch of consoling poetry that re-kindles the spark and illuminates even routines of life. How dull it would be, said Winnicott, if we were only sane. These words have helped me when, in the depth of depression, I have been unable to mourn.

A Very Special Love

When Evelyn and I were both at the Military Mental Hospital at Potchefstrom Province of Transvaal, South Africa, we had met on the bowling green where we were in competing teams. I have forgotten who won, it did not matter. We both won, both in the short and long run. Our quarters, the medics and the nurses, were in adjacent huts, separated by a high wire-mesh fence. When we could not drive out in a staff-car into the small town we managed to meet at night at a prearranged signal. It was that one or other, usually me, would whistle *So Deep is the Night*, a sentimental pop-tune at the time and had much to talk or not talk about to each other. When I returned after an outing – we all had to be in at a certain time always too early, of course – I went into the officers' bar to have a cool drink. One night the commanding officer and his wife were sitting there. She asked me whether I had just been home. How could I have been when I had no weekend leave and Johannesburg was over a hundred miles away? Innocently I said "no". As I undressed to go to bed I discovered the reason for her question. Evelyn's lipstick smeared all over my face and collar. My immediate superior, Major Alice Cox, was sent to investigate the disgraceful conduct. She was as thorough as I was obstinate. Evelyn and I met in future whenever possible at a small hotel on the road to Johannesburg called "Mimosa" where there were mimosa trees apparently always in sweet scented blossom. That they were really wattle trees made no difference. Alice took it upon herself to talk to my wife, Pat, "before it had gone too far". "It" already had. Soon afterwards the war ended and Pat started divorce proceedings when she realised I would not return from England. Evelyn and I lived together and got married as soon as we could and stayed together until her death parted us. Not without crises. But it was as fulfilled a marriage as any I have known or observed. At the wedding freesias took the place of mimosa, relations by scent. But freesias in flower last longer when taken home.

Love and the Age Gap

Age is not only chronological, it is also a variable bio-social datum with important psychological consequences. The most obvious of these are incest and childbirth. Our civilisation depends on outlawing incest and preventing popula-tion explosions. Incest, however, is not just limited to sexual intercourse or interferences between parent and child. Brother-sister incest occurs too as Thomas Mann so brilliantly described in his novel *The Holy Sinner*. That much holds universally but the degree of blood relationship that is acceptable between marital partners varies in the world according to religion and law. In the observations that follow I shall limit myself to the Western world and to "couples", both married and unmarried, of which I have been and still am one half.

In the case of a married couple the age gap usually implies that the man is older than the woman. I found that being of almost the same age is commoner in the young than later in life when the reproductive cycle of the woman and her best looks are on the wane. This being the general rule, the exceptions included first marriages or life-partnerships where at least one partner is over fifty and all the more individually interesting. If one partner has children from a previous marriage, with one or more are still living at home or is still in need of support, the whole scenario is different from that of a couple both recently married for the first time or a couple who never lived with a partner for any length of time up to the age of, say, forty-five. I have known both. So the social circumstances, including money, matter as much or more than the biological and intellectual. One has to remember too that marrying for love is a romantic, recent notion and therefore less tried and tested than the historically older commercial contracts. According to Tennyson, the Quakers have found the diplomatic solution, when they don't marry for money but go where money is.

I was first married at the age of twenty-five to a woman five years older. She had nursed me when I had measles and we had had a sexual relationship. I married her after our daughter was born and I left her although we had had a second daughter. We divorced five years later. My family had been very good to her after she brought our daughter to them and my mother especially while I was still in the army. I feel to this day as she was older and had more experience of the world, she should have been wiser. The age gap mattered and I felt trapped. But then again, I would not have had two lovely daughters giving me seven grandchildren and eight great-grandchildren at such a fairly early stage of life.

My second wife, Evelyn, was five years younger. It was the marriage to her that I mentioned which lasted twenty-six years. Evelyn died of cancer and our beautiful home broke up. The primary attraction had been of the kind I called "sameness".

My third wife was about the same age. We were living together but not without differences over gender (who was the man?). But we might have worked it out had it not been for her analyst. Hard as it is to believe, her much respected analyst, a woman, insisted – and I believe that this was true – that she should marry me and I "obeyed". A divorce followed two years later.

In couples of long standing the distinction I made between two kinds of primary attraction has usually evened out. Sameness and otherness are in an uncertain equilibrium. What is more, couples, all kinds of couples, who have known each other for a long time have built up an inner image or representation of one another on which that knowledge is based. They feel sure that it is so real and complete that they base their recognition and predictions on it. I do too. My describing it as an "inner" image is likely to cause irritation, because it throws doubt on the completeness of that knowledge, on its being the whole truth. Maybe what we know, the image, is shared with and thereby confirmed by others – family, friends and colleagues. The view I am taking is that this knowledge, while not untrue, is nevertheless incomplete; a selective image in that it has been built up by each partner who nevertheless cannot be unbiased nor without a "blind spot". Such images economise on having to take a fresh look and think. They facilitate one's daily dealings. Very convenient but incomplete and therefore misleading as one gets to know in moments of truth that shake the foundations as I experienced in my third marriage. In the others it was I who did the shaking. But anything that happens and is felt to be a catastrophe, robbery in my case, bankruptcy in others' or sudden serious accidents or illness, questions the foundation of the couple's relationship.

The age gap became important again when I began to live with Helga. I was seventy at the time, she twenty-six years younger. I loved her and proposed marriage after I had moved to Berlin. I had wanted it so that she should have a small pension. A consideration but by itself not a good enough reason. The primary attraction had been of the "otherness" type. It still is. Our age gap has become an additional difficulty. It is an objective fact that makes patience and tolerance a prerequisite to maintaining a bond that is more meaningful than living together in a marriage of convenience. A daily task. When it bears fruit it is like a minor miracle.

I can now recognise my own pattern of behaviour in matters of relationship that dates back to childhood and the relation with my mother after my father's death. I remained not only inclined to do what is expected of me but even to anticipate a woman's wishes, to please her and be loved for it. Then I begin to realise that this is the road to losing my autonomy. Angry and terrified I launch out on my own. Futile attempts, of course, if they involve lies. So much for my self-analytic point of view. A one-sided perspective, no doubt that cannot do justice to myself nor to my partner. But I cannot do better than remain a learner.

In exceptional circumstances our image of the other person is, as I said, shaken. We exclaim "but that is not like him/her". A previously unseen and unexpected bit of behaviour has broken through our fixed image of the partner, causing surprise, even shock. I include myself, when I quote the discovery of "marital infidelity" as a common example. It causes painful self-doubt in the "deceived" partner, a rift in the relationship and often divorce. Small comfort at the time that the image of the partner has now become more complete, more realistic. A better relationship than before has a chance to come into being. I have found repeatedly that in the marriages of long duration one of the partners, called "the erring spouse" in Victorian divorce cases, has occasionally more or less serious sexual relationships, while the other remains "faithful" or blind and long suffering. Men who go to prostitutes do nothing to shake their wives' image: nothing to do with love. A tad nearer to that would be "having a bit on the side" (German: *Seitensprung*). The same holds good for women, of course. I believe they manage to be more discrete and do not brag about their adventures.

Certainly, the shock that occurs during the lifetime of the couple is easier to tolerate than when it comes as a revelation after the partner's death, when time has run out for a conciliation between the old image and a potential new kind of loving relationship that includes one more bit of truth. My example of a not so exceptional circumstance should, of course, not be taken as if it were the cure for a married couple in need of a more realistic image of each other. Nor do I want to belittle the possible value the "other", the extra-marital love can have in its own right. The probability is that it started off with equally incomplete images of the partners. What will happen when reality shows its not so pretty face?

All the couples I have known of longer than twenty or more years standing have been married couples mostly with children but also without. I belonged to those with. The greatest threat, as I see it, is the partners' loss of autonomy. All of these I knew on a social, superficial level only, neither partner had been a patient of mine. My impression is that unanalysed couples often do better at staying together. No wonder, since coming to analysis at all indicates among many other possible reasons a striving for autonomy, an insistence on being or becoming oneself, but at a risk and not without a threatened loss of love and being on one's own, usually felt as loneliness. "Deserted spouses" either make that closer acquaintance with themselves or try to escape with the help of alcohol, drugs, promiscuity or even self-destruction – all very annihilative. But in most cases, time heals even though bitterness may remain. Clinging to another person may only repeat the pattern. If that is realised a new opportunity to come to oneself is open. This is a very individual matter but it is also a very real touchstone of personality. I am always in doubt whether to call it regrettable when couples of long standing evidently have become so interdependent that their individuality has vanished. Yet without some degree of adapting themselves to the other, they could not live together. If they would not support one another in daily life, in sickness or other calamities they would not be a couple. But adaptation that has become imitation borders on the ridiculous. One couple I knew, both in their fifties were making it hard for me not to burst into laughter when the partner who had not spoken would repeat the end of the sentence the other had spoken. A living example of "Little Sir (or Lady) Echo". But unwilling, or even deliberate imitation of each others' habits, manners and speech is common enough and more obvious to the onlooker than to the couple. It could be objected that no matter what my analytical perception and judgement may be, "as long as they are happy ...". True enough. Only when one of the seemingly inseparable couple dies can the other truly survive as a person whose former "other half" has become integrated or "inwardised" so that in the fullness of time a single yet whole survivor can emerge.

Having aired my own psychological views I hasten to emphasise the important role that the age of each of the partners is at the time of a possible or actual separation. It may even be a decisive factor in coming to a decision. Obviously, after twenty years of marriage neither of them can be all that young. Without being able to envisage making a future for themselves, including the possibility of finding another partner, they may prefer to put up with all the drawbacks of the present. "Better the devil you know ..." could either be wise or an excuse for inertia or anxiety about being alone. Finally, the presence of young children is often made use of for waiting until "they are old enough". Whatever that may mean. In my case I thought this would have been wrong reasoning. Anyway I preferred suffering a hefty dose of guilt feelings and longing for my daughters when I left my first marriage in South Africa and departed for England. My second marriage was the longest and best. The daughters became good mothers and wives and were successful women. Later as grown ups they understood and forgave me.

Should those who read it find any truth in this chapter, I would be glad but would ask them *not* to take it as a guideline. I had to make my own discoveries in this limitless field. They must too.

14
Not So Young in Berlin
(1986 to the present)

My living in Berlin falls into distinct phases. First there were the two years of commuting alternating with Helga's visits to London and mine to Berlin and joint holidays in France in the early 1980s. All that changed when we decided that this could not go on indefinitely and that jobwise it would be decidedly easier for me to come to Berlin. Language played only a minor part. My pronunciation and fluency of German was of course better than her very good English. But she had a pensionable job and was at the time deeply rooted in educational psychology, counselling and treatment. Transplantation would have been very difficult. Mine was comparatively easy as I had been asked by friends and colleagues to visit the local institute for psychotherapy to give seminars and do some supervision of trainees. So the big step was taken, I sold my house in Elaine Grove, Kentish Town, London and packed the more mobile of my goods and chattels, left some to Adrian, the others in boxes were given storage in my friend Andrew's cellar. The car sold, the day came and Helga's relatives and friends turned up in a light delivery van, we into her car and the Channel-Rubicon was crossed. At least that's how it appeared.

Now, seventeen years later, I have a nice home opposite a park in a pleasant part of Berlin. But when I am in London's West End where I practised for nearly forty years and also lived for nine, nostalgia overcomes me and lets me know those were the best years of a very full life. Living in Jordans we had made friends there, the husbands all being commuters like myself. With the exception of our neighbours, Michael and Frieda Fordham, they were in different professions. I liked that and Evelyn who was mostly at home and doing school runs made friends with the wives, visited retired single women, took part in village affairs like the orphanage and the amateur theatre group and was altogether very popular. I kept up some friendships after I moved to London and Berlin. Now all that is gone. Yes, "keeping in touch" but some separations are final. Two close friends who had been at our wedding in July 1992, Alan Edwards and Louis Zinkin, had died within nine months of each other; both were younger than I.

Reading my diaries now I realise that some of my reluctance to regard Berlin as my home town has lasted to this day, despite all the years that have passed. Of course it has lessened. During the first three to four years we visited England, mainly London, a lot of thanks was due to the generosity of friends, Coline and Anthony who lived in "The Parsonage", at Islington. As the name suggests it was a large house. But I still blush when I recall how much hospitality we accepted and how generously it was given. All past history. Only Andrew

Samuels, with his children and wife remains, an ever-faithful, ever-sparkling, heart-warming friend. Then there is the family, now all in London, my sons, two granddaughters, my brother's three children – I don't see enough of them and even less of a second cousin in Hastings. She it is, Miriam, who keeps the communication open between the far-flung family and we all know and like her for herself, in addition to her functioning like a good carrier-pigeon.

Being without any family of my own in Berlin where everyone I know has family is without a doubt the major factor that prevents me from feeling quite settled and at home here. In Berlin before the Nazis many of my father's relatives of an older generation had lived. The few who did not emigrate were murdered. My first and superficial acquaintance with the city dates back to a visit when my brother and I, in our early teens, had been invited to Uncle Joseph's and his wife's home at Falkensee, a suburb, where today many Berliners have their weekend cottages.

Berlin is an impressive city with its parks, lakes and woods within its borders and close by and its tree lined broad avenues and streets. The one thing Berlin has not got by comparison with London and that is a long history and tradition. No counterparts to the Tower, Tower Bridge, Westminster Abbey, Trafalgar Square; no Changing of the Guards. Berlin is more like a comparatively recent coalescence of villages. Although there is a "Mitte" there is no centre, no pulsating heart or even two, like London's City and West End. On the plus side there are relatively fewer traffic jams and the citizens are a friendly lot, easy to get into conversation with, compared with West End Londoners. Let that be my townscape and population-orientated reasons for finding Berlin so different having lived in London, my base for forty years. Looking at my diaries I notice that I clung for several years to the fantasy that I had not really left London. Helga and I had been regular customers on the car ferry from Hamburg to Harwich. We not only visited London but also Ireland and Scotland. I can say that although in the flesh I live in Berlin, in spirit and language no more than necessary. Even my professional papers remained first and mainly written in English. I do not dislike the special Berlin dialect, expressions and the intonation – it amuses me although it is not the German I knew as a child. My uncle, Joseph, had already noticed and written about the Berliner's readiness to raise their voices and get angry with each other in the street. And then, when you think they will come to blows, they suddenly come to an agreement and even joke. I found this characteristic unchanged. Of course this holds good more in the housing quarters than in the elegant shopping areas. Uncle Joseph in one of his books tells the story that puts it in a nutshell. He had set out to provoke the readiness of Berliners to have words in the street with raised voices. So when a coachman passed him, the cord of his whip carelessly dangling too near the sidewalk, my uncle shouted at him that the cord could easily have gone into his eye. But the coachman, not disposed to shout back, only answered "Yes, Mr Eye!"* and let the horse trot on with his whip dangling as before.

---

* It sounds funnier in German: "Jawohl Herr Auge!"

Why should I have to quote my uncle instead of relating my own encounters? Apart from my wife, who in this respect too is a true Berliner, I have not had many. I do not frequently go to market. If I do, I find the stalls are in the hands of foreigners. Unlike myself, they come from countries outside Europe. London's Cypriots are Berlin's Turks. The people who serve in shops are professionally polite. Colleagues are rarely Berliners. Or, if they are, this trait remains usually covered up. If it does not, I cannot write about it with the freedom I have if I write about complete strangers. The nearest I have come to having contact with Berliners who are not colleagues are the taxi drivers. I have had brief encounters with many. A small percentage of these were women. Again, mostly not born and bred in Berlin. Those who naturally have an eye on the tip which they might not get were they to let go of their quick-witted aggressiveness before the end of our drive. Besides I am too old now not to be shown respect, more than I would get in London, or any other place I have been to. All were quite easy to talk to but only a few spoke more than to answer my questions, how long they had been at this job, how many hours they were on shift. The answer varied from eight to ten hours.

I did not detect that the last driver had an accent, but he was listening to the BBC. Did he understand all that? Ja, do you understand it too, he asked. Yes, I am British. Silence. I told him that I had been living in Berlin for seventeen years. Silence. At the end of the journey, he said "I am British also". So much for my meeting Berliners. Another extraordinary type was tall and very thin. He owned a restaurant, he said in Zehlendorf, a good address in Berlin. Had lived in Spain for a long time, also in South America, was single. People eat far too much. An experiment had shown that professional sportsmen did just as well after thirty days of fasting. Many drivers were students supplementing their income, again a selected sample of the population. I am too old to live in a *Hinterhof* and get to know the *Kiez*, the Berlin word for the neighbourhood. So how can I come across Berliners like Uncle Joseph did, ordinary people. Are there any left?

I found that architecturally, too, Berlin beyond the touristy and representative parts had characteristic features of its own. In London's West End one finds mews, the stables and coachmen's houses behind the magnificent fronts where the well-to-do lived in a bygone glorious time. Berlins *Hinterhöfe*, courtyards, often more than one, were entered through the front of the houses that faced the street mainly in the poorer district. The courtyards where children could play gave light to the *Hinterhäuser* where there were enough floors to house a dozen or more families. All very cosy, everybody knows everybody and exchanges gossip. No metropolitan anonymity here. Where ordinary Berliners live they often form quite cosy communities, *Kiez*, hold street festivals, go to the still-surviving little shops, *Tante* (auntie) *Emma Laden*, know each other as if they lived in a village.

When I first came to London I was struck by the serried, odd-shaped chimneypots on the roofs of rows and rows of terraced houses, one for each fire place and stove. The bombs of the Second World War were not meant for those parts of London where the monotony of dark grey-slated roofs was broken by the orange-yellow clay of those chimney pots. From a heartless and purely aesthetic view one regrets that they were not. In Berlin I was struck by the unexpected appearance of red-brick, free-standing chimneys, needed apparently for light industry, interspersed among middling-to-poor domiciles, reaching up some twenty to thirty metres against the frequently blue sky. The geography and geology of the capital gives the landscape its fundamentals. A more or less north to south running valley left over from the last ice-age is now the river bed of the Havel on the western side. It flows through a series of lakes suitable for boating and bathing. A mixture of birch and fir trees is typical of the woods surrounding the lake. Another river, the Spree flows from the south-east through the town past the Reichstag, now Bundestag, and later flows into the Havel.

The geographical details I mention here are the result of my slow explorations and special interests, no guide book can replace the personal discovery. It took ages because I no longer drive a car nor have the time for endless bus-rides. Berlin and the Berliners remained a jigsaw puzzle for me. At last I now have an impressionist's picture of it.

Only once did I feel in tune with the rest of the population and that was when the infamous Wall came down in 1989, totally unexpectedly. It was really like long-lost brothers welcoming each other, the more so since the reunification had been brought about by the people themselves and not by politicians. For once the roles were reversed and the politicians had to obey. Their merit was that they did not resort to armed resistance and so violence was avoided. Of course, tears came into my eyes when I was with Helga and her relatives among the jubilant masses. The government in Bonn just as much as the allied occupying powers were taken by surprise. We, the residents are still paying the price. Quite literally. The loss of subsidies from the Bonn government has resulted in financial astringency and the bankruptcy of the East German economy has additionally imposed higher rates on the taxpayer.

When I think of the Berlin of today I still divide it into a before and after the wall and the sectors that divided East and West. The western part was again sub-divided between the allied powers into American, British and French sectors all with their military presence. Yet the whole of the western sector was surrounded by the part of Germany that was under Russian control. Westerly, beyond that, lay "West Germany" governed from Bonn.

When Adrian, my elder son, who was working with an English dance theatre in East Berlin, sought permission to come to visit me in the West he was refused. The official border posts one had to pass through included armed police, soldiers and unsmiling officials who thoroughly examined passports out of one's sight. I still have twenty-five marks in worthless East German currency which one was compelled to buy as one entered from the West. East Berlin itself, immediately behind the representative streets and buildings which served as shop-windows for visiting tourists, was in a state a miserable neglect. Streets full of pot-holes, plaster off the walls, paint off the window frames, no private telephones. Only high officials could send their staff to buy "luxury" food in the "decadent" West. One can still find many manufactured articles imprinted "Made in West Germany". I lived my first three years (1986–89) in the Berlin that was a political island. When that was withdrawn the city, used to spending lavishly, suddenly changed. It has not quite recovered yet.

Actually the "Wall" had been a grim institution with its barbed wire and watchtowers. In the ditch between its double walls, Berliners from the East trying to escape to the West were shot by the guards doing "their duty". Shades of the infamous concentration camps ("KZ") arise with these words.

Reunification of the people after forty years of separation takes longer than I would have expected. The difference in outlook of the older generation still shows in many ways. I notice it most in small details like the frilly curtains looking like petticoats of can-can girls, or perhaps our grandmothers. They distract the tourist's eyes from dwelling on the plaster that has fallen off the walls, window frames with the paint peeled off and the roofs in need of repair. But there can be no doubt about it, the centre of Berlin has shifted from the West to the East of the former wall, that is to where it had been before. So I had to re-orientate my inner map from the Kurfürstendamm to Unter den Linden.

All that would be too soberly-impersonal without mentioning some heart warming places – West and East – which I am still discovering. One is the Ludwig-Kirch-Platz and the streets with some elegant shops leading up to it. Here around the church are the gardens and spaces where children play with facilities for table-tennis, cafés with open-air terraces, trees as in so many of Berlin's streets. The East with its public buildings, university and museums has only been open to exploration since the Wall came down and has vastly changed and improved since. I like the narrow streets and corners of Mitte, where small art shops and galleries and restaurants invite exploring tourists to spend money and relax. Mind and stomach full, purse empty. But for my taste there is no more harmonious place than the Café Einstein in the West, with its Viennese atmosphere, newspapers, and glass of water that comes with the coffee. Apfelstrudel, warmish with vanilla sauce or cheese-cake done to perfection. Excellent service. A walled garden with fruit trees is open during the season. Outside in the street just a tad of prostitution all the year around.

Nor can I close a chapter of so many comparisons without mentioning the climatic difference. Berlin is dryer, the temperatures both summer and winter are more extreme than in London. And by comparison the hours of sunshine per year is 1,625 for Berlin but only 1,494 for London (according to Meterologischer Wetterdienst Berlin). One up for living in Berlin. My making comparisons shows that I am not completely at home here. But how else does one notice anything unless by comparing known with the new and unknown. Add to this that my special interest is in art exhibitions and a high standard of theatre. In both respects London is richer. I found Berlin's cultural forte to be on the musical side and in cabaret. The foremost orchestra, the Philharmoniker are world-famous. Cabarets are found in many places. Political satire and caricature is usually to the fore.

Berlin is still in the process of becoming a metropolis in Europe. Geographically it is too far east. It is neither a commercial nor financial centre. But then the whole of Germany is far less centralised and has only in comparatively recent times under Bismarck's chancellery in 1871 become a unified state, and still more recently a reunited capital. These are not only data, they affect the whole of the vast sprawling area of different architectural styles and epochs, also of old villages that have to some extent remained recognisable. Most obvious is the historical watershed between before and after the Kaisers. They built the most pompous buildings, including the *Bundestag*, reconstructed after the notorious fire which the Nazis had laid, pretending that the Communists had done so, to serve as signal to justify Hitler taking control and power over the whole administrative and military machinery of Germany. The scars one sees to this day on the columns of the building largely date back to the Russian siege at the end of the Second World War. The impressive transparent cupola which one can walk around giving a fine view over the city was designed by a British architect. The queues of people waiting to do so have so far been too long for my liking. Perhaps I am not curious enough.

15

Recent Travels

A Journey to St Petersburg, July 2000

Quite the most important discovery I made about travelling between major airports is that all have wheelchair service at the disposal of elderly people or disabled persons. There is time enough to ask for one if you are punctual at the check-in counters. They will notify the destination airport and the chair, with attendant, will be waiting for you at the gate when you get off the plane. Pulkova is the name of the Russian airline and the plane itself was not unlike the airbus used by western European countries for short hops. The difference in the seating was that I had much more room for my legs than the other airlines allow for ordinary (sardine) passengers. I thought at first that they had put me into business class, but that was not the case. The only other noticeable difference was the squareness of the stewardesses.

When we arrived after an uneventful journey, the weather was fair and the temperature about twenty-three degrees. The wheelchair was there and the porter helped me to collect my luggage, which I pointed out to him on the conveyor belt. Tatiana was present, fair and square, carrying a notice board with my name in Latin letters although I was prepared to read it in Russian. Local time was 14:25. I had left Schönefeld at 10 a.m. This is of course due to St Petersburg being two hours east of Berlin. The actual travelling time is only two hours fifteen minutes.

The car belonged to Valerie, the driver. It was at least twelve years old, but in relatively good condition, that is to say, the cover of the seating was not all worn out and there were handles on the doors and one could wind the windows up and down; by no means a foregone conclusion as I was to learn during my stay. Not infrequently there was no door furniture at all.

The road from the airport into town was excellent and obviously part of the "shop window". We passed some gigantic memorials. Other roads, for instance in the industrial parts, were like those in the GDR after 1989. In other words, full of pot-holes and just downright bad. But this I only discovered later, on the Sunday when Tonya and I, accompanied by Valerie, who also writes poetry, went out to Pushkin's boarding school near the village, also called Pushkin.

Two rather disagreeable surprises were waiting for me. One was Larissa's flat, where I was to stay, was on the sixth floor of a house with a view of a bridge across the Neva River that made me forget all the disadvantages. True, there was a lift. One had to go up some dirty stone stairs with a banister, a thin iron rail, then down again into the souterrain, where, unexpectedly in a corner there was an old-fashioned lift. It worked that day and we only had to go up one half-flight to Larissa's flat.

On entering the flat, everybody had to take off their shoes. This seems to be the local custom, "because our streets are not as clean as in Berlin". This was no overstatement, except, of course, for the main street, the Nevsky Prospect, part of the shop window. "Prospect" seems to be the word for avenue. It is the main shopping street which I got to know better. Larissa was small, end of forty, she spoke German as her second language. I gathered that she had once had a German boyfriend. She was an unhappy woman and made no bones about it, saying how difficult it was for a woman to live alone. Certainly she had barricaded herself against unwanted intruders. The main door to the flat consisted of heavy wooden planks fitted together; the main lock had to be turned four times. A minor lock only had to be pressed. Having succeeded in opening the door, one was confronted by an iron gate like a grill, which was locked by a horse-shoe-shaped lock like we use for bicycles. That having been negotiated, one was confronted by another door, which had some sound-proofing on the inside, which was – I nearly said "of course" – in tatters, with the wadding showing. The walls in my room were papered. Next to the window a huge piece of cement was missing, next to it was the prominent stopcock for the central heating. The view across the bridge over the river – with all the beautiful buildings, domes, spires, columns – was breath-taking. The curtains, consisting of two layers of gauze, one light green, one dark green, had to be pulled by hand to open or shut. But, on the window sill, there was an artistic collection of empty bottles of different shapes and sizes. This minor detail was highly characteristic. That is to say, art, whether pictures, architecture, or various exhibits, seems close to the heart of ordinary people, existing side-by-side with shabbiness and old-fashioned or even antique furniture. There were two gigantic armchairs opposite my bed, which was really the sofa and apparently without any springs whatsoever. I asked for a mattress and got an eiderdown as well as some kind of mat made of lamb's wool to put underneath the sheet, which was multicoloured so stains didn't show much. It could well have been a tablecloth. The cushion as well as the eiderdown was also covered by dark and multicoloured material. I thought at first, I can't sleep here, but I tried it out and fell at once fast asleep.

Another remarkable thing about the room was a mahogany Victorian table made to carry flowerpots, of which there were six different ones, all various leaves of green and obviously cared for. One beautiful piece was a kind of piano stool, which held another large plant. At the back of the room there was a table I used as a writing table and a heavy chair, with torn velvet upholstery, and behind that, a mirror. No wardrobe, but hooks and various coat hangers. For my shirts etc., I used shelves underneath the bookcase, which was of an ugly, modern design. The lighting at this time of the year was rarely needed, but there was, again, a hook on the wall at the right height to serve as a bedside light. After some doubts, I decided to stay. Larissa was, as advertised by Tatiana, a good cook and I had my first Borscht that evening. It was served cold at this time of the year. I had to make my "no onions" rule known here, as well as in all of the restaurants I visited, as I am allergic to onions.

Shortly after my rest, it was nearly 7 p.m. local time and I was scheduled to give my first two-hourly group supervision. I had hoped that they would leave me alone on the day of my arrival, but they insisted on getting their pound of flesh, i.e., me. The students, as the trainees were called, were a mixed bunch. There were only three for supervision in the first group, and the almost-simultaneous translation by Tatiana was, as far as I could judge, excellent. That evening I fell at once asleep shortly after they had brought me back home. Next morning I met my almost constant companions, Sergey and Max. They were eighteen years old, close friends and had an excellent sense of humour. Sergey was blonde and blue-eyed, like many Russians. Max was dark and much more foreign-looking, with high cheekbones and deeply set dark eyes. He was also the more introvert. Science subjects and mathematics were his thing, while Sergey had studied art and therefore knew his way around the Hermitage, which we visited on the first morning. The building is a vast palace in green and white on the outside with the columns and well-known architecture of many palaces and some churches. Lunch was ate in town, and then I had the group afternoon meeting at 5 p.m., which consisted of a new set of students. There were four, as on all the subsequent days. Only one of them was the same person, Julia, who had attended the first seminar. She certainly seemed to be one of the best. That is to say, she had at least an idea of what analysis is all about. Dinner that evening was out with Max, because I didn't want to have another tête-à-tête with Larissa and we went to a good restaurant, each paying their share. My favourite food turned out to be bliny, which consists of a crêpe (thin pancake), which one can have with all sorts of anything. I chose caviar which is probably classical. Red caviar is much cheaper than black. But even that dish costs only about $3.50. They brought us some awful wine, which, much to Max's embarrassment, I sent back for a better one.

The next morning, Saturday, I went with Max to the Nevsky Prospect and saw cathedrals. They all have two things in common: beggars outside lined up with their palms outstretched and lit candles inside. Max crossed himself and lit a candle. In contrast to Sergey, he seemed to be quite religious. But the attendance of people in all the churches and cathedrals was good. There is no seating in Russian churches. Nobody can fall asleep. I saw one or two monks and also a nun, with a sort of stove-pipe black headgear and gown, little of the face showing. Many priests, more beards than faces.

After the next supervision at 15.30 on the Saturday, I had a rest and at 6 p.m. the Manersky's, Sergey and Marina, a couple of between forty and fifty, called for me and we went to the programmed "cultural entertainment" in lieu of a fee for visiting lectures. It was in an old theatre; *Swan Lake*, a ballet I had seen many times before. The first Bolshoi company was touring. The performance was unexceptional. There were two embarrassing incidents. The first was that they had paid for an excellent seat for me on the balcony in a box, a German couple on tour were sharing it, while my hosts, had seats in the gods. Obviously because they could not afford better. There were two intervals. My friends were already waiting for me outside the box to take me up to the restaurant. We only had water and I suggested I would like to invite them to a glass of wine after the ballet. I noticed their resistance to the idea and it gradually dawned on me that they, being the hosts, did not want to be entertained by me because it would embarrass them if I paid in public. Eventually Sergey suggested that he would buy a bottle of wine for me and we would go up to my room and share the bottle there. Additionally, his honour was saved by his buying some peaches, for which he had paid out of his own pocket. Incidentally, Tatiana's welcoming gift to me had consisted of three bananas and one orange. The Manersky's and I had a very good talk about our mutual relations and our families until midnight. They were charming. She was the English speaker. They wanted to walk home; it would only take about half an hour.

The ages of their children were between seventeen and twenty, which is highly characteristic, as I noticed later. People tend to get married very young, in their early twenties, and have children very soon. Living together without at least a registry office marriage is socially not acceptable. A church wedding is better than only registry office. On the other hand, divorces seem very easily arranged and divorced couples are not necessarily hostile to each other. This early marrying applies to both sexes, although the man is usually a little older. This, as well as the shop window, the window-dressing, was exactly the same as in the GDR. Bad roads, shabby houses with the plaster falling off, small rooms, little food, no money, the German Democratic Republic had been closely modelled on what I saw in St Petersburg and probably applies to the whole of Russia. Tonya quoted one of their modern writers, who had put it simply "What Russia needs is roads and food."

The institute where I gave supervisions, with the exception of one Saturday when we met in my room, is a further example of this window-dressing. The official name, the East European Psychoanalytic Institute, is a grand and diplomatic title they have given themselves. The head of it is one Mikhail Reshetnikov, with whom I had what I can only call an audience on the last day, when I was virtually commanded by Tatiana, his devoted slave, to come to his office. Before I did, I had to go to the loo, which was a vast place with marble going right up to the ceiling, except in the corner where the actual john was. There was a wide gap in the marble, filled in with cardboard, through which a hose pipe went into the cistern of the lavatory. It was like the missing cement in my room, and I don't think anybody notices it much. While seemingly interviewing me, Reshetnikov only talked about himself and his achievements. A tremendous amount of self-glorification and "we too, only better than you," seems to be the Russian compensation for their poverty and anxiety about not counting for much in the international power game. When, during a pause, I said that I had served during the war in Africa as a medical officer, the reply from the chair behind the large desk was that he had served in three wars, starting off with Afghanistan and going on to some other "—stans". For good measure he added a train accident where he had supervised the psychological aid. He mentioned Hannes Dieckmann, who had been the head of the Berlin Institute, one-time chair of the IAAP and the author of several books on Jungian analysis. R. himself was President of the Psychoanalytic Association of all Russia. No, there were as yet no other institutes. In the course of my interview I mentioned that I would need a certificate saying that I had paid all expenses out of my own pocket in order to claim relief of income tax. Out went Tatiana, back she came carrying something that I could certainly frame and put on the wall, like doctors, analysts and lawyers do in America. However, the professor seemed considerate when he thought I might need a letter to show the custom's officer, in addition, of course, to the visa and the entrance and exit certificates I had got from the passport officials. On the spot, R. dictated a letter to obedient Tatiana in Russian to the effect that I had stayed as a guest at his house, including the dates of arrival and departure, because he thought the passport officer would want to know where I had stayed and what I had done. He read it out to me in English. The passport officer was not impressed and actually looked bored.

I had been in great doubt about this enterprise because I knew how dependent I was, not only because of the language and nobody in the street understanding English or German, but because of my handicap in walking, especially as far as stairs are concerned, which lead into the underground stations, which are also part of the shop window. Huge halls, marble and gold prevailing, and no advertisements on the walls. The stations were also very clean. All this to impress foreign tourists. To the same effect, the *St Petersburg Times* (in English) is handed out free of charge. My last social observation: I think the Russians are and have always been proud of the ornate luxury and the spectacle of their rulers and nobility. It is as if the Czar, the noblemen and landowners who lived in style, being waited on by serfs, as part of their possessions, represented no less than the deity on earth, like in the Roman Catholic faith the Pope represents Christ. Similarly, the pride in all this pomp and luxury of the rulers looked like a kind of compensation for their poverty and miserable lives of a serf. I told Tonya my view and she said that she had thought this herself and that there was probably more than a bit of truth in it. I think this attitude and ideology separates this eastern empire from the west European and American view of life, where it is open to anyone no matter of what rank, birth or social class to become a self-made person who mattered in the world as a token of which he or she was, if not very rich, at least well-off. Well enough off to own a car that wasn't falling to pieces.

No Russian, incidentally, travels in an official taxi if they can avoid it because it's too expensive. They stand in any of the major streets and hold out their hand. It usually does not take more than a few minutes before an ordinary car stops to pick them up. It's a black market and anyone with a car – no licence required – can join. In one old Volvo I travelled in, the rain came through the roof and the windscreen had a hole in it. The price is negotiated at the start. On one such trip, Max, Sergey and I had a completely crazy and probably drugged driver. After we got out we laughed with relief from the danger we had been in and the many collisions we had escaped.

The street scene was not very different from a west European town, say Amsterdam because of the canals. I was struck by the enormous diameter of the drainpipes. Made of tin they issue straight onto the pavement. I thought there must be flooding when the snow suddenly melts. Tonya confirmed.

People in the main streets were quite well-dressed, especially the younger generation. Taller than their elders. But not by as much as in Germany, I thought. Young girls, many quite slim, dressed mainly in black, frequently mini-skirts. Hardly any mobiles (German: "handies"; American: "cellulars"). Many people smoked.

The highlight of my journey came on one beautiful, warm and sunny Sunday when Tonya and I went out to Pushkin village and the nearby boarding school called the Czar's College. Next door was Catherine the Great's palace and the magnificent formal gardens. I chose to visit the college rather than the palace. No other visitors went to the college, with its airtight cells for the former pupils. Names over the doors. Many became famous. Everything in apple-pie order, including the classrooms' physics and navigation apparatus. A skilfully-drawn horse by Pushkin for which he only passed third grade. Afterwards we visited the nearby cemetery where many famous musicians and some writers are buried. The Victorian tombs with emblematic figures of assorted angels, saints, etc. forever praying for the departed or paying tribute to their genius. The whole ambience is reminiscent of Highgate Cemetery in London, where Marx is buried. Except that this one is totally flat and mournful.

Tonya, twenty-three, was the brightest "student" and best English speaker I met. No, she does not want to wait until she has finished her studies. She wants a baby now. Her boyfriend, a little older, works in the meat-product trade. Salary not too good. Maybe at thirty-three she'll start all over again. Not having the money for a PC she belongs to an email club just across her street. Time for each member is limited. We exchanged addresses and corresponded for a whole year by email.

Helga, as on so many occasions before and since, met me at the airport.

Morocco 23 January to 6 February 2001

Elias Canetti's book *The Voices of Marrakesh* although written in 1954 was still a useful introduction. As far as I could gather from a brief visit much of the essential structure had not changed. It also fitted in with the background of Islamic culture, Jewish quarters of towns and general poverty of the population. What had of course changed parts of the country was the tourist industry, especially noticeable in the hotel quarter of Agadir, gateway to Southern Morocco.

Even in Agadir the local population in places like the Café La Fontaine, Avenue Hassan II, far outweighs the number of tourists. In Marrakesh at the smart restaurant, Le Jacaranda, it was about half and half. In smaller towns still with their old quarters, the medinas, within their pink walls of baked clay, the tourists were a spectacle for the indigenous population, to be preyed on by begging, obvious in the form of hordes of barefooted children, hardly disguised by touting salesmen who tried to get one into their tiny artisan workshops. In the narrow streets one could barely escape their attention. They had the necessary words of German and I expect of English depending whatever kind of prey was being led by the Moroccan guide. Their own languages are Arabic and French, not *petit nègre*, but proper French taught at school, spoken by both children and parents, although I expect Arabic or Berber is spoken at home by the less educated. Koran schools seem popular, but general school attendance is not yet obligatory and will not be for several years yet. A developing country, apparently devoted to a King who can only ascend to the throne if he is married. The present one, Mohammed VI, is fairly young. "For Allah, King and Fatherland" is written in chalk in gigantic letters on several hills throughout the country. Do I smell revolution and Western-style democracy in the offing? According to one guide the population of Arab and Berber descent are all loyal to the King and there is no opposition.

A Moslem can no longer have four wives, even if he can show that he can keep them all. There seem to be stages of progress towards equality. To get married at all he must possess a certificate to the effect that he is single. To have a second wife, he must not only show that he can keep her but also produce the written permission of his first. I don't know how strictly all this is kept. In Marrakesh we were guided through a palace of a former Sultan. In contrast to its European counterpart it was completely empty of furniture but impressed through its Arab style architecture with inlaid mosaic of intricate patterns, varying between the geometric and flowery Arabesques, the former mainly in blues and white, the latter multicoloured flowery and joyful.

Impressive too was the large yard with a fountain in the centre, the Harem in spacious rooms for the women of the court on either side. At the far end was their common dining room, equally impressive in its architecture and decoration. The whole set up reminded me of a Chinese film, *The Red Lantern*, I had seen some ten years earlier in which a similar and cruel ownership of women at the command of an overlord had been the subject.

According to our guide there had been three categories of women – wives, maitresses, and concubines. I did not understand the difference between the last two, but one was meant to only last thirty or forty days. There was also a prayer room, one half being for women. I did not notice any difference between the emptiness of the two. Before entering any mosque the faithful have to ritualistically wash hands and face. Water alone is sufficient; no soap, no towels.

Both were also absent in the country "restaurant" where we had lunch situated in a stony desert. We had something to eat in the beautifully shady yard where our group had obviously been expected. They had made a concession by installing a European type of loo in addition to the Arab and French style of squatting places. But there were flies everywhere and I fell ill with acute enteritis early next morning and needed to be treated with antibiotics. We had to delay and reroute our departure.

It was in the afternoon of the desert trip I had one of the most memorable experiences in Morocco. This was the Oasis Ouijane. We had travelled there by jeep, no other vehicle could have stood up to the rigors imposed by the mountainous and rocky track. In the morning we had halted above the half-empty enormously-large dam and water reservoir. A sad sight reminding one that the greatest problem of the whole continent of Africa remains water or rather the lack of it. Where even a little rain had fallen as we saw on this trip there was a thin veil of green covering the otherwise yellow brown land. Some succulents and bulbs managed to live between the rocks.

After a bone-shaking, slow ride through a monotonous landscape, there suddenly appeared, shaking like an incredible vision the strong green of palm trees against the background of dun-coloured hills and the pinkish walls of houses. Is this what the explorer-sailors felt when after weeks at sea, with the water supply running low, at long last the cry "land ahoy" came from the look-out at the masthead, and this time it wasn't a whale. In both cases the colour green signalled water, relief, life. Shading palms, even olive trees and a small, lush meadow surrounded by trees. I felt so alive that I could assert myself against my painful knee and back. As we drew nearer it became clear that this oasis consisted of a whole village on very irregular ground with not only one but two springs. The water ran in carefully bordered rivulets between the houses. There was also a place for laundering. Women were doing the family's washing. The guide explained the system of sticks, stones and the shadow of a rock that indicated each family's day to use the laundry. As they saw us tourists looking down some of the women drew their veils closer over their faces. Were they afraid of the evil eye of the camera? Very likely. Many doors we saw on this trip were decorated with the sign against the evil eye.

Returning to the typical African and everlasting problem of water. There seems to have been plenty about in Agadir, because the hotel lawns and gardens were well watered. But – and this would have become a big "but" on a long stay – it was not of drinkable quality, so one constantly had to buy Sidi Ali spring water in large plastic bottles, be careful when cleaning one's teeth, and avoid salads and all uncooked food. *Thé à la menthe* (peppermint tea) is obtainable anywhere and at all times, poured out from on high through the spout of attractively shaped silvery pots. It has been boiled, of course and is a good and safe drink, only often too *sucré*.

The other highlight of our journey to Morocco was undoubtedly the Jemna el Fna, the central meeting place of Marrakesh. It was like something out of 1001 nights, like entering into an oriental fairytale. Although geographically speaking this part of the land lies further to the west than even Ireland. The place itself is large and irregular in shape. One becomes at once part of the multitudinous, colourful crowd. The first to surround us were about half a dozen water carriers in multicoloured hats and costumes from which bells, brass kettles and cups were hanging. Photographing them or anyone else who is conscious of it earns a few coins. (1 Dinhar = 11 Cents but it is worth a lot more. Red minitaxis, average distance in Marrakesh 5–10 Dinhar.)

There were also various small clusters of Moroccans, old and young, the men in their Djellabah of wool, mainly greens, browns, blues and purple all with peaked hoods. Sometimes I saw such a lone figure walking or standing still in the empty landscape. The hoods seem to offer protection against the sun as well as the cold at night in the desert, wind and sand. Many young women in the towns were now without veils, although their hair was usually covered by a shawl. The older ones traditionally in black from head to foot, slits only for nose and eyes. Many men with turbans of different colours, others with a red fez. Children barefooted, clothes often ragged, were prominent in all the small circles, eyes wide open in wonderment, mouths agape, as they were listening to the story teller. Not understanding a word did not prevent me from listening to the ancient art, almost hypnotised. Of course adults listened too, almost as fascinated as the children. In the middle of another little crowd there would be a snake charmer holding a dangerous cobra with its quickly moving split tongue bringing it close to his mouth. Another was holding a scorpion close to his eye. Then there were fortune tellers of course, mainly women with various small utensils and one little stool for the privacy of just one client at a time; same with the professional letter writers for illiterate customers. In the centre of the gathering place (Jemna) there were rows and rows of tables covered with white table cloths and benches on either side. Charcoal grills were frying and there were many other local specialities like the flan or round fresh bread loaves giving off a delicious smell. In all this hive of population small theatres too seemed to be on the go from early morning until late at night. The best was that the place with its unique lively atmosphere could not be photographed as a whole, only bits of it, which cannot convey the atmosphere with its smells, sounds and sights as a vibrant whole.

With all the poverty on the one hand and the strict religious segregation of the sexes on the other it is not surprising that prostitution should be rife. Living in a tourist centre I saw no obvious signs of it in the streets. But I gradually tumbled to it that a kind of sex-tourism was being practised in the hotels and shops. Helga and I noticed that one woman, a guest, was stroking the arm of a waiter in quite an obvious manner. When I went for a massage of my back, the masseuse locked the door of the cubicle quite ostentatiously which I found strange. When she started massaging while I was lying on my back from the toes upwards, I repeated that I had come for massage of my back, she said she would come to that later. But her finger tips strayed as if by accident up to my underwear; the same happened when I was lying on my belly. She was quite young, not pretty but enormously fat, desirable among Moroccan men. I only took notice of that when the following incident occurred on the day before our departure and some hours before I took quite sick with enteritis.

Helga had decided that the binoculars she had bought were too heavy and she wanted to give them away to the chamber maid but I suggested she should give them to one of the gardeners who were busy watering the lawn and hedges bordering onto our little terrace. She went out and stayed longer than expected. On return she told me what had happened. The gardener, a nice looking bearded man of around thirty did not even look at her present nor was he interested in her explanation why she wanted to dispose of it. Instead he began chatting and asked her whether she was alone and what her room number was. Helga told him that she was here with her husband. He nevertheless turned up a bit later, I suppose to inspect me, an old man – too old? He exchanged some polite words, all in French of course. A bit later he came back once more bearing a small bunch of freshly picked flowers to present to us both. He had already given her two small potted plants. "Moroccan" as he pointed out. They were succulents, sure not to survive out of doors in Berlin. Whether this was a kind of apology for his mistaking Helga's request or a way of enquiring whether his services would after all be required, I do not know.

After looking at the photos Helga had taken at my special request, it dawned on me that there had been a third highlight of the Moroccan holiday. I had quite overlooked it because there was no obvious connection between Agadir and my falling in love with the statues that adorned the beautifully designed and spaciously domed entrance hall of our hotel. The contrast between Arab and European architecture and design could not have been better resolved than in the way that the local architects had found. A prominent contribution were four nearly life-sized brass figures, two female, two male. They represented outdated European ideas of what Africans and ancient Egyptians looked like. The statutes' common function was to bear light. Arms raised above their heads they held torches that ended in flame-shaped, electric lightbulbs. What had attracted me and made me really fall for the figures was their late art noveau style. It recalled the years before I was born when art noveau had been the fashion.

My beloved dark brass ladies and gentlemen brought to mind a comparison with the illustrations of Ethiopians in Pigafetta's description of the Congo (de Bry 1598). In his travel book the features, figures and bearing of the local inhabitants one is introduced to look exactly like the men and women of European origin. Except that their half-naked torsos are draped in fanciful clothing, a mixture reminiscent of Roman togas and primitive loincloths, sometimes adorned with European headgear, other times with that of Red Indians. Hearsay had combined with the wish to introduce these aliens to the ignorant reader. The resulting mixture was as charming as it was misleading. Today we are no less enchanted when we smile at these fanciful illustrations that once represented the near-naked truth. Our smiles are like those of grown-ups when they look at a young child's naive drawings.

But I also wondered whether there was not more to it. I thought of the permanent tendency to combine curiosity and ignorance with sheer imagination and then to illustrate the product in order to make it convincing. A little knowledge grafted onto the completely unknown, in our time aliens from outer space, in earlier days called "noble savages". Another example is the confabulated illustration I found in an old travel book (1682) showing elephants with the body of large pigs and human eyes but with special emphasis on the great novelty, the famous trunk. A characteristic like darkness in the case of the statues of Agadir. All the rest is European fantasy, hearsay and eyewash. Or, again, the faked photos and blown-up headlines with which the gutter press feeds a sensation-hungry public. At bottom no change.

Such is my associative context to the third Moroccan highlight. None of it explains why this version of the Pygmalion legend should have taken such a hold of me that I wanted to take at least one of the statues home.

The German Spas (Kurorte): Bad Gandersheim

I had done well to pick the Diakonissen-Mutterhaus at the small Spa or Bad instead of a hotel or other type of accommodation. Looking for a place to stay while Helga was doing a nine-day trek along a well-known path through the mountains of Thuringia in East Germany. I had seen the illustrated Diakonissen (a Lutheran nun) Pension advertised in the brochure of the town of Bad Gandersheim, only three-and-a-half hours drive from Berlin and arranged a double room with all the comforts of a four-star hotel except for a minibar, of course, and the rule that one would have to keep one's room in order. "We are not a hotel." The snag was that I could have the room for one week only. But perhaps they could find me another for the second. As the days went by and that prospect grew dimmer Helga, who was still there, and I looked for alternatives among the hotels and *Kurkliniken* but what we saw was small and cheerless. Helga left and I spoke to Frau K, the wife of the resident Pastor. As the days went by she became more emphatic about their house being full up. The next day she came reinforced by her husband to tell me very kindly but definitely that I would have to move out. Together we went through the list of all the hotels in town knowing that they were not full up although this was the height of the season. None of them seemed to be as right as the accommodation I had here. They had even supplemented the room with a writing table and lamp, appreciating my wants. Obviously, we had come to an impasse. At that moment Frau K's mobile rang. She answered and I noticed how her face lit up as she exclaimed: "That is really a present!" What had happened was that the people who had reserved the very room I would have to vacate had cancelled. I nearly broke into tears of joy as a weight dropped off my mind. To think of moving into an uncomfortable anonymous place and all the packing and unpacking I would have had to do .... But that was only the rational consideration. I felt as if a small miracle had happened and said aloud "God tempers the wind to the shorn lamb". I had said it in English and the pastor, Herr K, understood but did not know the German equivalent. He said it was the language of Martin Luther. According to my dictionary it stems from a French proverb.

Another version of my theme losing-finding had occurred, another meeting with an "object" believed to be lost, but, oh joy, found again. It contributed to my *Kur* at least as much as the various physiotherapies.

Bad Gandersheim and the Lady in Red

She seemed to welcome it when I asked whether I could share the table which she had just snapped up before I could sit down at the Waldschlößchen, not a kilometre away from where I am staying. Dressed in red and discretely decorated with golden jewellery; her hair and spectacles were also golden. Everything tuned in.

The Waldschlößchen had been recommended by the taxi-driver for serving good German food. Maybe it was. Wiener Schnitzel soaked in fat, salad came with onions, mixed with beans and gurkins, red cabbage and beetroot which I hate. I had asked before "without onions". The red wine was undrinkable. At a German *Kneipe*, the nearest counterpart to a pub like this, one should always drink beer or a white wine. Everything was a mistake including coming here by taxi. But my walking radius is small these days, maybe five hundred metres.

Back to the red lady, over seventy, as she admitted later. She had been coming to Gandersheim for thirty years, three times a year. It seems to keep her slipped disc under control with the various therapies (*Anwendungen*) it offers. She also remarked that she had been good-looking but that was later, when she kindly took me home before returning to the Waldschlößchen and her white wine. She and her husband had retired from the business they had run in a south German town about three hundred kilometres away. She also likes Gandersheim because it gives her a break from cooking. Evidently it also gave her the opportunity to talk to strangers. Nowadays she always stays at the same pension in the old town, having previously stayed at one of the big hotels. She knew them all. While we were eating a very young man put himself next to her, almost snuggling up. He did not speak but repeatedly counted the coins in his new leather purse, as if he could make no sense of euros and cents. Looking at him more closely it became obvious that he was a half-wit as my companion confirmed. She had known him since his childhood. He belonged to the family who ran the pension where she stayed. It struck me afterwards that she did not mention any children of her own. Perhaps there weren't any. She also had been remarkably uncurious about me except for asking whether I was married. In the car on the way back to the Diakonissen-Gästehaus she said and as we shook hands "I have never been here, perhaps we shall meet again." I have forgotten what I replied but I am sure it was unenthusiastic. Yet I am very glad to have met her because without meeting her I could not have imagined how anybody could spend their lives like she had done. Not in my wildest fantasies, especially not with Bad Gandersheim as the earthly Paradise.

I saw her again when she passed me at the Seeklause. This was at a small *Kneipe* nicely situated by a small lake, with a fountain in the middle, where all they could offer at 8 p.m. was *Bockwurst*. This time she was wearing a red blouse, still unaccompanied on the way back to the car park. I thought thirty years is a long time in a woman's life. In a man's too, of course. But how can one find enjoyment in such monotony?

16
On Getting Very Old

The difference between being an old man and getting very old is enormous. I noticed the threshold at eighty-five. It is the last of all phases and no less drastic than the transition from childhood to puberty. The difference is, of course, that instead of growth there is constant loss and nothing that is wrong today will get better in time. No recovery from brittleness of bone, no improvement in loss of memory, hearing, sight and potency. But thanks to technology some remaining functions can be improved. Lens replacement by eye-operation enable me to see well and read even without glasses and hearing aids enable me to take part in conversation and enjoy music. The loss of subcutaneous fat and muscle tension causes folds and wrinkles; skin is colourless and in need of constant care; there is loss of hair and teeth. Eyes in their hollow sockets stare out of the mirror. The face and figure of a man who is merely old still show the characteristic features of the person he was and can quickly be recognised by those who have not seen him for some time. But seeing me again having become very old shocks people who have not met me for a few years. Decently, they hide it.

The best that can be hoped for is to slow down some of the decaying processes. Even that requires constant attention and sticking to a daily routine, planned sequences of action. Working out strategies for everything, even getting ready for the day and going to bed require deliberation. Self-discipline takes up mental space. Nothing that could formerly be left to automatic functioning and spontaneous action, such as walking and negotiating stairs, can be relied on. My movements must look as if done by numbers, staccato rather than legato. The person that had a name and a definite sex is turning into a neuter, an "it", like a new-born baby that is referred to as "baby" by those who look after it. When the baby grows into an infant he or she will be called by a name it will recognise as his or her own, an "I" that exists by itself. Not so a very old person who becomes more and more a relic to those he has to depend on until finally he becomes a nursing case like he was at the very beginning. Only now he won't "grow out of it".

Memory in old age deserves special mentioning under this heading. Losing memory and mind is everyone's fear after sixty-five. I have noticed small recent holes in mine like misdialling telephone numbers, omitting the last letter of a written word and worse still, forgetting the date or the time of an appointment. It's like the holes in a Swiss cheese that as such still has a coherent enough structure. All this part and parcel of getting very old. Nothing to be done about it. Noticing it, I take precautions such as slowly but surely closing down my practice, writing down memos to myself and actually *looking* at them, even if I think I know. The losing of things and mostly but not always finding them again has also become less enjoyable. The death of friends, all younger than I is more serious and brings about loneliness. They are irreplaceable, of course, each one of them is, but by now the whole category "contemporary" has vanished. I therefore appreciate and cultivate my young friends all the more and keep in close contact with my own offspring as much as I can but I hope no more than welcome.

Among the regular active measures I take is physical and memory exercise. Like one can train muscles, so one can train memory. Bilinguality, constantly translating, is one. I toy with the idea of brushing up my French or even learning a new language. I learn some favourite lines off by heart. Looking at old notes, papers I have written and photos taken prevents, temporarily, the holes from getting deeper or more numerous. A few windows even re-open. It seems that recalling the past is also good for what remains of the present mind. Not living on memories or "in the past". Keeping the present ability to remember the events of each day helps to be fully alive before night falls.

After all this gloom, have I found any advantages in getting very old? I would say, yes, with some important provisos. The first is that one is still able to distinguish clearly between past and present, between fantasy and reality. Most importantly between the person or persons one has been at various stages of life and the person one has become, all the limitations and burdens included. That is the hardest. In short a panoramic view as well as a perspective is needed, one that makes me aware of: "You are standing here!" A lot of humility is required to undergo the change from having been in charge to becoming more and more dependant. Once accepted I can, occasionally, become aware of and be grateful for what is left. Best of all, I can make what time the routines of the day leave available for my hobby, drawing and painting. And writing, of course.

Another condition for finding anything good in being very old is the full admission of having become unreliable in cognitive data such as times and names. Although people's names have always been a weak spot this has become worse. Memos must not be lost and have to be looked at or people have to be there to remind me, because the whereabouts of memos need remembering as well. The mental exercises I mentioned I think of as exercises for the ramifications between neurones ("dendrites") in the brain. Doing it requires all the self-discipline I can muster. Fear of decay helps. The reading of old letters and diaries of days long ago make me aware of how selective my memory is and how much it depends on the emotional charge and tension between the past event and the moment of trying to remember, in short, the associative link. I regard the collected material evidence of the past as useful for writing a biography. But it is the recollections that are needed for bringing to life once more everything that was in danger of falling into one of those holes. Reconnecting past with present, who I was, the image I had of myself in those days and then linking that *avatar* with my present appearance in the mirror. Remembering means mourning, says Freud. True as this is, I find that it also stimulates what is left of the brain's activity in the present. Looking into the past then becomes so much more than reminiscing or only mourning. If consciously controlled, it is a vitalising activity of the psyche right now.

The Mental Attitude to Very Old Age

Jung's concept of the "self" is a help here that I would not like to do without. In its briefest and most relevant form it is based on the unity of body and psyche or "somato-psyche". That unity exists from birth to death but it is the body that has the first and the last word. In between the extremes of age the psyche determines to a large extent the well-being or sickness of both. As part of the body the brain degenerates in old age and forgetting becomes part of the loss that is irretrievable. No "finding" in the end, except by noticing the end.

As at any other time of life so at this late stage my memories are associated with emotions, many unpleasurable. Memory gaps are partly, but only partly, caused by Freudian repression; as an autonomous kind of "not wanting to know" it is both powerful and tricky. The represssion of painful (traumatic) memories and their replacement by wish-fulfilling dreams and fantasies and even by bodily symptoms constitute the very spring from which psychoanalysis took off in the hope to cure by lifting amnesia and repression and helping the patient to face unpleasant realities.

How in practice does the "self" help? The short answer is by taking itself into account. If one considers the emphasis with which our Western society insists on the importance of the "I" or ego and its achievements and successes, meritocracy, the individuality of the person, not only regardless of nationality, race, religion, and even more so of the class and circumstance into which a person is born, it becomes easier to understand the drawback of too much individuality. It leads to isolation, rootlessness. Never before has there been so much mobility. Not only travel but go and live anywhere at any time. I have done my bit of that. Very rich people have houses in several distant places as the whim takes them. But roots are a different matter, the better appreciated as age advances. There the self comes into its own. It can neither be divorced from its home in the body nor its dependence on links with other individuals, relatives, friends, neighbours. In short, the self in each person must find a reflection in the community of others. It is both individual and collective. Jung put it simply when he told me that he drew the attention of sightseeing visitors to the greengrocer at the corner. I think that all our highly-prized individuality is a reaction to previous generations that, in the main, lived collectively, immobile, rooted to the spot, died where they were born, generation after generation. Virtually like tribesmen and women.

Associated ideas come to mind. Has the communication branch of technology become so important because we have neglected truly communicating with one another? The world has shrunk, we speak of "global". Not in the same class as being in closer contact. Another thought is whether wars in the long run have the unforeseen end to cut communications in order to create new and better ones between the former warring parties.

I want to come back to the self as a counterbalance to the overblown and omnipotent ego in its splendid isolation. The self speaks loudest when through disease, accidents, or sudden crises. Or through the death of a beloved person when the doors of perception are opened and one knows again what is and what is not important for staying alive. But the self also makes itself felt in less dramatic moments, when, for example a decision has to be made and the ego's wishes and desires combined with reason point very clearly one way but something we call an intuition in another. But that I believe is something else again. Although it is also "irrational", not based on anything one could explain, intuition is not linked so deeply with the body as the self demands. It is better expressed by a "gut feeling". Jungians know a lot about the self that manifests in the form of symbols, like Eastern mandalas as objects of meditation, or interpret the role of the self in a myth or a fairy-tale. Perhaps it is my disposition and medical training that determine my particular view of the self. I become aware of it in social settings, for instance large gatherings of people. But also when I am alone or listen to music, especially the organ, trumpets, or a choir. But with all the enthusiasm among analytical psychologists (Jungian analysts) about the *numinosity* of the self, it would be a very dangerous entity were it not counterbalanced by the ego and the continuity of being and of conscious control. I would fall down the stairs, if, as a very old man, I would rely on my body as it was with its past mobility, instead of taking care of each step. The ego's controlling break is now needed. Without it the self would better be regarded as an ornament by Westerners, other than mystics, who extrapolate the self outside the body as transcendent God.

The value described in Jungian literature regarding the balance between ego and self would be meaningless were it not for the warming source of love. This remains the essential vitamin at this late stage of life just as much now as at any time. I have been extraordinarily lucky in that respect. Of course, it takes two, a giver and a recipient, so I can take some credit. Narcissism as described earlier as a couple united in one person, all the more needed during the many hours very old people are alone, is only a substitute for feeling oneself loved by another person. I would like to think that in spite of all my innate aggressiveness I have been a natural taker and giver of that vitamin. The united couple shown in alchemical illustrations is, according to Jung, one of the symbols of the self in its united and unifying capacity, the very opposite of anonymous sex. Another expression for Balint's "harmonious interpenetrating mix-up".

My enumeration of the few advantages of very old age would be incomplete without restating the very good luck I personally have enjoyed by having been shown love. This concerns not only by the younger generation, but also by my late wife Evelyn and in my marriage with Helga; but also by my children and grandchildren as well as by colleagues and friends, all much younger than myself. At the time of writing a committee of the Berlin Institute for Psychotherapy has gathered to prepare the celebration of my ninetieth birthday. I have become something of a living relic, not like the photos of our pioneers that adorn the hall of our institutes. There are few of my near contemporaries who have been so honoured.

17
Memories and Remembering

My writing about childhood has confirmed something I suspected. The more you cast your mind back, the more you can concentrate on the "memories", images, smells, phrases, tunes, and associated feelings, the more details surrounding the conscious memories can be recollected and brought back to life. I remember the gas mantle in the kitchen and the "plop" sound when a little chain was pulled that made the glimmer become a bright yellow light. I found it exciting. The ice-chest in the corridor and the dank smell of it. The blue-grey earthenware pots in the larder where eggs were preserved in a kind of jelly and another one for cooking fat. This was during and after the First World War when I was little and food was scarce. The padlocked larder was kept locked against the jocular threats of our neighbour, the lawyer.

The more I remember, the more memories come flooding back. It is as if satellites were orbiting around each planet of recollection. Moons around these planets become visible with each new incandescence of recollection. I suspect that the solar light in this analogy is reflected by the objects but emanates from the concentration in the mind of the beholder. Of course, it was easier when my brother and I could reminisce together about our childhood and could complement and check each. He could not remember the death of our father, which happened when Erwin was only three. All the tension, my mother's despairing cries, my aunt trying to comfort her and showing me his dead body. Clear in my recollection is that his eyes were closed. She said he was in heaven. I had my doubts.

One might have expected a less detailed recollection or none at all of an experience that would, according to psychoanalytic theory, rank as traumatic. I shall come back to the point.

Recollections without analysis of the unconscious have convinced me that one can bridge the gap between past and present, if one sets out to do so. The recollections may not all be exactly what really did happen. But they are sad and alive, just as much as I am living now as I write this down. Of course there must be distortions of the real events. But my recollections are good enough for me. What is more, in twenty years of analysis they did not have to alter.

Another approach. When I look at a clear night sky above, I look into the past. I know in my head that the source of the light, the actual event, the "big bang" that gave rise to our universe happened maybe five thousand million light-years ago. A length of time that is beyond my comprehension and therefore only a datum. But that does not make any difference to my immediate feeling of wonder and awe, a feeling that inspired Kant to write his famous lines about "the starry heavens above me". Yet I do have a vivid memory of the night skies in the desert that I can call up and bring back right now as I write. I know that the memory will last the rest of my life. Impressed on my mind is this awe-inspiring symbol of eternity. Only abstract thinking tells me that it all started at one time and will end at another.

I do care about the "facts", the objective, verifiable truth of my story in as much as it can be ascertained. I also care about the neurophysiological advances and psychological experiments about how memory works. But how to set about selecting and writing down those recollections that ran parallel to modern history and tell something about the "me" at the time and strike a chord in the mind of other people who want to know "what it was like". In short, can a life be transformed into an autobiography in a way that will strike the chords of co-experience. Will they still vibrate when the book has been closed?

There have to be narratives chiming in with existing knowledge of the times referred to, but my story is illuminated by the manner of recounting and the persons I address myself to, family as well as friends and the public. The miniature events woven together make an all-over pattern that is colourful enough to reach the level on which a reader can co-experience. But my priority must be to record the events of my life that I feel were important and the too private ones that can be left out without diminishing the all-over design that speaks of my life's experience and reflections.

I admit that there is vanity in writing about oneself. But not only today's vanity, also the hope for a tiny morsel of immortality, however illusory. In addition there is the genuine desire for stock-taking before closing down, a sort of thanks-giving and, again, curiosity: what was it all about? Trying to make sense, give meaning and so round it off. Happiness, or the opposite, does not play the most important role here. It's the fullness, the range, the colour that make me grateful for a long life, no matter how painful it may end.

It is not so very important whether my attempt at an autobiography is based on all the facts, no holds barred, that filled my life past and present. The real issue, is something beyond the flattering feeling of familiarity and empathy with my narrative and reflections. This something that must be the hope of all writers of poetry, fiction or autobiography. The hope that the work will be read as a whole that makes sense.

Now to the actual work. First the raw material and the collecting of it. There are the expected and the unexpected sources. Photographs, letters, tape recordings, maybe the old gramophone records and newer discs, my diaries and dreams recorded in journals, presents and their givers, stones collected haphazardly, minerals, fossils, shells, maps ancient and modern, all these function as tangible mementos of times gone by, theirs as well as mine. Evidence of my animism.

At the junction of re-arousal of memory by both thought and emotion, I find that books take a very special place. Looking at my shelves I picked out those that were read with great enthusiasm when first bought and recalled now. On the professional but not purely professional side there was William James' *The Varieties of Religious Experience* (1902) with the range of his knowledge, theological as well as psychological and the simplicity of his style, no wonder the book became a classic. Jung's *Die Psychologie der Übertragung* (1946),

(The Psychology of Transference). It is based on his study of alchemy and a picture series in particular on which Jung bases his argument that the transformations an analysand undergoes in the course of an analysis are an analogue of the transmutations the alchemist observes when he tries to transform base metal into gold. That attempt proved to be too ambitious. I believe that the highest aim of a Jungian analysis, individuation, is equally so.

As for my hobby and fiction books R. V. Tooley's *Maps and Map Makers* (1949) was the best guide in a large field. In my memory there is no clear distinction between the illustrated books about early world images purporting to be maps, and the many tall art books. Cézanne had been my late wife's, Evelyn, and my favourite when we first came to London and saw the aquarelle of *The Gardener Vallier*. Two books remind me of that time, the fifties. One is Thomas Mann's *The Holy Sinner* which has remained my favourite novel. It is about brother–sister incest. Second comes James Hogg's *The Memoirs of a Justified Sinner*. A perfect study of being possessed or paranoid; eerie like Henry James' *The Turn of the Screw*. Third and nearer our time would come Georges Simenon's novel *Les Anneux de Bicêtre*, about a man's recovery in hospital from a stroke and Iris Murdoch's *The Sea, the Sea*, about a retired narcissistic actor haunted by the vision of his once youthful idealised girlfriend. Among the recent German fiction books Patrick Süsskind's *Das Parfum* takes pride of place. A man born in the most unfortunate circumstances one can think of develops an obsession to use human sweat for the production of a perfume. For that purpose he has to kill his victims. It is an orgiastic celebration of the obsession with the sense of smell and at the same time a revenge taken on humanity for his own misery. He, the perfume-maker, incidentally, has no smell of his own. Much like the man without a shadow.

William Blake's poetic genius combined with his art and graphic works have remained among the books I return to and once shared with friends and colleagues. A few patients had the same preference as I noticed when they quoted his verse. It reminds me of my long working hours spent at the unusually shaped almost octagonal consulting room 11 Devonshire Place, London.

The surroundings and objects, particularly presents that expressed loving feelings at one time are powerful reminders of the past. They bring back a whole host of details that otherwise I would be unable to remember. The moment of recollection bridges the gap of time. Nostalgia is inevitable but I think necessary to bring back the reality of time past. Loss to be borne. But what about the old pop-tune that comes unbidden, out of the blue and builds a nest in my ears where it stays quite a while before letting me go. Very often I succeed in discovering the present context into which the tune, the words or someone's name, fits. It often had to do with love, sometimes with anxiety, babies, sickness and death. Or a line quoted in connection with a devout biblical citation like: "All is vanity" or "For everything its season". They help to bear the certainty of ultimate loss, inevitable ageing and death.

Another form of short term memory is so inaccessible to voluntary recall that it seems to be in a class of its own. It has neither words nor images. It feels as if part of the body, say my fingers or feet had their own memory. My feet may carry me to the right place quite often when I don't know what I am looking for. When I get there I can remember what it was. My legs remember bicycling which I had not done for decades. My fingers remember what to do on the computer that I could not have put into words to explain to somebody else. Without taking neuro-physiological and psychological experiments into consideration, self-observation has convinced me that there is more than one memory. The second one works like an alarm system that supervises and nudges the first when it does not do the job and is on the point of forgetting. This second circuit comes into operation with an uneasy feeling "there was something else" and goes on prodding until the first has done its job.

According to Freud we "forget" our trauma, cannot remember painful scenes because we habitually try to avoid dis-pleasures and psychic pain. Instead of which we develop amnesias, or create fantasies, illusions or false recollections to cover up and counteract the pain that would have accompanied the wholesome but unenjoyable truth, which psychoanalysis can restore in exchange for the patient's acceptance of the ordinary miseries of life. But the lifting of the amnesia that we use, the forgetting or inventing of screen memories to hide the truth, is not the whole, not even the most important factor in the "cure" of neurotic symptoms as psychoanalysts once thought. Nowadays the developing relationship between analyst and patient is regarded as the nub of the matter and called working in the transference. The echo in the analyst's feelings is called countertransference. I agree up to the point where the individual personalities of the analytic couple play a decisive part in the outcome of the enterprise.

To come back to my main point, memory as the conscious focussing on some fragment that has come to the forefront of one's vision and demands to be given a context, like the catchy tune that is reluctant to leave before I know why it has intruded and give it due space. This means deliberately looking at memories and memoirs that were traumatic in the past and have been covered up pathologically by repression into unconsciousness, as Freud's trauma theory would have it. Helpful as it is in the treatment of hysteria, nobody's memory or forgetting is entirely determined in this manner. On the contrary, I am convinced that by far the greatest part of what I have forgotten is not repressed but is or was simply not available because not required for living now. If remembered it would be lumber to today's tasks. I maintain that most of what I have forgotten is open to recall by purposeful concentration or by accidentally coming across things which together with the associated memories has been deliberately called up. Of course, psychoanalysts would argue that the purpose of concentration was also unconsciously determined. Because of my omnipotence, I regard memory as consciously determined by myself (the ego). But why should psychoanalysis shun the joy there is in remembering and discovering fresh links between past and events unaided. Could there not be truth and value in the realm of consciousness that is necessary for understanding how the present situation has come about. Even reliving the past through my present recollections can provide energy, giving fuel for living now, because memories become part of my being here and now, despite all the pain, mourning, nostalgia or shame that accompany many of my recollections.

As I focus my memory on scenes that come to mind in connection with material objects or people, events, images I happen to find more and more links. My uncle in the photograph will not only be a name. His habits, manner, pipe and figures of speech, laugh, cough, sneezes and smells, her hat, or hairstyle, dress; above all, the ways we felt about and spoke to each other – what our relationship was like when we first met how it went on or stopped. Given time and space for rediscovery I could go on and on. Reminiscing? Yes, but also more thoughtfully switching back to the person I myself was then, to the place I and the other came from and the ways we lived at that time and went from there.

The potential endlessness of my associations is one reason that makes selection inevitable. The criteria for my not having any are rightly the subject of psychoanalytic theory. But the opposite is also true. Conscious intention like writing a biography and concentrating on it can re-awake forgotten memories. For instance how Uncle Joseph made up to our children's nurse.

I happen to be particularly liable to forget the name of persons I know quite well. But say I remember the first letter or a part of the name that is "on the tip of my tongue". For example the letter "M" or a word, like "Verdi". I don't let go but focus my mind on such clues. Nothing else. Suddenly a bit later it is back: "Monteverdi". It is as if you had a hair by which you can pull back the whole name, a street or a setting and gradually the whole context has reformed itself. Easy, says, the psychoanalyst, it was all there in the pre-conscious. "Maybe", I answer. "You always have a term for it, but does it explain or change anything other than that you feel in command of the situation?"

Another example: when the name of my Aunt Toni comes back and I allow myself to dwell on her memory, a whole string of not so pleasant memories come back, not as associations but as images and sensations I experience now. The crackling of the newspaper she read at breakfast, the smell of her cigarette, lit before she took off to the lavatory. Or the smell of urine around the bed of her neglected, very much older, husband. The whole of the scene becomes as vivid as if it were now. It commands attention like a film I am watching. I maintain that it had been deeply unknown and forgotten before and am convinced that it is a true recollection, recalled by deliberate concentration rather than by analysing my unconscious.

Two questions emerge from these reflections.

Is the division conscious–unconscious pre-ordained or man-made? This question is not meant to be rhetorical, I do want to leave the answer open. Starting with the division of body and mind (soma-psyche), we surely have created it to study two aspects of our being in detail. Similarly, I think about the border between conscious–unconscious as a hard and fast one because we need it in our analytic practice. I have enlarged upon this point in the chapters "On Training within a Human Context and "Meeting Famous Colleagues and Other Notable Figures". Terms like "transitional" and "inter-" that lower the fence that in analytical practice is useful up to the point of becoming thoughtlessly overused.

Can memory be so deeply encoded in the brain that it becomes inheritable? Experiments on the weaver bird in South Africa confirm the idea of inherited memory. The bird is the "weaver bird" because it weaves an intricate nest of grass and twigs. It is bell-shaped hanging upside down with the opening underneath, so that snakes cannot get at the eggs. Four generations of birds were reared in artificial surroundings that made it materially impossible to build the traditional nest. The fifth generation, brought up in freedom, built it again, faultlessly. I speculate that this pattern of behaviour is encoded in the birds' brains and therefore comparable to Jung's pattern of behaviour or archetype, the collective unconscious of humans.

True, there are worlds of difference between the bird's and the human brain. Psychologically, it involves the influence of emotions, their neurophysiological transmission and how memory operates via certain areas of the brain hence also enters my biographical reflections. The question of inherited memory traces refuses to go away.

Looking back I get an impression and feel of a man whose peculiarities are laid out before I became "me". You who read this see him in miniature, as through the wrong end of a telescope. Although the field of vision is limited, a multitude of miniatures when run together make a pattern characteristic of the person. In the end it spells out "the race is run, your time has passed, soon *you* will be like a forgotten dream". To get the message across the unbelieving me, I had to spool the film back and run it through again and again up to the crossroads where past and present join. Seeing it bears comparison with seeing the starry sky, as past, present and future all at once. The act of living usually separates us from that view because of the daily necessities and changing circumstances. Such as in my case osteoarthrosis and living on the second floor, a combination which threatens increasing immobility or having to move.

Re-viewing, recalling memories, touching memorabilia can create the illusion that the one-time participants are still around. No wonder it has taken such a time and an autobiography to help to get the message across: they are all gone the old familiar faces and your time is almost up. No future, except you look at your offspring and for the short time while you continue to be in the minds of people who have known you. Maybe there is a tiny morsel of the present still to be tasted. But let it be clear, I say to myself, someone else's turn now. And after that yet another generation. A glimpse of eternity before final darkness.

Writing now that my ninetieth birthday has been celebrated "Between Losing and Finding" is becoming an ever more apt title for these memoirs. As often as not the "lost" object, the one that is the most wanted just at this moment is not really lost, nor even mislaid. On the contrary, it is just where it should be, only my anticipation that it could be lost, blinds me to its presence. Say I wanted to look up a word in the dictionary. It is not even mentioned – or so it appears. Following my own rules about such situations, I can escape a minor panic. When I look again, I find the word is where it should be, plain as a pikestaff.

A neurotic symptom? Certainly; the diagnosis comes together with a whole host of psychodynamic interpretations. All they do is to comfort me because they tell me somebody else, other pseudo-losers have been here before. At least I am not alone with my madness. A much younger friend and I discovered per chance that we suffer and enjoy such daily events in exactly the same manner. I do not know what psychopathology we have in common. It makes no difference to our friendship nor to the different ways we live. The losing-finding syndrome is an incurable part of the essential me. And the finding is usually so wonderful, the meeting the object again so joyful that it fills me with a sense of gratitude. So, taking it all in all, I would not want to be cured, even if it were possible. A "cure" could even spoil the fun I find in writing. Thinking about it professionally the title of one of Michael Balint's books, *Thrills and Regressions*, comes to mind as the one that describes the situation best. Never mind that I remain addicted to thrills. How boring life would be without such excitements.

So far I have been lucky to escape more or less the usual forgetfulness of old age. I can be pretty sure of that because when I notice the disappointment or astonishment of younger people that I have *not* forgotten their names in different contexts. Mischievously I sometimes play at having forgotten. At the official celebration of my ninetieth birthday I gave this irrepressible misbehaviour a good airing. Having listened to the eulogies which are an equally inescapable part on such occasions, I told only my friend Andrew what I would do. It was to act the part of a very old man having already lost his mind and memory. When the time came to reply and make a short speech that I had written down I got up, fumbled about in my pockets, could not find it and turned to my wife: "Where is my speech?" She, poor thing, did not have it. "Have you given it to Andrew?" "Andrew, have you got it?" He, straight faced: "I have not got it." Renewed prolonged fumbling in pockets. The guests became worried about the oldster in his embarrassment until, suddenly, like the rabbit out of the conjurer's hat, I drew the speech out of another pocket. Most of the audience having been taken in, clapped with relief. Claudia, who had not been deceived, told me afterwards I had not been panicky enough. So still something to learn before trying my hand at play-acting. It had been fun, but I also felt slightly ashamed because I had allowed my imp to mislead my friends. If I had put my tricking them into words they would have been: "Your eulogies speak only about a part of me. Look what I have just done." My excuse for the trickery is that I had just noticed myself that when writing I increasingly often leave out the last letter of a word. Yet another sign that I have not got much further to go. So I must get on and finish this book.

Seeing what is happening as if one were a character in a play as well as the onlooker, I notice that I often combine the parts of my two aunts in one. The one who loses, the other who finds. Between the two exists a tense emotional relationship, not necessary to divide it into conscious–unconscious parts. My being able to describe their relationship in psychodynamic terms would not alter anything. It merely helps the analytic observer to feel in charge of the unknown. For the purpose of finding a meaning it would be better to look at it as an amusing play. It avoids conflict without escaping it.

Borrowing the eyes of another person to find the lost object is often successful. But then finding and welcoming the object back is lost. Pure gain is when I borrow my secretary's eyes to keep me and my notes in sufficiently good order to complete writing this book.

18
Still Searching

All my life I have searched for some faith. Not necessarily a religious faith. More like trust. No doubt, I shall go on for the rest. I found synagogues, churches and all places designed for worship uninspiring, especially when prayers, singing congregations or other rituals were in progress. Too much performance, too much theatre, all organised "lift up of hearts" had embarrassed me already in childhood. Such faith as I found of lasting value is largely determined by aesthetics. The god-like part of humans I see reflected in the arts; the specifically human quality in love. The architecture of the buildings can fill me with a sense of wonder even awe, so can the stained glass windows and the coloured light filtering into the dark interior, the mosaics on the floor, beamed ceilings, maybe with chandeliers, the warm flame of candles and organ music that vibrates in my chest have the same effect as the beautiful voices of the boys' choir at King's College Chapel, Cambridge. All these can move me to tears. So can a procession, especially when in traditional costume like the one I saw at the *fête des filets bleus* in Brittany. I am equally moved by an individual lost in devotion, like a Jew, head bowed, the whole body wrapped in his prayer shawl, as he will be when he is buried. Or listening to the sheep's horn as it is blown on the Day of Atonement emitting a shrill and eerie sound, image of the voice of God telling his people in the desert of his presence. The sight of a Hindu woman propitiating Ganesa by prayer and offering food; an African by the graveside of his ancestor also offering food; Buddhist monks sitting straight-backed in meditation, single minded, trained by daily discipline. I feel both moved and warmed by the Friday evening Jewish ritual and ceremonial family-meal when the family and strangers that happen to pass through are invited to take part in the ceremonious meal that ushers in the Sabbath, when all worldly matters come to stand still. A ritual suffused with love.

Freud would have seen all these acts as childish acts based on an illusion and born out of the need for an eternal father who has survived murder by his sons. His interpretation cannot be disproved but I doubt whether it contains the whole or even the most relevant truth. The longing and searching for some being or a cause more important than one's own survival and vulnerability seems to be inherent in mankind. Whether it is sought in an established religion, a political aim, scientific research or an ideal like the united human family. I see all of these as searches for a mystical union between love everlasting, the mortal individuals and their search for something of highest imperishable and most valuable good. I do not want a general view, philosophy, or *Weltanschauung* as much as a sharp focus, something that can become burning, acting like the centre of a magnifying glass that gathers the sun's rays to a central point with which one can burn (hence German: Brennglas). No doubt the central point is also dangerous when it consumes the whole person. I have seen it as paranoia, rightly called "monomania".

When I was a child between ten and twelve I looked for signs of life on Mars, no doubt having read science fiction. In times of crisis and in old age I find some comfort in my continuity in the form of genetic inheritance and most of all in what I call the Godhead inside me that does not primarily judge by "good" or "evil". The Buddhist's priority of freedom from desire is closer to my ideal, although I cannot imagine that I shall ever get there as long as I am truly alive. Communal worship seems to deprive me of the communion I seek with my god who is the indefinable end of all knowledge that Bion refers to as "O" in order to give a neutral designation to the unknowable final sum of all knowledge.

Yet I appreciate the value of organised religion in the form of charity, as long as it does not threaten non-believers or the 'other' believer, anyone outside their own confession. But I also believe that William James (*In the Varieties of Religious Experience*) was right when he wrote that the only cure for alcoholics is religion. The danger of converts is their becoming crusaders. Soldiers of God. George W. Bush, president of the USA, is the outstanding example in our time.

All the various humanitarian nursing associations, ambulances, hospitals and hospices that offer shelter and care for refugees and outcasts regardless of creed and colour redress to some extent the vicious persecutions and murder committed by many organised religions that know themselves to be more right than others and feel provoked by their very existence. To make matters worse the other as "non-believer" is often of different racial origin which becomes additional and often more important grounds for hatred and violence, as I can attest in the case of anti-Semitism that I have witnessed rather than personally experienced.

The adherents of the "right" religion feel it their duty to bring the non-believers into the fold by persuasion and missionising rewards. Or, if that is not enough, by violent means. All these abuses alone support my claim that there are "others" who have the need to continue in a search for which there is no ultimate point of arrival. Nobody has ever tried to convert me. I suppose they sensed that there was nobody to convert as I disagreed with none. I merely have my doubts about the benefit I would derive from any organised religion. I prefer an in-dwelling or "immanent" God.

Who then are those others, like myself, who place their trust in the void of self-oblivion rather than the image of an external "transcendant" God and the substantial organisations and traditions built around it by the adherents to what James calls "The Religion of the Healthy Minded". Bion as psychoanalyst refers to the majority of believers without a trace of contempt as "The Establishment". In my searches I knew early on that I did not belong there. Now I can formulate positively that my longing is to become one with the No-thing, better understood as oblivion. But that word is as easily misunderstood just as Jung's distinction between the ego (the "I", the Freudian "Ich") and the "self" is. The ego makes plans and decisions, is in command of logistics, the "self" is an autonomous body–mind unity on which the ultimate co-operation with or divergence from the "ego" depends. In the mystical experience, the "I" of everyday life is temporarily superseded by the self because it is in union with it or, as I would say, with "God" but I can equally call it union with the "All". James discovered this state by experimenting when he inhaled nitrous oxygen (laughing gas). Alcoholics and drug takers presumably search for it by losing their "I" and its controlling rational, limiting reality. They try to get to the blissful unification by a short-cut by blotting out the "I" (becoming "blotto"?). The problem is that I also want to return to the "I" that I know as myself, constantly searching as well as desiring to satisfy my other instincts.

In my various searches I found less dangerous approaches, some more pedestrian than others. The more out of the way events that just happen like the fortuitous meetings I had with people who knew more about my hobby with maps than I do. All this "greater than I" is more extreme in mystics who have experienced "transport" or ecstasis. James tells us that all mystics are agreed that the experience cannot be communicated. I owe the knowledge that in the Middle Ages there were also some women-mystics, to my late and long-term friend, the writer Monica Furlong. She had like myself a leaning towards mysticism but combined it with church-going and even revolutionising the church by fighting for women to become ordained as priests.

Jung and Bion also retained a foot in both camps, in that they thought of themselves as both scientists as well as mystics. Both quote such well known mystics as the German Meister Eckhardt and the Jewish David Luria. Among modern English mystics I found Evelyn Underhill who wrote *Essentials of Mysticism*.

I have wondered why "mystical" is and has for over a hundred years been a term of reproach, if not contempt. In a world that awards the highest praise to measurable scientific achievement "mystical" constitutes a heresy. When accurate measurement, precise definition and repeatability by experiment mark the pinnacle of communicable science, anything "mystical" must be anathema because by its very nature it can neither be measured nor communicated. To the mystic the incommunicable state of knowing is revelation. The word mystic was originally exclusively used in connection with religion but has become applicable to anyone who claims to make a striking disclosure. And so it is with mysticism, originally confined to the religious experiences of well-known mystics, it can now be applied to special situations which inspire a sense of awe to an extent that a new unity, an altered awareness of reality, and a conciliation takes place of the past with the present. It is as if, again in James' words, "all the opposites of the world were melted into one". Every time it is the newness of the experience called mystical that matters. The mystic is not, in any sense, a "funny". James quotes Martin Luther, a down-to-earth person, who in his life as a monk had the experience of seeing the scriptures in an entirely new light and straightaway felt as if he were new-born. "It was as if I had found the door of Paradise thrown wide open." He it was, who, according to legend, threw the famous ink-pot at the wall where the devil had appeared. The ink-pot legend describes, in my view, more a visionary than a mystical event. Reacting excitedly to a vision brings it close to what we are used to seeing in psychotic states. Why then the reproach of confusion or vagueness that is so commonly attached to "mystical", in the sense of deliberate "mystification", in other words trying to cover something up or even to deceive.

I want to speculate how this disparaging aura surrounding mysticism has come about. For one, anything that is unusual or uncommon about another person is suspect to good citizens who know right from wrong. Why, they may ask, cannot the mystic be like other people? And, indeed one cannot *learn* to become a mystic if, as James puts it, one is born a "healthy-minded, sky-blue" optimist. There is further the similarity I mentioned between a mystic with his fleeting sometimes visionary experience and some psychotics who describe what they see or hear, things and voices that we, who live in sober reality, consider as delusions, therefore insane. To protect ourselves, a *cordon sanitaire,* a safety zone against becoming infected by madness has to be thrown around such people. We used to lock them up. Now we use chemical straight-jackets. Or, if they are otherwise "quite nice" and tame persons, it may be sufficient to keep one's safe distance.

As psychiatrists and analysts we are already suspect of being a little mad. Maybe that is why I have never spoken about my own single but possibly mystical encounter. There may well be others like myself who think it wise to keep their mouths shut. When I tried to reach that state by silence and meditation in a retreat, nothing happened. Likewise with the help of yoga and appropriate breathing and meditation. That was when I was in my fifties. In those days too it was my habit to get up between five and six in the summer months and to sit in my dressing gown with a first cup of tea on the bench under the pear tree. Long shadows over the lawn, the air dew-fresh, birds in dawn-chorus, in the distance shots at intervals in the cherry orchard to keep the birds away. In half an hour the milkman's van will come rattling up the drive. Suddenly, there is complete silence, even the air stands still. I feel myself transposed, as if into another world where time stands still. This may have lasted only a fraction of a second or a couple of minutes until I was back, the surroundings and sounds all there as before. Only I was not, because I knew I had seen beyond the reality I knew and appreciate so well. I also knew that I would never forget that moment. Never again did I experience anything like that and now think of it as nature-mysticism. The nearest I can compare it with was when during my war-time service I had once gone out alone into the semi-desert and felt wonderfully and absolutely alone, lost in timeless silence. The "as if" in my singular experience is sufficient indication of the actual event being indescribable.

Books and writing remind me that there are also profane ways of reaching one-ness by total dedication to a single subject. During the time of my yoga attendances I met a person whose life of study and academic achievement in a single subject filled the centre of her being. This was Frances Yates of the Warburg Institute and Collection, London. The Renaissance with its pre-scientific Hermetic and Cabalistic (as she spelt it) tradition was the centre of her universe of which Giordano Bruno was an eminent exponent. Remarkable as a prescientic figure he nevertheless credited the Copernican revolution of the universe. Yates' dedication made her person one with her knowledge and research. Her enthusiasm was infectious. I am glad to have met her.

I also had to ask myself what, in the end, has remained Jungian in my point of view and me as a person in search of a centre. I appended answers to an imaginary questioner about the practical difference between Freud and Jung and came down on the side that agrees with the importance of the personalities involved in the transactions between each specific analyst–patient–couple. I restate it here as my *credo* that without there being a fundamental liking between the analytic couple that will withstand all temperatures and storms, neither psychoanalysis nor analytic psychotherapy works.

I would put further as my inheritance from Jung, tolerance vis-à-vis other forms of psychotherapeutic treatment, notably Freudian psychoanalysis. Jung's avowed attitude has certainly not been reciprocated by psychoanalysts nor by the more right wing of Jung's followers. After all there is competition involved, as there is between faiths, which militate against tolerance. It is all the more remarkable that in London a Freud–Jung discussion group of analysts has been meeting for many years without coming to blows.

Jung's "Psychological Types" I found of limited usefulness. "Introvert" and "Extravert" have become labels in ordinary language. Like all originally technical terms they become worn and meaningless by over usage. As a means of quick superficial orientation however this pair of opposites has remained useful. On closer acquaintance the "other" more often than not becomes a mixture of both, just like myself. The same holds good, only more so, for Jung's further classification of persons into feeling, thinking, sensing and intuiting types. True, one may be more obvious than the other. But as I got to know people in depth I found that it is doing injustice to look at anyone as the personification of a type because it limits my leaving space for unexpected and individual exceptions.

Closely associated with my coming to grips with Jungian thinking is the highest rung of the ladder of any person's development "Individuation". Not to be mistaken for individualism, I take it to mean that an inner balance has come about between all that is unique and characteristic of me the individual who is also aware that he depends on being in touch with others. The process that leads to individuation is hard to put into words. Words alone are inadequate. Jung resorted to religious, including Eastern, symbols, notably the *mandala*. He also made allowance for patients who may be better at expressing themselves by nonverbal modes of communication, for instance painting or movements such as dance. I like drawing or just scribbling spontaneously.

In real life, as I know it, both professionally and socially, the mixture of contradictory features in every person is commoner than appears on the surface. Analysis offers a surprising view into another person's psyche – and one's own. I quote Shakespeare in Mark Anthony's final eulogy of the murdered Caesar:

His life was gentle and the elements
So mixed in him that Nature might stand up
And say to all the world "This was a Man!"

"So mixed" I take to mean contradictory, even paradoxical.

I return to the beginning of the chapter when I say that I share Jung's high regard for the holy but must repeat that I do not specifically mean religious, as the theologian Rudolf Otto did, whom Jung quoted in connection with the concept "numen" or the "numinous", a word that is used to express the spiritual power attached to the participation in an event, originally of a religious nature. At the lower end of an imaginary scale, it can be a thrill or a shudder, while the upper is known as awe-inspiring, overwhelming. To make a special allowance for states of being simply overwhelmed and speechless is more Jungian than Freudian. The *forte* of the latter is to explain all phenomena in dynamic technical terms. At the end of all my searching including having been in psychoanalysis four times, I have not found that the interpretations have changed me as much as have some living numinous illuminating moments shared in analysis. They occur of course in ordinary life, such as being present at a birth and death. These awe-inspiring moments are peak experiences. Combined with the verbal-explanatory principle such experiences have given me a stereoscopic view and perspective on the day-to-day problems of living.

Another way of searching is by writing, spontaneous or planned. Planned pre-supposes that mental processes such as fantasies, thoughts, reflections, dreaming and discussing have preceded the process. Now the utmost concentration is required. The necessity of giving it constant attention goes on all the time, no matter what else I may be doing in a routine way. It is as if I were inside the subject of my particular focus at the time, not just concerned with it. It is also in me, comparable maybe to a baby in the womb. Some women have told me that they never feel so happy as when pregnant. I feel safe when in my comparable state. Nothing and nobody can rattle me. When I was young I could not understand how a woman could like pregnancy: such a drag to walk about with an enormous belly. Now I can. An undeniable centre is given. Even if it is devouring her, she is giving life, the embryo is giving her a new expectation of life. In contrast to writing where I must take the chance that the product will already look dead the next day. The people around me get angry. "You are in a world of your own and have not listened to a word I said!"

Over and above the losing, searching and finding of my keys or purse and the book that was there only a moment ago, there are these other kinds of searches that go on, although I often could not tell what I am seeking. If asked I would hesitate before I could find the words with which to formulate a reply because I would first have to find the words to exactly describe my aim. If the short answer should be "God", "love", "my vocation" or "death" my questioner would think I am mad or else they press for details which I have not got available. Stuck between vague or complex explications, I look for detailed examples. There aren't any that would express exactly what I mean or do not invite further questioning. God for example. Must he be found in religion? If a deity, which one? What address? – Or "Death". No question. But how seriously do we believe it when hale and hearty?

The searching as such is a far more difficult activity to describe than the search for a lost or mislaid object. It is not an activity in the same sense as trying to find an object I lost. It happens without conscious intention like looking up a word in the dictionary. It happens when I am in a passive receptive frame of mind, a passive exploration, like falling in love or finding a teacher or a guide, priest or psychotherapist. Or a cause, political, scientific, social. Some seem to find their centre or focal point in an enduring marriage and surrounding family. One does not exclude the other. In my case, I could not have done without my marriage to Evelyn and am now dependant on Helga's goodwill towards the old man. Yet a "belief-system" has remained central to my being and still feeling alive. Not just for the daily routines and work but to my very relationship to the world as far as I know it and extending beyond. A belief-system that gives a viewpoint just like a religious person sees the world as God's creation or the natural scientist as the result of a combination of physical and chemical processes, or, like the poet Blake, who could see "the world in a grain of sand". But whether I am religiously, analytically, scientifically or poetically minded, my focus remains a central unifying belief in which I must trust, never forgetting that it is only one among many. I may think mine is the truest and making the best sense although I must admit that it cannot be the whole story. My formerly most important viewpoint, analysis, has acquired rivals in art and literature. Actually, they get on quite well together, I enjoy their diversity and hope to combine all three within my social and historical context.

Whatever my belief-system may be, it cannot altogether replace religion. There is something so primary or primitive, about religion that no belief-system can take its place. Mine is not organised and has no label. I had already introduced it when I wrote about my reaction to a devoutly religious person whose sight can give me "holy shudders". The names Quakers and Shakers express it too. There are a lot of other experiences, a birth or a murder, that can fill me with awe or make me stand aghast. Usually it has something terrifying about it, like coming upon an accident, hearing of the sudden death of a young person; but also joy when I hear of someone I like who has had a windfall, has come into a lot of money from not knowing where to turn. I smile immediately. Prosaically I have to add that my face also relaxes into a smile when I turn the shower from cold to hot.

A terrifying or thrilling event gives me gooseflesh, makes me pale, gives me the shivers, makes my hair stand on end – but these and all bodily reactions are only *linked* with what I believe in. Physiology may observe and even measure in a rough and ready way what goes on emotionally. Darwin and his illustrated *The Expression of the Emotions in Man and Animals* (1872) showed that the same facial muscles are used, for instance in expression of anger in cats and humans. The human emotions were illustrated by actors or photographs of small children. That seemed to be enough to classify the work as scientific. More recently Francis Crick, discoverer of the double helix structure of DNA wrote that accurate measurement was the enemy of vitalism. That word would include my "belief-system". As for Darwin the "how", not the question "why", was what mattered. The more you discover how things work, the more "why" becomes redundant. For me both are of equal importance but I am by nature inclined towards the philosophical "why".

The kind of objectivity of the "lie-detector" once used in American court cases has been found unreliable because the belief-system functions as a unity and cannot be divided into psyche and soma. It is convenient to call it "psychosomatic" but it was there before that term came into fashion as the totality of the human being plus something else. What, if anything, is it? By biblical tradition "the breath of life" that God breathed into the otherwise ready clay-figure of Adam. It is without substance nor is it localisable; commonly referred to as "spirit" or atmosphere. I have known moments when I felt inspired, at other times I felt de-spirited.

Whichever way it takes me, I want to know more about the source of this spirit and for what reason it affects me. One danger on such a search is the spiritualists who hold their séances looking for the thrills of the miraculous, a form of soothsaying, part of the vast realm of magic and superstition. But spirit is without substance and like Jung's synchronicity without causal explanation. It was easy for me to understand and even sympathise with the Freudian antagonism to "all this mumbo-jumbo". Psychoanalysts in the past were making Jungian mythology into "mystical", in this way enlisting everyman's suspicion, as if it meant nothing less than deceitful, forgetting in this context that by making frequent use of the "Oedipus complex" Freud was giving a mythological name to a clinical observation and theory. A prominent psychoanalyst after him (Bion) went further when he not only used other myths like "The Confusion of the Tongues" at Babel and even quoted mystics, Jewish and Christian, in support of his hypotheses.

Although I said "no" when asked whether I am religious I left out that I am in sympathy with the mystics and their common aim to be united with God. My version is with the total being in me, that I can sense without naming it. So if I call out to God, it is also to the unknown Self within. Evidence of its existence comes through when the somato-psychic unit functions in unforeseen but reliable ways. It may be evoked by extremes of pain, pleasure, or emotions like anger that suddenly flair up and burst the dam of controlled behaviour. All have been regularly followed by the relief of having come through. Now I am fully alive, not just ticking over. Although the feeling itself may be indescribable it can be shared. An exceptional voice at the opera makes one's soul vibrate. It is that which comes as close as a religious feeling or a shock.

There are however minor forms of unification without any religious aspect. Like those caused by swings or the big dipper at the fairground, children love them especially. Simulation of danger without real risk. All scream with pleasurable anxiety. My late colleague Balint referred to thrills and regressions. Thrills certainly. Regression, I must question. If he limits the meaning to happenings like falling out of a tree like a baby-monkey and being caught at the last possible moment, I understand him. If Balint includes the highly evocative ritualistic events and the other emotional peaks I quoted in support of my belief-system, then the psychoanalytic concept of regression as a return to a previous state of development, meaning childhood, is too narrow for my liking. Although psychoanalysts will concede that everyone has occasionally the need to sleep, dream, have fantasies, regress, like the Catholic Church allows carnivals, the aim of analysis according to Freud remains all the same the patient's giving up the pleasure principle for the reality principle – accordingly, life is earnest, if not downright grim.

Finally, where does my body-soul mysticism stand in respect of good and evil? I have to ask myself, before anyone else will, are you not just self-seeking, forgetting about your neighbours, not caring about the rest of mankind when really you are self-absorbed, imagining that you are seeing, or even being God? To all these and similar legitimate questions I would answer: Maybe. I shall attend to that in a moment. Only my searching and occasionally finding, if only by catching a glimpse that will last, comes first. It is a MUST, or an instinct. So is waiting for death after ninety, to dissolve all traces of grandiosity, simplicity found.

Appendix

What is the Difference between Freud and Jung?

In the past I have often been asked this question by lay people. That it is still being asked shows that both kinds of analysts, that is psychoanalysts and analytical psychologists, who claim the two pioneers as their ancestors are still known as 'Freudians' and 'Jungians'. Analysts themselves recall their origins less often than in the past which suggests that there have been successors and developments in both kinds of analytical practice. I shall return to the question by giving the most concise description of the difference I can think of.

To describe the difference I must start with what the two have in common. Briefly, it is the rediscovery that there exists a region in our minds which is, and remains, most of it, most of the time, unknown to ourselves. Invisible like electricity, we can only infer its presence from the manifestations. An example. We cannot 'see' the blind spot in the field of our vision but a simple test shows it is indisputably there. In this case the anatomical reason for the blind spot is easily demonstrable. In the case of the mental region that analysts call *unconscious*, such proof is by definition impossible. Were it possible, we could no longer use the term. So it remains a concept and we have to rely for evidence on our understanding of certain phenomena. These are there in plenty once the concept is allowed for. People who pride themselves on their self-knowledge and control find it hard to swallow that they harbour fantasies and motives for their actions which might not be morally and socially acceptable were they known to themselves. So now we have two reasons for part of the mind remaining unrecognised, unconscious. One is the impossibility of knowing it all, the other not wanting to know. Since Freud's time public resistance to that idea has decreased without, however, vanishing. It remains unpalatable when it concerns not certain others, but oneself.

Why then should anybody want to pry into the unconscious? Both Freud and Jung were children of the nineteenth century. And so was Darwin, the giant among explorers whose work stamped it as a golden century of exploration in natural science. Exploration of the mind can be seen as a parallel. The *Zeitgeist* exerted a strong influence on all kinds of research. Freud in turn was influenced by the French doctors Charcot and his pupil Janet who practised hypnosis and demonstrated its striking effects on patients. On his return to Vienna, Freud started to practise hypnosis too but soon switched from the flamboyant demonstrations of the French colleagues to a more and more scientific approach to the patient and discovered laws according to which the conscious and unconscious mind interacted. When, for instance the instinct-driven fantasies of the patient were intolerable as socially acceptable behaviour, the fantasies and desires had to be repressed. The energies required were then not available for love and work in daily life. I believe that Freud's failures with hypnosis were a further spur to follow his scientific bend rather than the French fashion of the day. However, some influence of this earlier method of psychotherapy is still noticeable in the patient lying on the couch listening to the unseen analyst's voice during psychoanalytic sessions. Jung did not use the couch and remained visible to the patient.

With this historical sketch as a background I am now ready to return to the differences. Freud's epoch-making *Die Traumdeutung* (1900), (The Interpretation of Dreams) has remained his most fundamental work because he used the already existent concept of the unconscious to build up a systematic structure of interacting parts of the psyche for the use of treatment of neurosies. This was to become fundamental for psychoanalysis. Jung, by eighteen years his junior, visited Freud in Vienna and was most impressed by the older colleague who knew, as he said, more than he did. He had worked mainly with psychotic patients at the mental hospital in Zürich and became Freud's pupil. For several years they worked in close contact and travelled together on a lecturing tour to America. Freud regarded Jung as his "crown prince" until they parted in animosity, which has affected their followers to this day. Although their fundamental difference was centred on opposing views regarding the significance of symbols, I believe that their differences can be best understood if we look at their methods of interpreting products of the unconscious, such as dreams and fantasies. The common aim of interpretations remains that it should enable patients to become more aware and make allowance for what was truly going on in their unconscious mind. This, in turn, is expected to free the energies previously needed not to take notice of (repress) painful events in the past and elaborated by fantasy causing a variety of the neurotic symptoms. Positively expressed the patient should, after repression has been lifted and reality accepted, be free to enjoy a more fulfilled life. The only proviso being that the patient could tolerate some painful truths as a fair exchange.

Let this be a sketchy outline of the Freudian position. Jung takes the opposite point of view. Make the patient aware of his personal contribution to his present complaints. By all means. But guide him also to the riches of his unconscious mind, his share in the culture of mankind as a source of the dormant energy and creativity which give meaning to the individual's life where before there was emptiness. However, this can't be done until the patient has also become aware of his *shadow*. By this term Jung refers to the ever and in everybody present (hence archetypal) unconscious, including unpleasant characteristics which we so easily see in others (project into others) instead of integrating these into one's image of oneself or self-image. It is the old biblical story of the mote and the beam.

We see that both the Freudian and the Jungian disciplines aim at easing suffering and emptiness by truer and greater self-awareness. Now to the crucially different ways of getting there, that is the methods of getting from lesser to greater consciousness of the unknown part of the mind. Let us take a hypothetical snippet of a dream as an example. The first thing is to assume that we don't know what it means and why we should dream it and also that no off-the-peg explanation exists that acts like a *passepartout* and can be looked up in a book or on the internet.

No analyst worth his salt would interpret a dream if he did not know the essential details of the dreamer's existence, such as age, sex and circumstances. The abstract model I shall use here is shorn of all the details that would surround the life of a real dreamer/patient. In my example I shall assume that it is a young man.

Let us further assume that my imaginary psychoanalyst is told the following dream: *"I was lying alone in warm sunshine on the banks of a river. An elderly woman came along. She had not noticed me until she nearly stumbled over me. She told me off for being in her way. That was the end."*

The first method of interpretation makes use of the dreamers *associations*. It means that he is asked to let details of the dream link up with the first thing that comes into mind.

Association method

Dream: "Banks of a River", see text above. The dreamer associates:

"The town where I was born was on a river.
↓
We moved from there when I was four.
↓
I remember my mother often going to funerals after my father had died. She said I was her sunshine, the only joy she had.
↓
It was always too cold to swim in the river.
↓
It's cold here. May I have a blanket?
↓
I can't think of anything else. I'd rather you ask me some questions."

Psychoanalyst's Interpretation

The patient's associations would lead to the conclusion that the *manifest* dream contains a hidden message, a latent content behind the manifest dream as recounted. It might run as follows: The dreamer is in a depressed state and has been so from his unhappy childhood on. Although he was his mother's, the elderly woman in the dream, joy she may also have felt that he was in her way since she had to bring him up single-handed for which she had to work hard. This prevented her from finding a new partner. Or, more likely, since the patient is the dreamer, she was in *his* way which he did not allow himself to know as she was his only parent and he depended on her. Let this be the psychoanalyst's interpretation of the dream's hidden message. Additionally, the wish-fulfilling part, warm sunshine, expresses the dreamer's longing for warmth and relaxation and perhaps an indolent dependence. Psychoanalytic colleagues would regard the sunshine as an illusory compensation for the cold reality. I think both kinds of analysts would interpret the dreamer's request for a blanket as an indication that the patient had also developed a positive relation to the analyst, a positive transference, which reflects the transferred image of a protective mother that enables the dreamer on the couch to turn to his analyst. I believe both kinds of analysts would see this aspect in the same way.

Analytical Psychologist's (Jungian) Interpretation

Now let us look at the same dreamer telling his dream to a Jungian, to an "analytical psychologist", sitting most likely in a chair opposite him or her. That at least is the "classical" position. Nowadays many also use the couch or let the patient choose.

In my personal comment on the imaginary psychoanalyst's interpretation, I have already indicated the analytical psychologist's *method* of arriving at an interpretation, which is called *amplification*. It means that interpretation starts by leaving the manifest dream have its own untranslated say. The psychoanalytic interpretation was, as we assumed, based on recognising the pleasure principle, lying in the sun, and bringing "the reality principle", cold, loneliness, purposelessness into consciousness so that it can be worked on by the subsequent transactions between patient and analyst.

The Jungian method, "amplification" means not only leaving the dream intact, but making it more ample, richer, fuller. How can this be done? Much is left to the interpreter's individual style and once again the individual dreamer's person and circumstances as well as the analyst's diagnostic assessment but the general answer would be by engaging in a dialogue. In the course of this and depending on the dreamer's non-verbal responses including his facial expression and voice, he will try to emphasise that both sun and water are essential elements of any form of life as is also having a mother. He will certainly try to find out what else the dreamer expects, how he hopes to get it and what has he so far done about it. In other words his active interest in the patient and his relationship to his mother and the world outside will be outspoken. He assumes that the patient's unconscious speaks in the form of symbolic images rather than hides wish-fulfilling, pleasure principle determined elements that would lead away from reality.

The Jungian analyst may by his participation have encouraged the dreamer sufficiently to come out of his shell and say something about the gloomy-depressed and cold side of his life, about the lack of love, or hate and perhaps about his feeling of hopelessness. If he feels it indicated the imaginary Jungian analyst may draw attention to the river flowing into the ocean, the symbolic equivalent of the vast unconscious container, the archetypal Mother, in which the patient has a share.

Different as the two psychodynamic routes to dream interpretation are, by association or by amplification, different as the thinking behind these methods is and as incompatible as the theoretical edifices that have been built on these appear, the gulf has gradually lessened. Representatives of both directions meet and find that they are all treating the same patients to whom it is essential to establish the close confidential contact without which there can be no therapy. The form and style of contact is the psychodynamic product of two personalities and are therefore not as predictable by objective determinants as our administrators wish. The most we can do is to have an informed guess about which combination of patient and analyst might be the most fruitful.

By giving this *ad hoc* constructed example of the two methods of interpretation based on two different perspectives of the unconscious I hope to put the interested questioner in a better position to further explore the work of both Freud and Jung and obviously their followers. He or she might even sample for themselves whichever method would suit them best. My own opinion is that the personality of the analyst is at least as important as the "school" he belongs to. I can say this because I am myself the offspring of a "mixed marriage", having had both Jungian and Freudian types of analysis.

Glossary

Different technical subjects are referred to in this book. This list is of the author's personal definitions.

Active imagination – Jung's term for association but this time it starts from an image which may be a picture. By concentrating on it and by contemplation, it expands into other images and may change the mood of the beholder. The term is not restricted to visual images, it equally refers to verbal images as in metaphors or auditory images or by movement as in dance.

Amnesia – Not having a memory of a past event. As used by Freud this is due to not wanting to know or "repression". The reason being that the event or period was painful, even "traumatic". Psychoanalysis can raise much of the "forgotten" event to the level of consciousness again.

Analytical Psychology – Jung who had been a pupil of Freud's was to become his "crown prince". But he became a heretic who was later accused of anti-Semitism. They fell out over their different views on symbols. For Freud a symbol was a cover-up for anything that was really "instinctual". For Jung the symbol meant something in its own right. Later he discovered that there was also a "collective unconscious". He meant that in addition to their personal unconscious, people were also influenced by the unconscious that was "in the air" by which I mean the influence of the spirit of their times, people's upbringing and national or racial biases and prejudices, influenced further by the media, advertising, politics, religion, social and material advantages, even fashions.

Anima/animus – Jung's special Latin terms to indicate the personification of the unconscious feminine part of a man's mind projected into a "She" and vice versa, animus in the case of women the masculine part projected onto a man. Both have special erotic and sexual attractive qualities which can however turn into being repulsive.

Animism – Takes places when we attribute human life to things or animals. The "medicine" (charm or totem) that the West African wanted to pacify (see chapter "Sailing as to War, the War Years, Victory") was an animism. Animal lovers are often animists.

Archetype – Jung is usually associated with this word and certainly the first to use it as a technical term. However, in different contexts the word has gained different significance. There is a theory of archetypes. Thus anima/animus, see above, are archetypes. In my practical work I think of archetypal behaviour as something that is typical of a certain role in a drama or on stage, except this is not played but serious presence. Thus people are not archetypes, although they sometimes seem as if possessed by an archetype and behave accordingly. Thus we know our roles as good or bad mothers and fathers, sons and daughters, lovers, husbands and wives, doctors and patients etc.. "Good" does not mean much more than in accordance with expected behaviour and "bad" against it but our, the onlooker's or reader's, emotions react spontaneously in sympathy or antipathy with what we perceive and judge accordingly. Archetypal behaviour and our reaction to it is one-sided and extreme.

Atavar – Hindu word that has entered our literature. Originally referring to the different appearances of a God, like Zeus who could in classical Greek mythology became a swan. I use it when I see myself in photos or diary notes of the distant past and recognise myself with astonishment.

Balint groups – Founded by Michael Balint, psychoanalyst, who wanted to bring about that the general practitioner and other doctors too would find their job more interesting, if they could listen to the patient's words not only as symptoms but also from the socio-psychological angle and in emotional perspective. Patients too benefit and feel themselves with all their complaints recognised as human beings and not just as carriers of symptoms that need diagnoses and treatment.

Counter-transference – The analyst's automatic reaction to the patient's transference, see below. It originally had a derogatory significance, something that should not be there but Jung took it as being naturally there. In the mid 1930s psychoanalysts too detected that, when recognised(!), it was a useful instrument in the practice of analysis.

Denial – Refusing painful reality. One of the mechanisms of defence.

Drive – Is not always positive, can also be destructive, in that case it is related to the "death instinct".

Ego – English analytical language, the equivalent of "I"; German "Ich".

Electro-encephalogram – Comparable with the better known electro-cardiogram (ECG), this one (EEG) measures and records the tiny currents that are produced rhythmically as the heart beats and the circulation flows through the body.

Eros – The Greek name of the God of love and used in poetry. More frequently used is the adjective "erotic", see chapter "Reflecting on Various Kinds of Love".

Great mother – Jung's special term for the archetypal mother who creates and destroys. There are many statues of the Hindu goddess Kali as she dances on corpses, emphasising her destructive aspect. The life-giving side is accentuated by her breasts.

Identification with the aggressor – Freud's special term for the paradoxical fact that one can identify with the person who attacks one.

Incest – Well known as something that happens from time to time and is outlawed. Analysts more often than others use it when the relations between the sexes are too intimate considering the age gap or the social circumstances, also when the relation between the participants does not permit it.

Individuation – Jung's term for a person becoming what he really is, i.e. ego plus self in balance. A slow process. Not to be mistaken for being individual.

Inflation – When a person becomes too big for his boots.

Mandala – A symmetrical configuration of a circle with other geometric figures. Used for contemplation, usually in Zen Buddhism. Jung painted several of his own.

Mechanisms of defence – It is the ego that defends itself against being hurt in a variety of ways. This happens quite automatically hence "mechanism", against being hurt (traumatised). Inflation could be one, denial another, "identification with the aggressor" (see above) a third.

Mystical/mystification – Derogatory terms used when a person cannot understand what is going on and suspects he is being hoodwinked.

Mythology – The major role in Freud's developmental theory of sexuality is based on the Oedipus myth. Jung recognises this but regards other myths as equally important.

Narcissism – Unjustified pride (vanity) and self-love. Some of this is necessary. The exclusion of love for others impoverishes. Actors and artists are often narcissistic.

Neurology – A medical specialty referred to nerves and the knowledge of the whole nervous system including the brain. Not meaning anything "psychic". If it does it is called "psycho-somatic".

Neuropsychological – A composite word like "psycho-somatic", really self-explanatory. Both halves together indicate that they are really inseparable, we can say psychoneurological or somato-psychic to indicate which is the primary aspect at the time.

Numinosity – It is a state of mind of *Ergriffenheit*. The dictionary translates it as being "moved" or "stirred" but that is too weak. Being gripped and overwhelmed would seem closer. It used to be applied in a purely religious sense. Jung uses it for the archetypes power unalloyed, i.e. before it has met an ego that can modify it.

"Object" – Used in analysis much like aim or target, e.g. the object of my love is ... and then comes the name that has emotional significance. It could also be hatred or anger. Analysts talk about someone's love- or hate-object.

Paranoia – Persecutory mania. The paranoid person may appear quite normal in all other respects, hence the old term "mono-mania".

Para-psychology – Comprises a large field on non-scientific and mainly future predicting practices, e.g. telepathy, astrology, chirology, etc.

Persona – The mask of the Roman actor. Metaphorically used by Jung, this is the role we play in public life according to the person we would like to be, are expected to be, pretend to be. A pseudo-person.

Pleasure principle – see reality principle.

Pre-genital/infantile sexuality – Freud stipulated that sexuality started in infancy but was not targeted at first on specific sexual organs. Thus he referred to an oral and anal "erogenous" zone as preceding "genitality".

Projection/to project – Much like in the cinema we all project, like a projectile in a gun, what is in us into the world outside and often onto or into another person. Especially all that we do not want to be, e.g. dishonesty. We project the shadow (see below). Jesus' story of the mote and the beam in the eye fits here.

Psychiatry – A medical specialty. Meaning specifically the knowledge of the psychoses and treatment of these, e.g. schizophrenia. Such treatments are usually physical with emphasis on tablets given by mouth or injections.

Psychoanalysis – Coined by Freud who wanted it to remain an exclusive term but it did not. Today it is practised according to various other psychoanalytic authors like Melanie Klein or Lacan, all acknowledging the importance of the unconscious part of the mind and its translation into consciousness with the help of words.

Psychology – Claims knowledge of a wide range of subjects divided into the psychology of learning, memory, children and other age groups or branches such as industry and markets. In fact it can be applied to people including all mammals and their activities. Psychological is often used as the opposite of physical.

Psychotherapy – This is the widest term of all mentioned here for it includes all kinds of therapy not only analysis but also therapies that do not make use of the concept of an unconscious mind. Behaviour therapy or gestalt – or, occupational therapy or social therapy. In fact the psychological foundation of any therapy. Love remains the best therapeutic ingredient but is not without risks.

Psychotic – Insane. Diseases like schizophrenia or severe depression are extreme examples but there are times in which we are all a bit mad or psychotic. Shakespeare's: "The lunatic, the lover, and the poet, are of imagination all compact ..."

Reaction formation – This is also an ego defence. It is used when, as one would expect, a person who has been hurt by another instead of being angry, converts anger into the opposite, let us say professes to like or even love his tormentor. People who have been abducted begin to make friends with the abductors, as in the Stockholm Syndrome.

Reality principle – Used by Freud as the opposite of the **pleasure principle** that is we seek pleasure in order to avoid reality. "Reality" is Freud's ideal.

Regression/to regress – Literally going back to a place I have come from. For Freud it meant going back from being grown up to behaving like a child. Under the influence of alcohol we all regress.

Reparation – In analysis it means trying to repair a previous damage when one realises what one has done. One makes reparation mainly in order to relieve guilt feelings and to have a clear conscience again.

Repression – In psychoanalysis means not wanting to remember something that has been painful. It is one of the ego defences. The job of the analyst is to undo repression and so being able to recall a "traumatic" incidence.

Schizophrenia – The commonest mental disease, it often starts between adolescence and adulthood when a person can still recover. It is the commonest mental disease or psychosis. Popularly it is a "split mind". More often than not it can only be controlled rather than cured. But even that means that more frequently than in earlier days the schizophrenic can live outside an institution. Some schizophrenics are dangerous.

Self – The self as a particularly Jungian concept is an archetype and in contrast to the ego is not under one's control. Much of Jungian theory is built around the self and its symbols. For practical work I regard it as indicating the whole of the person, body and mind. In analysis one learns to listen to the self and get to know the feel of it. The older one gets the more one has to pay attention to the self.

Shadow – According to Jung only the ego throws a shadow. The shadow comprises all the unwanted parts of oneself put together as one dark configuration, see Oscar Wilde's *The Picture of Dorian Gray.*

Squiggle game – Winnicott's special diagnostic tool consists of something like a spontaneous drawing. Children can do it better than adults. The squiggle game is what Winnicott played with children. He asked them to do the first squiggle, he continued on the same piece of paper so it became a combined squiggle. They talked to each other while the hands did the squiggle.

Supervision – Is part of the analyst's training when he or she is in training analysis and has begun to see their first patients. He has to report at regular intervals to one of the "training analysts", the supervisor.

Symbol – The bone of contention between Freud and Jung, see above. Jung was concerned with the intent of the symbol, that which it aimed at. So it can be interpreted in many different ways. Symbols arouse affects.

Symbolic (understanding) – Understanding symbols. This is not a purely intellectual understanding by means of words.

Synchronicity – Jung linked different physical and psychological events not by the principle of cause and effect but by a common root, namely "meaningful coincidence". A well-known example: Two people walking together in the street talk of a third, their mutual acquaintance. Then, suddenly and unexpectedly that person comes walking along towards them. The two say, "how strange, we were just talking about you", or, if they are on familiar terms, they might say "talk of the devil". They leave unsaid: "and there he appears", which is based on an old superstition. Jung's clinical example is that of a patient telling him a dream of an Egyptian scarab, when another beetle, the nearest European relative, knocks against the window pane. Conclusion: The realm we call the Unconscious possesses something like magnetic attraction. We cannot explain or analyse the phenomena by cause and effect reasoning. (See chapter "On Training within a Human Context".)

Thanatos – The god of death in Greek mythology. Used by Freud as the opposite of Eros.

Training analyst – An analyst who has been elected by colleagues of his institute to take on new candidates for analysis as students for training and supervision. Students are called "trainees".

Transference – See also counter-transference. A most decisive instrument in the process of analysis and its outcome as it has to do with changes that occur in the analysand (patient or trainee) which are noticed by the analyst. It is loosely positive or negative, with reference to the emotional aspect of her/his transference. For psychoanalysts the patients' transference is based on the feelings they had towards their parents, therefore a mother- or father-transference. In analysis the quality of the picture or image is now attributed to the analyst, be it love or hatred or a mixture of the two, ambivalence. In every case it must be sorted out so as to become balanced and realistic.

Jung looks at the transference from the animus/anima angle, see above. That means it is closer to the gender than the bodily sex of the parent. He bluntly says a boy's first anima is his mother. So inner reality has priority over outer. Clearly Jung was an introvert (see typology, below). So was Melanie Klein, a psychoanalyst.

Transitional object – Winnicott's term for the first thing that the infant finds and accepts in his development from being attached to the breast or nipple towards reality outside. It is not a given substitute but something found, usually a flannel or corner of a pillow the infant discovered by himself and values as his own. Winnicott thought that, for the adult, Art, Religion and Philosophy have comparable qualities. Hence also transitional phenomena.

Trauma, traumatic – Used in analysis for any serious and lasting damage done to the psyche. The more so when it has been "repressed", see above.

Type/typology – In Jung's classification based on observation supported to some extent by experiments. The best known are in the first category extravert and introvert. They are further subdivided into four: thinking and feeling, sensation and intuition. After that it becomes more complicated. I orientate myself by the typology and take no further notice of it during my analytical work.

Unconscious/collective unconscious: The concept of an unconscious part of the mind, it is older than Freud's use of it for therapy. Whereas Freud always means the personal unconscious, Jung's concept is that there is also a collective unconscious. This addition is now slowly gaining ground. It influences the socio-cultural sphere in which all of us are born and live. See also mythology.

Chronology

1913   Born in Düsseldorf 8 February.

1930   Matriculated (A-levels) at Hindenburg Gymnasium.

1930–33   Medical Student at Bonn and Freiburg.

1933   Emigrated to South Africa.
Continued medical studies at Johannesburg
(University of Witwatersrand).

1937   Graduated.

1938–39   Locums in the country.

1939   First paper in *South African Medical Journal.*

1939   Geraldine born in England.

1940   Married "Pat" (Patricia Bannister), Simonstown, Cape Province.

1940–46   Served as medical officer in the South African Army Medical
Corps.

1941   Helen born in Cape Town.

1946   Demobilisation Loan. Emigrated to England.
Postgraduate Studies in Psychiatry, London.
Diploma in Psychological Medicine.
Qualified in Child Psychiatry.
Training analysis.

1949   Married "Evelyn" (Joan Evelyn Clark).

1951   Membership of the Society of Analytical Psychology.
Lived at 25 Regent's Park Crescent, London.

1952   Adrian born in London.
Practised as analyst in Devonshire Place, London.

1953	Training analyst. Moved out to Jordans, near Beaconfield, Bucks.
1955	Yvonne, our three-months-old baby, drowned.
1957	David born at Beaconfield.
1971	Met Andrew Samuels as trainee.
1976	Evelyn died.
1977	Sold "Old Ways" Jordans, moved to Montague Street, London, and had practice there.
1978	Married Helen Besemeres (Australia) in London.
1981	Divorced Helen.
1984	Met Helga Anderssen (Berlin).
1986	Moved to Berlin. Member and training analyst of the C. G. Jung Institute Berlin. In private practice.
1992	Married Helga in Stroud, England.
2003	Private and official celebration of ninetieth birthday at Berlin with delegates of the Society of Analytical Psychology, the International Association of Analytical Psychology, London and Professor Andrew Samuels.

Publications by Fred Plaut

About eighty professional published and fifty unpublished papers.

A few publications on cartography:

"General Gordon's Paradise" in *Encounter* June/July 1982.

Phantasiekarte in *Lexikon zur Geschichte der Kartographie* 1986, Deutike, Wien.

Books

Analysis Analysed 1995.

A Critical Dictionary of Jungian Analysis 1986
co-author with Andrew Samuels and Bani Shorter.

Index

Bold page numbers indicate an entry in the Glossary

Abraham, Karl, 95
active group therapy, 90
Active imagination, **161**
Adler, Gerhard, 62, 67, 68, 83, 85, 89, 94
administrators, 73
affairs, love, 113
African National Council (ANC), 25
Africanders, 24
age gap, 114, 115
Agadir, Morocco, 129, 131, 133
aggressor, identification with, **163**
alchemy, 142
alcoholics, 149
amnesia, 143, **161**
amplificiation, 159
analysis
    and self-knowledge, 60
    and fees, 60
    familiarity, atmosphere of, 61
    fees and secrecy, 69
    educational, 75
    cultural influences, 81
    and autonomy, 116
Analysis Analysed, 71, 74
analysis sessions, frequency, 78, 79
    analysis, 83
analysts, income of, 69
analytical psychologist, 159
analytical psychology, 83, **161**
analytical psychotherapy, 83
Andreas' art class, 103
anima/animus, 77, **161**
animism, **161**
anti-Semitism, 148
    in Germany, 17, 20, 25
apartheid, 24
archetype, 71, 84, **161–2**
architecture, arabic, 133

asbestosis, 33
Association of Jungian Analysts, 62
    associations, 158
Astor, James, 71
Atavar, **162**
Aus Tsing-Tao entkommen, 13
autobiography, 141
Ayot St Lawrence, 52

Bad Gandersheim, 133–5
balimo, 37
Balint groups, 88, **162**
Balint, Enid, 88
Balint, Michael, 88, 139, 146, 154
Bannister, Pat *see* Plaut, Pat
Bantu, 25, 36
Basuto, 37–8
Beckett, Samuel, 64
belief-system, 153
Belisha beacon, 50
Bennet, E.A., 67
Berlin
    bankruptcy, 122
    climate, 122
    compared with London, 119, 122
    Russian siege, 123
Berlin Institute for Psychotherapy, 139

Berlin Institute of Analytical Psychology, 91
Berlin Wall, 25, 121
Berliners and anger, 119
Bernhard (uncle), 26–7
big bang, 140
Bion, W.R., 85–7, 95, 97, 148, 149, 154
    and Melanie Klein, 86
    and DSO, 86
bisexuality, 111

black market, 51
Blake, William, 142, 153
blind spot, 156
Blumenstraße, 9
Boers, 84
Böll, Heinrich, 112
Bonn, 19
    government, 121
books, 141
Böttger, Claudia (secretary), 146
Brender, Clara, 6
British Journal of Medical Psychology, 59
British Psychological Society, 88
brother, relationship with, 9
Bruno, Giordano, 150
Bührmann, Vera, 91–2
Bush, George W., 95, 148
buskers, 51

Café Einstein, 122
Californian mode, 90
Canetti, Elias, 129
Cape Coloureds, 32
Cape Town, 7
Carroll, Lewis, 106
cartobibliography, 98
Cecil Avenue, 47
Cézanne, Paul, 142
Chang, Chinese magician, 41
Charcot, Jean-Martin, 156
charity, 148
Charlie (cousin), 20, 26
Child Guidance Clinic, 107
Child Guidance Training Centre, 52
childhood abuse, 11
Clark, Cosmo, 52
Clark, James, 52
Clark, Joan Evelyn (future wife), 48,
    49, *see also* Plaut, Evelyn
    arrived from South Africa, 51
class distinction, 50
Coco de Mer, 100
cognitive psychology, 73
commuting, 53–4
competition for patients, 70

concentration camps, 17
conscious–unconsious, 144
couch, the, 68, 78, 157, 159
counter-transference, 77, **162**
couple relationship, 105
Cox, Alice, 46, 48, 114
creativity, 81–2
Crick, Francis, 153
"crossing of the line", 21
Czar's College, 129

"Dad's Army", 13
Dannhauser locum, 35
Dart, Professor Raymond, 30
Darwin, Charles, 153, 156
Das heitere Plaut Buch, 14
Day of Atonement, 147
death, waiting for, 155
decimalisation, 50
defence, mechanisms of, **163**
denial, **162**
Der Stürmer (newspaper), 20
Der Völkische Beobachter
    (newspaper), 20
deserted spouses, 117
Detmold, 1, 8, 14
Deutsche National Partei, 18
Deutsche Volkspartei, 18
Devonshire Place (consulting rooms),
    53, 90, 95, 96, 142
Dieckmann, Hannes, 127
Dieckmann, Hans, 91
Dingaan's Day, 24
Diploma in Psychological Medicine,
    57
Dolly (cousin), 26
Doris (au-pair), 53
drawing technique, 103
dreams, 38, 157
    interpretation of, 158
dream-snake, 78
drive, **162**
drug takers, 149
Dunera, 41
Düsseldorf, 20

East European Psychoanalytic
    Institute, 127
Eckhardt, Meister, 149
ECT see electro-shock treatment, 59
Edwards, Alan, 118
ego, the, 94, 148, **162**
    ego and the self, 139
Elaine Grove, 118
electro-encephalogram, **162**
electroshock treatment, 59
Ella (aunt), 1, 3, 47
Eloff Street, 29
Encounter (magazine), 98
"epistemepholic instinct", 106
Ernst (friend), 13
Eros, **162**
Erwin (brother), 1, 10, 19, 36, 41
    witchdoctor interview, 36–9
Escombe Avenue, 27, 28, 40
Esselen community, 90
Evelyn, *see* Clark, Joan Evelyn and
    Plaut, Evelyn
evil eye (camera), 131
exercises for the mind, 137
extravert, 151
Eysenck, Professor Hans, 58

faith, 147
family tree, 6
family-meal, Jewish, 147
fantasies, 157
father *see* Plaut, Hermann
fee-paying patients, 79
fees, 60
Festival of Britain, 53
Fierz, Heinrich, 92
Fierz, Marcus, 92
Fordham, Frieda, 61, 84, 101
Fordham, Michael, 60, 61, 62, 67, 68,
    71, 77, 89, 94
forgetting names, 144
form filling, 74
Francis Edwards (shop), 96
Franz, Marie Louise von, 92
Freiburg, 18, 19
Freud Museum, 64

Freud, Anna, 64, 94–5
    and Melanie Klein, 68
Freud, Sigmund, 59, 60, 61, 62, 63,
    65, 66, 68, 72, 74, 77, 78, 82,
    85, 87, 137, 143, 147, 151,
    154
    different from Jung, 156–60
Freudians, 156
Frey, Toni, 92, 93
Furlong, Monica, 109, 149

Ganesa, 147
gardening, 47, 142
Gay, John (*The Beggar's Opera*), 58
gender, 111
General Medical Council, 31, 76
German Jewry, 18
God, 37
Godhead, 148
"Golden Flower", 78
Gordon, General Charles George, 100
Grand Union Canal, 52
grandmother, 2, 3, 47
great mother, **163**
Greenwich, 51
Gymnasium, 16

happiness, pursuit of, 60
Harley Street, 67, 76
Harrods, 50
health insurance schemes, 68
heaven, 140
Henderson, Joe, 91
Herrigal, Eugen, 64
High Veld, 48
Hill End Hospital, 59
Hill End, St Albans, 51–2
Hill, Denis, 58
Hille-Bille, 14
Hitler, Adolf, 16, 25, 123
Hobson, R.F. "Bob", 57
Hogarth Press, 52
Hogg, James, 142
Hokey-Cokey (dance), 52
Holocaust, 17
homosexuality, 108

Hutsback, Judith, 94
hypnosis, 156–7

I-Ching, 64
identification with the aggressor,
    95, **163**
identity and language, 80
Immorality Act (South Africa), 25
incest, 105, 108, 114, **163**
    brother–sister, 114, 142
individuation, 92, 142, 151, **163**
infantile sexuality, **164**
inflation, **163**
Institute of Psychoanalysis, 62, 68
    secret committee, 62
institutions, microcosm of, 46
insulin-coma treatment, 59
insurance companies, 73, 74, 75,
    79
introvert, 151

Jacobi, Jolande, 93
Jacobi, Mario, 93
Jaffé, Max, 42
James, Henry, 142
James, William, 141, 148
Jemna el Fna, 131
Johannesburg, 26
John (batman), 43
Jones, Ernest, 62, 85
Jordans, 13, 53, 60, 89, 100
Joubert Park, 28
Joubert, General Petrus Jacobus,
    28
Journal of Analytical Psychology,
    94
Journal of Medical Psychology, 88
Julia (student), 126
Jung, C.G., 62, 64, 65, 66, 67, 68,
    71, 77, 78, 81, 83, 92, 109,
    113, 138, 139, 141–2, 145,
    148, 149, 151, 152, 155
    relationship with Freud, 84
    different from Freud, 156–60
Jung, Emma, 84
Jungians, 156

Kaffirs, 26
Kant, Immanuel, 140
Kew Gardens, 50
Kikuya tribe, 43, 44
King's African Rifles (KAR), 42, 45
King's College Chapel, 147
Ki-Swahili lessons, 43
kitchen-mimicry, 92
Klein, Melanie, 83, 85, 94–5, 106
    and Anna Freud, 68
Krankenkassen, 75
Kriegskinder, 12
Kwazulu, 34

labyrinth, the, 74
Laden, Osama bin, 95
Lady in Red, 134–5
Lambeth Walk (song), 51
language and identity, 80
Larissa, 124–6
Latin, spoken by Africans, 45
Layard, John, 94
Leaky, Richard, 46
Leibwächter ("bodyguards"), 62
Lewis, Aubrey (professor), 57
Liberty's (shop), 20
lie-detector, 153
Lina (aunt), 7
location, 99
locums, 32, 34, 35
Lokitang, 45
Lola (analyst) *see* Paulsen, Lola
London blitz, 121
London fog, 50
London, post-war, 50–1
"losing things", 1
love
    and sexuality, 105
    without sex, 109
    affairs, 113
    commercial contract, 115
Lucas, Dr (solicitor), 9
Luckner, Graf von, 13
Luria, David, 149
Luther, Martin, 134, 149
Lyon's Corner House, 53

macho man, 111
Maida Vale Hospital, 58
Mali (aunt), 1, 2, 7, 16, 19, 27, 31, 32, 47
mandala, 85, 151, **163**
Mandela, Nelson, 24, 25, 28
Manersky, Maria, 126–7
Manersky, Sergey, 126–7
Manfred (uncle), 1
Manichaen, 84
Mann, Thomas, 114, 142
Mansfield Gardens, 64
mapping, 74
marital infidelity, discovery of, 116
Marrakesh, 129
masturbation, 105
Maudsley Hospital, 52, 57, 67, 86
Max (student), 126
May, Karl, 14
McLuhan, Marshall, 65
meaningful coincidence, 64
mechanism, 95
mechanisms of defence, **163**
Mecklenburg Square, 52
medication, 87
Meier, C.A. "Freddy", 92
Melville, Herman, 74
mementos, 141
memories, 140
memory, 143
  in old age, 136
microcosm of institutions, 46
Middlesex Hospital, 58
Military Mental Hospital, 113
Miller, Emmanuel, 58
mine dumps, 29
Miners' Compensation Act, 33
miscegenation laws, 32
Moby Dick, 74
molimo, 37
money, 75
Montague Street, 55
Moody, Robert, 67, 94
Morocco, 129
Moslem and wives, 130
mother *see* Plaut, Friederike

mother-tongue, 80
mourning, 55
Murdoch, Iris, 142
Mussolini, Benito, 45
mystical/mystification, **163**
mysticism, 149–50
mythology, **163**

Nanyuki, Mt Kenya, 42, 43
narcissism, 109, 139, **163**
Natal, 34
National Health Service, 52, 75
National Insurance (British), 75
National Party, 47
National Socialism, 16
Nazism, 16–18
Neo-Friburgia (student club), 18
Neurological Hospital, Queen's Square, 52
neurology, **163**
neuropsychological, **163**
Nevsky Prospect, 125, 126
Nietzsche, Friedrich, 112
Nina (labrador), 55
note taking, 80
No-thing, 148
Ntlama, Louisa, 37
numerology, 92
numinosity, **164**

Oasis Ouijane, 130
"object", **164**
Oedipus, 77
officers' mess, 48
Ogilby's map, 96
Olifantshoek locum, 34
orgasm, 111, 112, 113
Orwell, George, 68
otherness, 106, 112
Otto, Rudolf, 152

Papadopoulos, Renos, 93
paranoia, **164**
para-psychology, **164**
Park Crescent, 53
Parkhouse, Archie, 29

Parkinson's laws, 59
passport, 19
    British, 51
patient, late arrival of, 66
Patterson, Colonel, 27
Paulsen, Lola (analyst), 52, 60, 77
payment for piecework, 75
Payne, Sylvia, 95
pea-soupers (London), 50
penetration, 111
Perls, Fritz, 90
persona, **164**
Petticoat Lane (market), 51
pharmacological therapy, 59
Phillips, Adam, 87
Physikum, 19
Plaut, Abraham (grandfather), 2, 3
Plaut, Adrian (elder son), 12, 14, 53,
    55, 100, 101, 108, 118, 121
    in East Berlin, 121
Plaut, David (younger son), 100,
    101, 108
Plaut, Erwin (brother), 27, 140
Plaut, Evelyn (second wife), 13, 50,
    53, 94, 100, 101, 102, 108,
    113–14, 115, 118, 137, 142,
    153
    dies of cancer, 55
Plaut, Faith (sister-in-law), 11
Plaut, Fred
    visits father's grave, 6
    death of father, 7–8, 57, 140
    mother's infidelity, 8
    nightmares, 8
    birthplace, 9
    father substitute, 11
    mother's disappointment in, 11
    emigrated to South Africa, 19
    "home", 20
    leaves mother and brother in
        Germany, 20
    escapes from Germany, 20
    arrival in South Africa, 23
    loan from Aunt Mali, 31
    locum doctor, 32
    attends post-mortem, 33

    has illegitimate child, 40
    marriage to Pat, 40
    climbs Mt Kenya, 44
    duodenal ulcer, 46
    birth of Helen, 46
    apprenticeship in psychiatry, 46
    moves to Johannesburg, 47
    interest in psychiatry, 47
    meets Evelyn, 48
    divorce from Pat, 48
    first analysis, 48, 61
    move to England, 49
    in love with Evelyn, 49
    analysis with Lola, 52
    divorce from Pat, 52
    birth of Adrian, 52
    commuting to London, 53
    death of Evelyn, 55
    inability to mourn, 55
    career choice, 57
    paper on electroshock treatment, 59
    guilt over leaving Pat and children,
        60
    chooses Jungian, 75
    and language, 80
    meets Jung, 83
    and religion, 85
    letters to Jung, 85
    Maudsley or Tavistock, 86
    and Enid Balint, 88–9
    friendship with Michael Fordham,
        89
    and the Zinkins, 90–1
    visit to Zürich, 92
    edits *JoAP*, 94
    and map collecting, 96
    Paradise, 97, 99, 100, 135
    elected FRGS, 98
    gardening at Jordans, 100–1
    death of baby daughter, 101
    and roses, 101
    joins art class, 102
    met first daughter, 107
    and lesbian wife, 111
    and love affairs, 113
    marries Evelyn, 114

relationship with mother, 116
moves with Helga to Berlin, 118
and Berlin taxi-drivers, 120
and travelling, 124
and Larissa's flat, 124
supervision in St Petersburg, 126
visits Morocco, 129
ninetieth birthday celebrations, 139
speech at ninetieth birthday, 146
mystical experience, 150
Plaut, Friederike "Reike" (mother), 1,
   3, 5, 19, 27–8, 140
mourning, 6
made childrens' clothes, 10
Plaut, Geraldine (elder daughter), 11,
   40, 58, 89, 107
Plaut, Helen (third wife), 90, 107
Plaut, Helen (younger daughter), 11,
   29, 41, 58
Plaut, Helga (fourth wife), 4, 102,
   103, 115, 118, 121, 129, 132,
   133–4, 139, 153
Plaut, Hermann (father), 5–6
Plaut, Joseph (uncle), 4, 7, 14, 119,
   144
singer-songwriter, 14–15
admired sister, 15
Plaut, Pat (first wife), 32, 40, 46, 114
Plaut, Paul (cousin), 57
Plaut, Yvonne (daughter), 101
"Plaut–Paradise", 97
Plautus, Maccius, 83
pleasure principle, 59, **164–5**
pornography, 98, 112
Portobello Road (market), 51
Post, Laurens van der, 84
post-analytic era, 72
Postmasburg, post-mortem at, 33
Potchefstroom (psychiatric hospital),
   46, 48, 113
pre-genital sexuality, **164**
pregnancy, 152
Prieska locum, 33
Primrose Hill, 52
projection, **164**
prophylactic medicine, 38

psychiatry, **164**
psychoanalysis, 83, 87, **164**
psychoanalytic concepts, 68
psychoanalytic group, 86
Psychoanalytic Institute, 71, 95
psychology, **164**
psychotherapy, **165**
psychotic, **165**
Ptolemy, 96–7
Pushkin, Alexander, 129

Quakers, 55–6, 153
Queen's Square Hospital, 58

Randfontein locum, 36
reaction formation, 56, **165**
reality principle, **165**
regression, **165**
religion, 148, 153
reparation, 56, **165**
repression, 56, **165**
Research Institute for Analytical
   Psychology, 92
Reshetnikov, Mikhail, 127
Rickmann, John, 59, 60
Robert's Heights, 47
Rommel, 47–8
roots, 138
Rosa (aunt), 7
roses, 101

Saddam Hussein, 95
sameness, 106–8
Samuels, Andrew, 93, 118–19, 146
schizophrenia, 59, **165**
Schmisse, 18
Second World War, 5
Seddon, James, 94
self, the, 139, 148, **165**
self-discovery, 60
self-love, 110
Sergy (student), 126
servants in South Africa, 23
sex
   and spirituality, 112
   without love, 110

sex *continued*
  on anniversaries, 110
sex-tourism, 132
sexual perversions, 63
sexuality
  and love, 105
  infantile, 110
  pre-genital, 110
Seychelles, 100
shadow, **165**
Shakers, 56, 153
Shakespeare, William, 151
Shaw, George Bernard, 52
Sikusoka, 42
Simenon, Georges, 142
Simonstown, 41
smoking on trains, 54
Smuts, General J.C., 28, 46–7
Social Services (British), 52
Society of Analytical Psychology, 61,
  66, 67, 71, 89
  AGM, 62
Society of Friends *see* Quakers
Society of Jungian Analysts of
  Northern California, 91
sources for autobiography, 141
South Africa
  racial laws, 23
  social distinctions, 23
  Governor-General, 24
  parliament, 46
South African Air Force, 47
South African Embassy in London,
  24, 25
South African Medical Corps, 41
South Bank (London), 53
Speakers' Corner, 51
spirit, 154
Squiggle Game, 65, 87, **166**
SS *Gloucester Castle*, 20, 40
St Antony, 2, 3
St Ebba's, Epsom, 58
St Mark's Crescent, Regent's Park, 52
St Petersburg Times (newspaper), 128
St Petersburg, 124
Staatssexamen, 30

state control, 74
Stein, Leopold, 94
stethoscope, prestige/magic of, 36
stolen fruit, 110
Sullivan, Barry, 50
supervision, **166**
Susi (poodle), 55
Süsskind, Patrick, 142
swastika, 16
Swiss Cottage, 61
symbol, 157, **166**
symbolic understanding, **166**
syncronicity, 84, **166**

Tatiana (student), 124, 125, 126, 127
Tavistock Clinic, 58, 67, 86
Thanatos, **166**
therapy, analytically-orientated, 59
time and women, 102
Toni (aunt), 7, 26, 144
Tonya (student), 124, 127, 128, 129
Tooley, R.V., 96, 142
townships, 28
training analysis, 75
training analyst, **166**
transference, 63, 69, 71, **166–7**
  groups, 71
  dreams, 83
transitional object, **167**
trauma(tic), **167**
Tree Tops Lodge, Kenya, 51
Truth and Reconciliation Commission,
  24
type/typology, **167**

Uganda Field Ambulance, 42
  and Italian bombers, 45
Uncle (Onkel) Joseph *see* Plaut,
  Joseph
unconscious phenomena, 64–5, **167**
unconscious, the, 64, 74, 79, 156, 157,
  167
  demystification of, 66
  worship by Jungians, 71
Underhill, Evelyn, 149
Union Castle Line, 21

Union of German Mothers, 12
United Party, 47
Ürdingen barracks, 8

vanity in autobiography, 141
Vater ist im Kriege, 12
Verbindungen, 18
Voortrekkers, 24

waiting lists, 75
Wajir, 45
Waldschlößchen, 134
Wanderers, 28
war, declaration of, 40
Warburg Institute and Collection, 150
water, lack of in Africa, 130, 131
"we" lost out to "I", 78
weaver bird experiment, 145
Wehrenhagenstraße, 3, 4
well-polished mirror (Freud), 60, 62
Weltanschauung, 147
Wheelwright, Joe, 89, 91
widow bird, 34
Willingshausen, 6

Wilson, Harold, 50
Wimbledon, 14
Winnicott, D.W., 62, 65, 87–8, 95
witchdoctor's bones, 37
witchdoctors, 36
witchdoctor-students, 37
Wolf and Heller, 6
women and time, 102
Woolf, Virginia, 52
worship, communal, 148

Yalom, Irwin D., 72
Yates, Frances, 150
yoga, 64, 150

Zanzibar, 42
  bazaar, 41
Zeitgeist, 156
Zen Buddhism, 64
zero meridian, 51
Zinkin, Hindle, 90
Zinkin, Louis, 90, 118
Zürich hard-liners, 78
Zürich school, 77